COLLECTED WORKS
OF RENÉ GUÉNON

Studies in Hinduism

RENÉ GUÉNON

STUDIES
IN HINDUISM

Translated by
Henry D. Fohr
Edited by
Samuel D. Fohr

SOPHIA PERENNIS

GHENT NY

Originally published in French as
Études sur l'Hindouisme
© Éditions Traditionnelles 1966
English translation © Sophia Perennis 2001
All rights reserved

Series editor: James R. Wetmore

For information, address:
Sophia Perennis, 343 Rte 21C
Ghent NY 12075

Library of Congress Cataloging-in-Publication Data

Guénon, René
[Études sur l'Hindouisme. English]
Studies in Hinduism / translated by Henry D. Fohr ; edited by
Samuel D. Fohr.—2nd ed.

p. cm. — (Collected works of René Guénon)
Originally published: Paris : Éditions traditionnelles, c 1966.
ISBN 0 900588 69 1 (pbk: alk. paper)
ISBN 0 900588 70 5 (cloth: alk. paper)
1. Hinduism. I. Fohr, Henry D. II. Fohr, S.D., 1943– III. Title.
BL1210.G813 2001
294.5—dc21   2001001098

The Publisher wishes to give special thanks to
HENRY D. AND JENNIE L. FOHR
for their generous support, without which this edition
would not have been possible.

Contents

EDITORIAL NOTE

THE past century has witnessed an erosion of earlier cultural values as well as a blurring of the distinctive characteristics of the world's traditional civilizations, giving rise to philosophic and moral relativism, multiculturalism, and dangerous fundamentalist reactions. As early as the 1920s, the French metaphysician René Guénon (1886–1951) had diagnosed these tendencies and presented what he believed to be the only possible reconciliation of the legitimate, although apparently conflicting, demands of outward religious forms, 'exoterisms', with their essential core, 'esoterism'. His works are characterized by a foundational critique of the modern world coupled with a call for intellectual reform; a renewed examination of metaphysics, the traditional sciences, and symbolism, with special reference to the ultimate unanimity of all spiritual traditions; and finally, a call to the work of spiritual realization. Despite their wide influence, translation of Guénon's works into English has so far been piecemeal. The *Sophia Perennis* edition is intended to fill the urgent need to present them in a more authoritative and systematic form. A complete list of Guénon's works, given in the order of their original publication in French, follows this note.

The present volume consists of articles published posthumously in 1966, to which has been added (as chap. 12) Guénon's separate study *La Métaphysique orientale*. This latter is the text of a lecture delivered at the Sorbonne on December 12, 1925, first published in *Vers l'Unité* (Paris) in 1926, and then by Les Éditions Traditionnelles (1939, etc.); several English translations of this lecture have appeared: in the journal *Tomorrow* (Winter 1964), in *The Sword of Gnosis* (Penguin, 1974), and as a pamphlet entitled *Oriental Metaphysics* (Hanuman Books, 1989). A translation of *Études sur l'Hindouisme* by Ian Kesarcodi Watson, omitting the book's extensive review section, was published in 1985 by Navrang of New Delhi.

Guénon frequently uses words or expressions set off in 'scare quotes'. To avoid clutter, single quotation marks have been used throughout. As for transliterations, Guénon was more concerned with phonetic fidelity than academic usage. The system adopted here reflects the views of scholars familiar both with the languages and Guénon's writings. Brackets indicate editorial insertions, or, within citations, Guénon's additions. Wherever possible, references have been updated, and current English editions substituted.

The present translation of the chapters is based on the work of Henry Fohr, edited by his son Samuel Fohr. The extensive section of reviews was translated largely by Cecil Bethell, who also provided the indexes. The entire text was checked for accuracy and further revised by Marie Hansen. For help with selected sections and proof-reading thanks go to John Herlihy, Patrick Moore, and William Quinn. A special debt of thanks goes to James Crouch for his help with bibliographic references to the A. K. Coomaraswamy reviews. Owing to the number of times Coomaraswamy's name appears, it has been abbreviated to 'AKC'.

The sources of the original French articles collected in this book are as follows: chap. 1, *Voile d'Isis*, March 1930; chap. 2, *Le Monde Nouveau*, June 1930; chap. 3, *Voile d'Isis*, October–November 1933; chap. 4, *Voile d'Isis*, August–September 1935; chap. 5, *Voile d'Isis*, October 1935; chap. 6, *Voile d'Isis*, November 1935; chap. 7, *Études Traditionnelles*, August–September 1937; chap. 8, *Études Traditionnelles*, August–September 1937; chap. 9, *Études Traditionnelles*, March 1940; chap. 10, *Études Traditionnelles*, July–August 1947; chap. 11, *Cahiers du Sud*, Special No. 'Approches de l'Inde', 1949. The Appendix contains lists of all article and book reviews.

The Works of René Guénon

1

Ātmā-Gītā

In our most recent work we alluded to an interior meaning of the *Bhagavad-Gītā*, which, when it is considered from this
point of view takes the name *Ātmā-Gītā*,[1] and since we have been
asked for some account of this subject, we think it will not be without interest to give one here. The *Bhagavad-Gītā*, which is an epi-
sode from the *Mahābhārata*,[2] has been translated so many times
into Western languages that one might think it must surely be well
known to all, but this is not the case at all because, to tell the truth,
none of these translations gives any evidence of real comprehension.
Even the title itself is generally rendered somewhat inaccurately as
'Song of the Blessed One', whereas in reality the principal meaning
of *Bhāgavat* is 'glorious' or 'venerable'. The meaning 'blessed' may
sometimes be applicable, but only in a very secondary way, and one
that is in any case quite inadequate in the present case.[3] *Bhāgavat* is
in fact an epithet that applies to all divine aspects, and also to those
beings considered particularly worthy of veneration;[4] the idea of
happiness, which moreover is ultimately of an entirely individual
and human order, is not necessarily contained in it. There is nothing

---

1. *Spiritual Authority and Temporal Power*, chap. 5.

2. We recall that the two *Itihāsas*, that is, the *Rāmāyana* and the *Mahābhārata*,
forming part of the *Smriti* and therefore having the character of traditional writings, are something altogether different from the simple 'epic poems' in the profane
and 'literary' sense customarily attributed to them by Westerners.

3. There is a certain relationship between the roots *bhaj* and *bhuj* which can
lead to confusion; the latter, of which the primitive meaning is 'to eat', expresses
above all the ideas of pleasure, possession, and happiness; conversely, in the former
and its derivatives, such as *bhaga*—and especially *bhakti*—the predominant ideas
are those of veneration, adoration, respect, devotion, or affection.

4. Buddhists naturally give this title to Buddha, and the Jains, similarly, to their
Tīrthaṅkaras.

astonishing in the fact that this epithet is applied especially to Krishna, who is not only a venerable figure but as the eighth *Avatāra* of *Vishnu* really corresponds to a divine aspect; but there is still something more to consider here.

To understand this, we must remember that the *Vaishnavite* and *Shaivite* points of view correspond to two great paths befitting beings of different natures. As a support in raising itself toward the supreme Principle, each takes one of two complementary divine aspects from which they derive their respective designations, transposing it in such a way that it is identified with the Principle itself, envisaged as without restriction and beyond all determination or specification whatsoever. This is why the *Shaivas* designate the supreme Principle as *Mahādeva* or *Maheshvara*, of which it is properly an equivalent of *Shiva*, whereas the *Vaishnavas* designate it by one of the names of *Vishnu*, like *Nārāyana* or *Bhāgavat*, this last being used in particular by a certain branch whose representatives for this reason are called the *Bhāgavatas*. There is no element of contradiction in all of this; the names are multiple, like the paths to which they correspond, but these paths all lead more or less directly to the same goal. Hindu doctrine knows nothing comparable to Western exclusivism, which insists that one and the same path must suit all beings equally, without taking any account of the differences of nature that exist among them.

Now it will be easy to understand that *Bhāgavat*, being identified with the supreme Principle, is by this very fact no other than the unconditioned *Ātmā*; and this is true in all cases, whether this *Ātmā* be envisaged in the 'macrocosmic' or in the 'microcosmic' order, according to which point of view one wishes to adopt. Obviously we cannot think of repeating here all we have said elsewhere on this subject;[5] what interests us most directly at present is what we might call the 'microcosmic' application, that is to say the application to each being considered in its particularity. In this respect Krishna and Arjuna, respectively, represent the 'Self' and the 'ego', or the personality and the individuality, which are the unconditioned *Ātmā*

---

5. For this and for what follows, the reader is referred especially to our work *Man and His Becoming according to the Vedānta*.

and *jīvātmā*. From this interior point of view, the teaching given by Krishna and Arjuna is that of supra-rational intellectual intuition, whereby the 'Self' communicates with the 'ego' when the latter is 'qualified' and prepared in such a way that this communication can be effectively established.

We should point out, since this is of the greatest importance for the matter at hand, that Krishna and Arjuna are represented as mounted upon the same chariot. This chariot is the 'vehicle' of the being envisaged in its state of manifestation, and it is Arjuna who fights while Krishna drives without fighting, that is, without himself engaging in the action. In a very general way the battle in question symbolizes action in a form appropriate to the nature and function of the Kshatriyas, to whom the book is especially addressed.[6] The field of battle (*Kshetra*) is the domain of action wherein the individual develops his possibilities, but such action in no way affects the principial being—which is permanent and immutable—but concerns only the individual 'living soul' (*jīvātmā*). The two who are mounted on the same chariot are thus the same thing as the two birds spoken of in the Upanishads: 'Two birds, inseparably united companions, live on the same tree; one eats the fruit of the tree, the other looks on without eating.'[7] Here again, although with a different symbolism representing action, the first of these two birds is *jīvātmā*, and the second is *Ātmā* unconditioned, and it is the same again for the 'two who entered the cave', mentioned in another text[8]—so that, if these two are always closely united, it is because they truly are but one with regard to absolute reality, for *jīvātmā* differs from *Ātmā* only in an illusory way.

---

6. It is to be noted that this meaning is also quite precisely that of the Islamic conception of the 'holy war' (*jihād*); the social and exterior application is here only secondary, as is evident from the fact that it merely constitutes the 'lesser holy war' (*al-jihād al-asghar*), whereas the 'greater holy war' (*al-jihād al-akbar*) is of a purely interior and spiritual order. [For these two 'holy wars' Guénon used the forms *jihad seghir* and *jihad kebir* respectively. ED.]

7. *Mundaka Upanishad*, III.1.1; *Shvetāshvatara Upanishad*, IV.6.

8. *Katha Upanishad*, I.3.1. The 'cavern' is no other than the cavity of the heart, which represents the place of the union of the individual with the Universal, or of the 'ego' with the 'Self'.

To express this union there also exists the remarkable word *Nāra-nārāyana*, which is directly connected to the *Ātmā-Gītā*. We know that *Nārāyana*, 'he who walks (or is carried) on the waters', is a name of *Vishnu* applied by transposition to *Paramātmā* or the supreme Principle, as we said above, the waters here representing formal or individual possibilities.[9] On the other hand, *nara* or *nri* is man, the individual being inasmuch as he belongs to the human species; and there is reason to note the close relation that exists between this word and *nāra*, which designates the waters,[10] although to develop this point now would draw us too far afield from our subject. *Nara* and *Nārāyana* are thus respectively the individual and the Universal, the 'ego' and the 'Self', the manifested state of a being and its non-manifested principle; and they are reunited indissolubly in the compound *Nāranārāyana*, sometimes spoken of as two ascetics living in the Himalayas, and so recalling more particularly the Upanishadic text just mentioned above, in which the 'two who entered the cave' are at the same time designated as 'dwelling on the highest peak'.[11] It is also said that in this same set, *Nara* is Arjuna and *Nārāyana* is Krishna, these two mounted on the same chariot being always, under one name or another according to the symbolism employed, *jīvātmā* and *Paramātmā*.

These pointers allow us to understand the interior meaning of the *Bhagavad-Gītā*, a meaning in respect of which all the others are finally only more or less contingent applications. This is especially true of the social meaning, in which the functions of contemplation and action, relating respectively to the supra-individual and the individual, are considered to be those of the Brahmins and the Kshatriyas.[12] It is said that the Brahmin is the type of fixed or

9. In the Christian tradition, the walking of Christ upon the waters has a meaning exactly comparable to the same symbolism.

10. Perhaps among the Greeks the names Nereus and Nereides—that is, water nymphs—are not without some connection with the Sanskrit *Nāra*.

11. Here we have an indication of the symbolic relationships between the cavern and the mountain, to which we have had occasion to allude in *The King of the World*.

12. We have developed this point of view particularly in *Spiritual Authority and Temporal Power*.

immutable beings (*sthāvara*), and that the Kshatriya is the type of mobile or changeable beings (*jangama*).[13] One can easily see the analogy between these two classes of beings, on the one hand, and on the other, the immutable personality and the individuality that is subject to change, and this immediately establishes the link between this meaning and the preceding. What is more, we see that even where it is particularly a question of the Kshatriya, the latter, perhaps because action is his proper function, is taken to symbolize individuality of whatever kind it may be, which is necessarily also engaged in action by the very conditions of its existence, whereas the Brahmin, by reason of his function of pure contemplation or knowledge, represents the superior states of the being.[14] Thus we may say that every being has within itself the Brahmin and the Kshatriya, but with a preponderance of the one or the other of these two natures according to whether its tendencies draw it primarily toward contemplation or toward action. We see by this that the scope of the teaching contained in the *Bhagavad-Gītā* is far from being limited to the Kshatriyas taken in the proper sense, although the form in which that teaching is expounded is particularly appropriate to them; and if Westerners, among whom the Kshatriya nature is encountered much more frequently than that of the Brahmin, were to understand traditional ideas—as they formerly did— such no doubt would be the form most immediately accessible to them.

13. The totality of beings is sometimes designated by the compound *sthāvara-jangama*.

14. This is why the Brahmin is designated as a *Deva* on earth, the *Devas* corresponding to supra-individual or non-formal (though manifested) states; this designation, which is rigorously correct, seems never to have been understood by Westerners.

2

THE SPIRIT OF INDIA

THE opposition of East and West, reduced to its simplest terms, is basically identical to that often held to exist between contemplation and action. We have already dealt with this subject many times, and have examined the different points of view from which the relationships between these two terms may be envisaged—that is to say, are they really contraries, or not rather perhaps complementaries, or, yet again, should they not stand in a relation of subordination rather than one of coordination? Here then we can do no more than summarize these considerations quickly, indispensable though they are for anyone seeking to comprehend the spirit of the East in general and that of India in particular.

The point of view that consists in purely and simply opposing contemplation and action to one another is the most exterior and superficial of all. The opposition does indeed exist in appearance, but it cannot be utterly irreducible; besides, one may say as much for all contraries, which cease to be such as soon as one rises above a certain level, that wherein their opposition has all its reality. Whoever says opposition or contrast thereby says disharmony or disequilibrium, that is to say something that can only exist from a limited and particular point of view, for in the totality of things equilibrium is made up of the sum of all disequilibria, and whether we like it or not all partial disorders converge in the total order.

In considering contemplation and action as complementary we place ourselves at a point of view already more profound and more true than the preceding one, because the opposition is therein reconciled and resolved, its two terms in a certain way balancing each other. It is then a question of two equally necessary elements that mutually complete and support one another, and that constitute the twofold activity—interior and exterior—of one and the same single being, whether it be each man taken individually or humanity envisaged collectively. Such a conception is assuredly more harmonious and more satisfactory than the first, yet if one held to it exclusively there would be a temptation, by virtue of the correlation thus established, to place contemplation and action on the same plane, so that one would need only strive to maintain the balance between them as well as possible without ever raising any question of a superiority of one over the other. Now this question always arises, and we can say that the antithesis of East and West consists precisely in the fact that the East maintains the superiority of contemplation over action whereas the West—and especially the modern West—on the contrary affirms the superiority of action over contemplation. Here it is no longer a question of points of view, each of which can have its own justification and at least be accepted as the expression of a relative truth, for since a relationship of subordination is irreversible, the two conceptions are really contradictory and thus exclusive with respect to each other, so that one is necessarily true and the other false. We must therefore choose, and perhaps the necessity of making this choice has never before been so compelling, or so forceful and urgent, as in the present circumstances; and it may perhaps become even more compelling in the near future.

In those of our works to which we alluded above[1] it was argued that contemplation is superior to action, just as the immutable is superior to change. Since action is only a transitory and momentary modification of being, it could not have its principle and sufficient reason within itself, and if it is not joined to a principle that lies beyond its contingent domain it is but pure illusion, which is to say that the principle from which it draws all the reality of which it is capable—both its existence and its very possibility—can only be found in contemplation, or, if one prefers, in knowledge. Similarly,

---

1. *East and West, The Crisis of the Modern World,* and *Spiritual Authority and Temporal Power.*

change in its most general sense is unintelligible and contradictory—that is, impossible—without a principle from which it
proceeds and which, by the very fact that it is its principle, cannot
be subject to it, and is thus necessarily immutable; this is why in the
ancient West Aristotle affirmed the necessity of an 'unmoved mover'
of all things. Now it is evident that action belongs to the world of
change, of 'becoming'; knowledge alone allows of leaving this world
and its inherent limitations, and when it attains the immutable it
thereby possesses immutability itself, for all knowledge is essentially
identification with its object. This is precisely what escapes the comprehension of Westerners, who so far as knowledge is concerned
envisage something merely rational and discursive, and therefore
indirect and imperfect, something that could be called knowledge
by reflection, and to an ever-increasing degree do not even value
that inferior knowledge except in the measure that it can directly
serve practical ends; engaged in action to the point of denying all
that goes beyond it, they do not realize that for want of a principle
action itself thus degenerates into an agitation as vain as it is sterile.

In the social organization of India, which is but an application of
metaphysical doctrine to the human order, the relationships
between knowledge and action are represented by those of the first
two castes, the Brahmins and the Kshatriyas, of which knowledge
and action are respectively the proper functions. It is said that the
Brahmin is the type of fixed beings, and that the Kshatriya is the
type of mobile or changeable beings, so that all the beings in this
world are principally related to one or the other according to their
nature, since there is a perfect correspondence between the cosmic
order and the human order. It is not of course that action is forbid-
den to the Brahmin, or knowledge to the Kshatriya, but in such
cases this occurs as it were by accident and not essentially; the *svadharma* or the proper law of caste, in conformity with the nature of
the being to which it belongs, lies in knowledge for the Brahmin and
in action for the Kshatriya. Thus the Brahmin is superior to the
Kshatriya as knowledge is superior to action; in other words, the
spiritual authority is superior to the temporal power, which in recognizing its subordination to the former will be legitimately, that is
to say truly, what it must be; otherwise, by separating itself from its

principle, it will only be able to function in a disordered way and will go fatally to its ruin.

To the Kshatriyas normally belongs all outward power, since the domain of action is the outer world; but that power is nothing without an inner principle—one that is purely spiritual—that incarnates the authority of the Brahmins, and in which it finds its only valid guarantee. In exchange for this guarantee, the Kshatriyas by virtue of the power they wield must assure the Brahmins the means of accomplishing their proper function of knowledge and teaching in peace, sheltered from disturbance and agitation. This is what is represented by the figure of *Skanda*, the Lord of War, protecting the meditation of *Ganesha*, the Lord of Knowledge. Such are the normal relationships between the spiritual authority and the temporal power; and if they were always and everywhere observed, no conflict could ever arise between the two, each then occupying its proper place in the hierarchy of functions and beings, a hierarchy strictly in conformity with the nature of things. We can see that the place reserved for the Kshatriyas and consequently for action, although subordinate, is very far from negligible since it includes all the exterior power, at once military, administrative, and judicial, that is synthesized in the royal function. The Brahmins need only exercise an invisible authority, which as such may be unknown to the masses, but which is nonetheless the principle of all visible power. This authority is like the pivot about which all things turn, the fixed axis around which the world accomplishes its revolution, the immutable center that directs and regulates the cosmic movement without participating in it—and it is this that is represented by the ancient symbol of the *swastika*, which for this reason is one of the attributes of *Ganesha*.

It is appropriate to add that in any particular application the place necessarily accorded to action will be greater or lesser according to circumstance, something as true of peoples as it is of individuals, for while the natures of some are above all contemplative, those of others are above all active. And there is undoubtedly no country where the aptitude for contemplation is so widespread and developed as it is in India, which is why the latter may be considered the representative par excellence of the Eastern spirit. Among

Western peoples on the other hand it is quite certain that an aptitude for action predominates among the majority of men, and that even if this tendency were not as exaggerated and deviant as it presently is it would nevertheless persist, so that contemplation could never be more than the affair of a much more limited elite. This however would suffice for a return to order, for unlike material force spiritual power is in no way based on number, but at the present time Westerners are truly but men without caste, none among them occupying the place and function best suiting his nature. And let us not deceive ourselves: this disorder is spreading rapidly and seems to be gaining ground even in the East, which is still affected only in a very superficial and much more limited way than might be imagined by those who, knowing only more or less Westernized Easterners, do not suspect how little importance they really have. Nonetheless there is a real danger, which despite everything is at risk of increasing, at least for a time. The 'Western peril' is not an empty expression, and the West, which is itself its own first victim, seems to wish to drag all of humanity down to that very ruin with which its own error threatens it.

This peril is from action that is disordered because deprived of its principle, such action being in itself but a pure negation that can lead only to catastrophe. Some will say however that if such a thing exists it is because this very disorder must finally return to that universal order of which it is an element just as all the rest, and from a higher point of view this is rigorously true. All beings, whether they know it or not, whether they wish it or not, depend entirely upon their principle in all that they are; disordered action is itself only possible through the principle of all action; but because it is unaware of that principle, because it does not recognize its dependence thereon, it is unregulated and without positive efficacy; and if one may put it so, it possesses only the slightest degree of reality, that nearest to illusion pure and simple, precisely because it is furthest from the principle in which alone absolute reality resides. From the point of view of the principle there is only order; but from the point of view of contingencies disorder exists, and in what concerns earthly humanity, we are in an age where this disorder appears to be triumphing.

One could ask why it is so, and the Hindu doctrine, with its theory of cosmic cycles, furnishes an answer to this question: we are in the *Kali-Yuga*, the dark age when spirituality is reduced to a minimum by the very laws of development of the human cycle, which bring on a sort of progressive materialization through different periods, of which ours is the last, here taking 'human cycle' to mean the duration of a *Manvantara*. Toward the end of this age everything is confused, the castes are mixed, the family itself no longer exists. Is this not exactly what we see around us? Must we conclude from this that the present cycle is effectively drawing to its close and that we shall soon see the dawn of a new *Manvantara*? One could be tempted to believe this, particularly in view of the increasing speed at which events are rushing forward, but perhaps the disorder has not yet reached its final pitch, perhaps humanity must descend yet further into the excesses of a totally material civilization before it can begin a reascent toward the principle and toward spiritual and divine realities. But this is of no great consequence: whether it be a little sooner or a little later, this descending movement that modern Westerners call 'progress' will reach its limit, and the 'dark age' will come to an end; the *Kalki-avatāra* will then appear, he who is mounted on a white horse, bearing on his head a triple crown (token of sovereignty over the three worlds) and holding in his hand a sword flaming like the tail of a comet. The world of disorder and error will then be destroyed, and by the purifying and regenerating power of *Agni* all things will be re-established and restored in the fullness of their primordial state, the end of the present cycle being at the same time the beginning of the future cycle. Those who know that it must be so cannot, even in the midst of the worst confusion, lose their unwavering serenity; regrettable though it may be to live in an age of trouble and or nearly universal darkness, they cannot be affected by it in their inner nature, and this is what constitutes the strength of the true elite. Undoubtedly, if darkness should continue to spread, this elite could be reduced to a very small number, even in the East; but it suffices that some few preserve true knowledge in full so that when the time will have been accomplished, they be ready to save what can still be saved of the present world in order to form the seed of the future one.

At present, the East alone can fulfill the role of conserving the traditional spirit, with all that it really implies when understood in its most profound sense. We do not mean to say the whole of the East, since the disorder encroaching from the West may unfortunately reach it in certain of its elements, but it is only in the East that a true elite still survives, in which the traditional spirit is to be found in all its vitality. What remains of it elsewhere is reduced to exterior forms whose significance has for the most part already been long misunderstood, so that if something of the West can be saved this will only be possible with the aid of the East; yet even so, to be effective this aid will have to find a base of support in the Western world—but about these possibilities it is difficult to furnish precise ideas at present.

However that may be, in a certain sense India alone out of all the East has a privileged position in respect of what we have in mind, since without the traditional spirit India would no longer be anything. Indeed, Hindu unity (we do not say Indian unity) is not a unity of race or language, but exclusively one of tradition: they, and they alone, are Hindu who effectively adhere to that tradition. This explains what we were saying previously about the aptitude for contemplation being more general in India than anywhere else: participation in tradition is indeed only fully effective to the degree that it implies a comprehension of the doctrine, and this doctrine consists primarily of metaphysical knowledge since the principle from which the rest derives is to be found in the purely metaphysical order. That is why India appears more particularly destined to maintain to the very end the supremacy of contemplation over action, to set up through its elite an impassible barrier against the encroachment of the modern Western spirit, to preserve knowledge of the permanent, the immutable, the eternal intact in the midst of a world agitated by incessant change.

Moreover, it must be understood that it is the principle alone that is immutable, and that the applications to which it gives rise in all spheres may and even must vary according to the circumstances and the age, for whereas the principle is absolute, its applications are as relative and as contingent as the world to which they relate. Tradition allows adaptations that are indefinitely multiple and various in their modalities, but all these adaptations, providing they are made rigorously according to the traditional spirit, are nothing other than the normal development of certain of the consequences contained eternally in the principle; in every case it is thus only a matter of making explicit what was hitherto implicit, and so the basis, the very substance of the doctrine, always remains identical under all the differences of exterior form. The applications may be of all kinds; such are notably not only the social institutions already mentioned, but also the sciences, when they are truly what they should be; and this illustrates the essential difference that exists between the idea of these traditional sciences and that of the sciences established by the modern Western mind. Whereas the former take all their value from their connection with metaphysical doctrine, the latter, under the pretext of independence, are narrowly locked in upon themselves and can only attempt to press on ever further, although without reaching outside their narrow domain or extending its limits a single step, in an analytic movement that could continue indefinitely without any advance in the true knowledge of things. Is it by some obscure feeling of this powerlessness that the moderns have come to prefer research to knowledge, or is it simply because this endless research satisfies their need for an incessant agitation that claims to be an end in itself? What could Easterners make of these vain sciences that the West tries to offer them when they themselves possess other sciences incomparably more real and vast, sciences by means of which the least effort of intellectual concentration teaches them much more than all these fragmentary and scattered views, these chaotic masses of facts and notions that are only strung together by more or less imaginary hypotheses laboriously erected only to be immediately overturned and replaced by others that are no better founded? And let no one attempt to compensate for all their shortcomings by boasting inordinately of the industrial and technical applications which have resulted from these sciences, for no one dreams of contesting that they do at least serve this level of practical utility, even if their speculative value is illusory; but this is something that would never truly interest the East, since it places too little value on such altogether material advantages to sacrifice its spirit to them, knowing as it does the immense superiority of the point of view of contemplation over that of action, and that all passing things are as nothing compared with the eternal.

For us then the true India is not that more or less modernized—that is to say, Westernized—India as dreamed of by some young people educated in European and American universities who, however proud they may be of the altogether exterior knowledge they have acquired there, are nonetheless completely ignorant from the Eastern point of view in spite of their pretensions, which constitute the very opposite of what we mean by an intellectual elite. The true India is that which remains ever faithful to the teachings transmitted by its elite over the centuries; it is that which fully preserves the deposit of a tradition reaching back higher and further than humanity; it is the India of *Manu* and of the *Rishis*, the India of Srī Rāma and Srī Krishna. We know that this was not always the region designated by this name today; there is even no doubt that since the primordial Arctic sojourn spoken of in the *Veda* it has successively occupied many different geographical locations, and will perhaps occupy yet others; but this matters little, for it is always there where the seat of this great tradition whose maintenance among men is its mission and its raison d'être is found. In the uninterrupted chain of its Sages, its *Gurus* and its *Yogis*, it subsists through all the vicissitudes of the outer world, as unshakable as *Meru*; it will last as long as the *Sanātana Dharma* (which we could translate as the *Lex perennis*, with as much accuracy as a Western language permits) and it will never cease contemplating all things through the frontal eye of Shiva, in the serene immutability of the eternal present. All hostile efforts will finally be shattered against the single force of truth, just as clouds dissipate before the sun even if they have succeeded momentarily in obscuring it from our gaze. The destructive action of time lets nothing subsist but what is superior to time: it will devour all those who have limited their horizon to the world of change and placed all reality in becoming, those who have made for themselves a religion of the contingent and the transitory, for 'he who sacrifices to a god will become the food of this god'; but what can time do against those who bear within themselves the consciousness of the eternal?

3

𝒦UNDALINĪ YOGA

On several occasions we have mentioned the works of
Arthur Avalon (Sir John Woodroffe) devoted to 'tantrism', one of
the least understood aspects of Hindu doctrine. What is thus called
'tantrism', because it is based on treatises designated by the generic
term *Tantras* (and which is moreover much more widespread and
less confined within narrow circles than is ordinarily believed), has
in fact always been left almost completely to one side by orientalists,
who have been put off both by the difficulty of understanding it and
by certain prejudices—these latter moreover being only the direct
result of their incomprehension. One of the principal of Woodroffe's works, entitled *The Serpent Power*, has recently been republished.[1] We do not propose to offer an analysis of it here, which
would be almost impossible and of little interest besides (it being far
preferable that those of our readers who read English should refer to
the volume itself, of which we could give only an incomplete
impression), but rather to make clear the true meaning of its subject, without restricting ourselves to following the order in which
the material is expounded therein.[2]

It must first of all be said that we are not altogether in agreement
with the author on the fundamental sense of the word *yoga*, which,
since it literally means 'union', would not be comprehensible if it

1. *The Serpent Power* [Madras: Ganesh & Co., 1950, etc.]. This volume includes
the translation of two texts, the *Shatchakra nirūpana* and the *Pādukā-panchaka*,
preceded by the long and important introduction to which our study refers.

2. On many points we cannot do better than refer to our own work *Man and
His Becoming according to the Vedānta* for ampler explanations that could not be
reproduced within the compass of an article, explanations with which we must
consequently suppose the reader to be already familiar.

were not applied essentially to the supreme goal of all 'realization'. To this Woodroffe objects that there can be no question of union except between two distinct beings, and that *jīvātmā* is in no way really distinct from *Paramātmā*. This is perfectly correct, but although the individual is in effect only distinguished from the Universal in illusory mode we must not forget that it is from the individual that all 'realization' necessarily proceeds (the word itself otherwise having no raison d'être), and that from his point of view the latter presents the appearance of a 'union' that in truth is in no way something 'to be accomplished', but only a becoming conscious of 'that which is', that is, the 'Supreme Identity'. A term such as *yoga* therefore expresses the aspect that things assume when seen from the side of manifestation, which is obviously as illusory as is this manifestation itself; but it is inevitably the same with all forms of language since they belong to the domain of individual manifestation, and it is enough to be aware of this not to be drawn into errors by their imperfection, or tempted to see in it the expression of a real 'dualism'. It is only secondarily and by extension that this same word *yoga* can then be applied to the collection of various means set in motion to attain 'realization', means that are only preparatory and to which the name 'union' however understood could not properly fit; but in any case all this in no way affects what is in question here, for from the moment the word *yoga* is preceded by an adjective distinguishing it in some way, it is quite evident that it is only used to designate the means, which are multiple, whereas the goal is necessarily one and the same in all cases.

The type of *yoga* in question is related to what is called *laya-yoga*, which consists essentially in a process of 'dissolution' (*laya*), that is to say, of resorption into the non-manifest of the different elements constitutive of individual manifestation, this resorption being effected gradually according to an order rigorously inverse to the order of the production (*srishti*) or development (*prapañca*) of that same manifestation.[3] The elements or principles involved are the

---

3. It is regrettable that the author frequently uses—and in particular to translate the term *srishti*—the word 'creation', which as we have often explained is not suitable from the point of view of Hindu doctrine. We know only too well how many

tattvas, which *Sānkhya* enumerates as the production of *Prakriti* under the influence of *Purusha:* the 'inner sense', that is, the 'mental' (*manas*), joined to the individual consciousness (*ahankāra*), and, by the intermediation of the latter, with the intellect (*Buddhi*) or *Mahat*); the five *tanmātras* or subtle elementary essences; the five faculties of sensation (*jñānendriyas*) and the five faculties of action (*karmendriyas*);[4] and finally, the five *bhūtas* or corporeal elements.[5] Each *bhūta,* with the *tanmātra* to which it corresponds and the faculties of sensation and action that proceed from the latter, is resorbed in the one immediately preceding it in the order of production in such a way that the order of resorption is as follows: first, earth (*prithivī*) with the olfactory quality (*gandha*), the sense of smell (*ghrāna*), and the faculty of locomotion (*pāda*); second, water (*ap*) with the sapid quality (*rasa*), the sense of taste (*rasana*), and the faculty of prehension (*pāni*); third, fire (*tejas*) with the visual quality (*rūpa*), the sense of sight (*chakshus*), and the faculty of excretion (*pāyu*); fourth, air (*vāyu*) with the tactile quality (*sparsha*), the sense of touch (*tvach*), and the faculty of generation

difficulties are raised by the necessity of using Western terminology, which is as inadequate as may be for what is to be expressed, but we think that this word is nonetheless among those that could be easily enough avoided, and we ourselves have never found occasion to use it. While on this question of terminology, let us also point out the impropriety of translating *samādhi* as 'ecstasy', this latter being all the more irksome as it is normally used in Western languages to designate mystical states, that is to say something of an altogether different order, with which it must not be confused; its etymological signification moreover is 'to go out of oneself' (which suits very well the case of mystical states), whereas what the term *samādhi* designates is quite to the contrary a 'return' of the being into its own Self.

4. The word *indriya* designates both a faculty and its corresponding organ, but it is generally preferable to translate it as 'faculty', first because this is in conformity with its primitive sense—which is that of 'power'—and also because consideration of the faculty is here more essential than that of the corporeal organ by reason of the pre-eminence of subtle manifestation in relation to gross manifestation.

5. We do not really understand the author's objection to the use of the word 'elements', which is the traditional term in ancient physics, to translate *bhūtas;* there is no reason to be preoccupied here with the oblivion into which this meaning has fallen among the moderns, to whom moreover every properly 'cosmological' conception has become similarly foreign.

(*upastha*); fifth, ether (*ākāsha*), with the sonorous quality (*shabda*), the sense of hearing (*shrotra*), and the faculty of speech (*vāch*); and finally, at the last stage, the whole is resorbed in the 'inner sense' (*manas*), all of individual manifestation finding itself thus reduced to its first term and as it were concentrated in a point from which the being passes into another domain. Such then will be the six preparatory degrees that must be successively traversed by the one who follows this way of 'dissolution', freeing himself gradually from the various limiting conditions of individuality before attaining the supra-individual state where effective union with the supreme Self (*Paramātmā*) in Pure Consciousness (*Chit*) is realizable—a union, total and non-formal, from which 'Deliverance' (*Moksha*) immediately results.

To understand clearly what follows, it will be important never to lose sight of the notion of the constitutive analogy of the 'macrocosm' and the 'microcosm', by virtue of which all that exists in the Universe is found also in a certain fashion in man, which the *Vishvasāra Tantra* expresses in this way: 'What is here is there, what is not here is nowhere' (*Yad ihāsti tad anyatra, yan nehāstri na tat kvachit*). It should be added that by reason of the correspondence existing among all states of existence, each one of them contains a reflection of all the others in a certain way, which for example permits 'situating' in the domain of gross manifestation (whether considered in its cosmic totality or in the human body) 'regions' corresponding to diverse modalities of subtle manifestation, and even to a whole hierarchy of 'worlds' representing so many different degrees in universal existence.

This said, it is easy to understand that there are 'centers' in the human being corresponding respectively to each of the groups of *tattvas* enumerated above, and that these centers, although belonging essentially to the subtle form (*sūkshma-sharīra*), may in a certain sense be 'localized' in the corporeal or gross form (*sthūla-sharīra*), or, to put it better, with respect to different parts of the latter, these 'localizations' really being nothing other than a way of expressing correspondences like those just mentioned, correspondences that most truly imply a special link between such a subtle center and such a determinate part of the corporeal organism. In this way the six centers in question are related to the divisions of the vertebral column, called *Meru-danda* because it constitutes the axis of the human body, just as, from the 'macrocosmic' point of view, *Meru* is the 'World Axis':[6] the first five, in ascending direction, correspond respectively to the coccygeal, sacral, lumbar, dorsal, and cervical regions, and the sixth to the encephalic part of the central nervous system; but it must be clearly understood that they are not at all nerve centers in the physiological sense of this word, and that one must not in any way assimilate to different plexuses, as some have tried to do (which is moreover in formal contradiction with their 'localization' inside the vertebral column itself), for here it is not a case of identity but only of a relation between two distinct orders of manifestation, a relation sufficiently justified moreover by the fact that it is precisely by means of the nervous system that one of the most direct connections of the corporeal state with the subtle state is established.[7]

Similarly, the subtle 'channels' (*nādīs*)[8] are no more nerves than they are blood vessels; they are, one may say, 'the lines of direction followed by the vital forces'. Of these 'channels', the three principal ones are *sushumnā* (which occupies the central position), and *iḍā* and *piṅgalā*, or the two *nādīs* on the left and right, the first feminine or negative and the second masculine or positive—these last two thus corresponding to a 'polarization' of the vital currents. *Suṣumnā*

6. It is rather astonishing that the author did not point out the connection between this and the symbolism of the Brahmanic staff (*Brahma-danda*), the more so as he alludes on several occasions to the equivalent symbolism of the caduceus.

7. The author rightly points out how erroneous are the interpretations ordinarily given by Westerners, who, confusing the two orders of manifestation, try to reduce everything in question to a purely anatomical and physiological point of view: the orientalists, ignorant of all traditional science, believe that it is only a case of a more or less fanciful description of certain corporeal organs; the occultists for their part, if they do admit the separate existence of the subtle organism, imagine it as a sort of 'double' of the body subject to the same conditions as the latter, which is hardly more exact and can only end in grossly materialized representations. And regarding this last remark, the author shows in some detail how far the conceptions of the Theosophists, in particular, are from the true Hindu doctrine.

8. In *Man and His Becoming*, Guénon uses the word 'arteries' in referring to the *nādīs*, rather than 'channels'. ED.

is 'located' along the interior of the cerebrospinal axis, extending to the orifice that corresponds to the crown of the head (*Brahma-randhra*); *iḍā* and *piṅgalā* lie outside this same axis, around which they intertwine in a sort of double helical coil ending respectively at the left and right nostrils, and thus linked to the alternating respiration of the one nostril to the other.[9] The 'centers' we have mentioned are situated along the course of the *sushumnā*, or still more exactly within it (for it is described as enclosing two other, even narrower, concentric 'channels' called *vajrā* and *chitrā*);[10] and as *sushumnā* is itself 'localized' in the medullary channel it is quite obvious that there can be no question of any corporeal organs whatsoever.

These centers are called 'wheels' (*chakras*), and are also described as 'lotuses' (*padmas*),[11] each having a definite number of petals (radiating out in the interval comprised between *vajrā* and *chitrā*, that is, within the first and around the second). The six chakras are: *mūlādhāra*, at the base of the vertebral column; *svādhishthāna*, corresponding to the genital region; *manipūra*, to the umbilical region; *anāhata*, to the region of the heart; *vishuddha*, to the region of the throat; *ājñā*, to the region situated between the two eyes, that is, to the 'third eye'; and finally, at the top of the head, around the *Brahma-randhra*, is a seventh 'lotus', *sahasrāra* or the 'lotus of a thousand petals', which is not counted among the *chakras* because,

9. In the symbol of the caduceus the central staff corresponds to *suṣumnā*, and the two serpents to *iḍā* and *piṅgalā*, the latter at times also being represented on the Brahmanic staff by the tracings of two helical lines coiling around each other in inverse directions in such a way as to cross at the level of each of the nodes that mark the different centers. In the cosmic correspondences, *iḍā* is related to the moon, *piṅgalā* to the sun, and *suṣumnā* to the igneous principle; it is interesting to note the connection that this presents with the three 'Great Lights' of Masonic symbolism.

10. It is also said that *suṣumnā* corresponds by its nature to fire, *vajrā* to the sun, and *chitrā* to the moon; the interior of the *suṣumnā*, forming the most central channel, is called *Brahma-nāḍī*.

11. The seven nodes of the Brahmanic staff symbolize the seven 'lotuses'; in the caduceus on the other hand it seems that the terminal knob is to be compared only to *ājñā*, the two wings that accompany it being then identified with the two petals of that 'lotus'.

as we shall subsequently see, as a 'center of consciousness' it is related to a state that is beyond the limits of individuality. According to the descriptions given for meditation (*dhyāna*), each lotus carries in its pericarp the *yantra* or geometric symbol of the corresponding *bhūta*, in which is the *bījamantra* of the latter, supported by its symbolic vehicle (*vāhana*); there too resides a 'deity' (*devatā*) accompanied by a particular *shakti*. The 'deities' that preside over the six *chakras*, and that are nothing other than the 'forms of consciousness' through which the being passes to the corresponding stages, are respectively, in ascending order, *Brahmā*, *Vishnu*, *Rudra*, *Isha*, *Sadāshiva*, and *Shambhu*, who moreover, from the 'macrocosmic' point of view, have their abodes in the six hierarchically superposed 'worlds' (*lokas*): *Bhūloka*, *Bhuvarloka*, *Svarloka*, *Maharloka*, *Janaloka*, and *Tapoloka*. Over *Sahasrāra* presides *Paramashiva*, whose abode is the *Satyaloka*; thus, all these worlds have their correspondences in the 'center of consciousness' of the human being, according to the analogical principle previously indicated. Finally, each one of the petals of the different 'lotuses' bears one of the letters of the Sanskrit alphabet, or perhaps it would be more accurate to say that the petals are the letters themselves;[12] but it would be of little use to enter into more detail on this subject at present, for the necessary elaborations will find their place better in the second part of our study, after we have explained what *Kundalinī* is.

Kundalinī is one aspect of *Shakti* considered as cosmic force; one could say that it is this force itself insofar as it resides in the human being, where it acts as vital force. The name *Kundalinī* signifies that it is represented as coiled about itself like a serpent, and indeed its most general manifestations are effected in the form of a spiral movement developing from a central point that is its 'pole'.[13] The

---

12. The numbers of petals are: 4 for *mūlādhāra*, 6 for *svādhishthāna*, 10 for *maṇipūra*, 12 for *anāhata*, 16 for *vishuddha*, 2 for *ājñā*, making a total of 50, which is also the number of the letters in the Sanskrit alphabet. All the letters are found in *sahasrāra*, each being repeated there 20 times (50 x 20 = 1,000).

13. See what we have said on the subject of the spiral in *The Symbolism of the Cross*, and recall too the figure of the serpent coiled around the 'World Egg' (*Brahmānda*), as also around the *omphalos*, whose precise equivalent we shall discover a little further on. [See *The King of the World*, chap. 9. ED.]

'coiling' symbolizes a state of rest, that of a 'static' energy from which all forms of manifest activity proceed; in other words, all the more or less specialized vital forces constantly in action in the human individuality under its double subtle and corporeal modality are only secondary aspects of that same *Shakti* which in itself, as *Kundalinī*, remains immobile in the 'center-root' (*mūlādhāra*), as base and support of the whole individual manifestation. When 'wide-awake' it uncoils and moves in an ascending direction, resorbing into itself the various secondary *Shaktis* as it crosses the different centers mentioned earlier, until it finally unites itself with *Paramashiva* in the 'lotus of a thousand petals' (*sahasrāra*).

The nature of *Kundalinī* is described as being at once luminous (*jyotirmayī*) and sonorous (*shabdamayī* or *mantramayī*); we know that 'luminosity' is considered as properly characterizing the subtle state, and also that sound plays a primordial role in the cosmogonic process. From the same cosmogonic point of view there would also be much to say on the close connection that exists between sound and light.[14] At present we cannot elaborate on the very complex theory of sound (*shabda*) and its different modalities (*parā* or non-manifested, *pashyantī* and *madhyamā*, both belonging to the subtle order, and finally *vaikharī*, which is articulated speech), a theory on which the entire science of the *mantra* (*mantra-vidyā*) rests; but we do point out that this is what explains not only the presence of the *bīja-mantras* of the elements within the 'lotuses' but also the presence of the letters on their petals. In fact, it must be clearly understood that here it is not a matter of letters as written characters, nor even of articulated sounds perceived by the ear, but of letters regarded as the *bījamantras* or 'natural names' of all the activities (*kriyā*) connected with the *tattva* of the corresponding center, or as the expressions in gross sound (*vaikharīshabda*) of the subtle sounds produced by the forces that constitute these activities.

14. On this point we shall only call to mind by way of a particularly striking concordance the identification established at the beginning of the Gospel of Saint John between the terms *Verbum, Lux,* and *Vita,* making it clear that, to be fully understood, it must be compared to the world of the *Hiranyagarbha.* [See *Perspectives on Initiation,* chap. 47. ED.]

Insofar as it remains in its state of repose *Kundalinī* resides in the *mūlādhāra chakra*, which, as we have said, is the center 'localized' at the base of the vertebral column, and which is the root (*mūla*) of *sushumnā* and all the *nādīs*. Here is found the triangle (*trikona*) called *Tripura*,[15] which is the seat of the *shakti* (*shaktipītha*); the latter is there coiled three and half times[16] around the symbolic *linga* of *Shiva*, designated as *Svayambhu*, covering with its head the *Brahma-dvāra*, that is, the entrance of *sushumnā*.[17] There are two other *lingas*, one (*Bāna*) in the *anāhata chakra* and the other (*Itara*) in the *ājnā chakra*, corresponding to the principal 'vital nodes' (*granthis*) the crossing of which constitutes what may be called the 'critical points' in the process of *Kundalinī-yoga*;[18] and finally there is a fourth (*Para*) in *sahasrāra*, abode of *Paramashiva*.

When *Kundalinī* is 'awakened' by the appropriate practices which we shall not take the time to describe here, it penetrates into the interior of the *sushumnā* and during its ascent successively 'pierces' the different 'lotuses' which unfold at its passing; as we have already said, when it reaches each center it resorbs into itself, the various

15. The triangle, as *yantra* of the *Shakti*, is always figured with the base above and the apex below; it would be easy to show its similarity with a number of other symbols of the feminine principle.

16. In passing let us note an analogy between these three and a half turns of the coil of the *Kundalinī* and the three and a half days during which, in various traditions, the spirit remains attached to the body after death, and which represent the time necessary for the 'unraveling' of the vital force that remains in the 'unawakened' state in the case of ordinary man. One day is a cyclical revolution corresponding to a coil in the spiral, and—the process of resorption always being the inverse of that of manifestation—this uncoiling is considered as summing up in a way the whole life of the individual, but the return is made going back along the course of the events that constituted it, to which we hardly need add that these ill-understood details have often given rise to all sorts of fantastic interpretations.

17. The *mandala* or *yantra* of the element *Prithivi* is a square, corresponding as a plane figure to the cube, whose form symbolizes the ideas of 'foundation' and 'stability'; one could say, in the language of the Islamic tradition, that we have here a correspondence with the 'black stone', equivalent to the Hindu *linga* as well and also to the *omphalos*, which, as we have shown elsewhere, is one of the symbols of the 'center of the world' [see The *King of the World*, chap. 9].

18. According to the state of development of the being, these three *lingas* also relate to the different locations of the *luz* or 'kernel of immortality' discussed in *The King of the World* [chap. 7].

principles of individual manifestation specially linked to that center, which, thus brought back to the potential state, are drawn along in its movement toward the superior center. These are so many stages of *laya-yoga*, to each of which is also related the acquisition of various 'powers' (*siddhis*), but it is important to note that this does not at all constitute what is essential, something we cannot overstress inasmuch as the general tendency of Westerners is to attribute to these kinds of things, as indeed to all 'phenomena', an importance which in reality they cannot have. Thus, as the author very correctly points out, the *yogi* (or more precisely he who is on the way to becoming one) does not aspire to possess any conditioned state, no matter how superior or 'celestial' it may be, no matter how elevated it may be, but aspires only to 'Deliverance'—for all the more reason then he cannot become attached to 'powers' whose exercise comes entirely from the domain of the most outward manifestation. He who seeks these 'powers' for their own sake and makes of them the goal of his development rather than seeing in them only simple, accidental results, will never be a true *yogi*, for they will constitute for him impassible obstacles hindering him from continuing to follow the ascending way to its final end. His entire 'realization' will therefore only ever consist of certain extensions of human individuality, a result whose value is strictly nil with respect to the supreme goal. The 'powers' in question are normally only regarded as signs indicating that the being has effectively reached a particular stage, in this way providing as it were an exterior means of assessment; but what really matters, at whatever stage it may be, is a certain 'state of consciousness' represented as we have said by a 'deity' (*devatā*) with which the being is identified at that degree of 'realization'; and these states themselves are valid only as a gradual preparation for the supreme 'union', which has no common measure with them since there can be no common measure between the conditioned and the unconditioned.

We shall not here repeat the enumeration that we have already given in the first part of this study of the centers corresponding to the five *bhūtas*, and of their respective 'localizations';[19] they relate to

---

19. It is important to note that *anāhata*, referring to the region of the heart, must be distinguished from the eight-petaled 'lotus of the heart', which is the abode

the different degrees of corporeal manifestation, and in the passage from one to the other each group of *tattvas* is 'dissolved' into the group immediately above, the more gross always being resorbed into the more subtle (*sthūlānām sūkṣma laya*). And lastly comes the *ājñā chakra*, where are found the subtle *tattvas* of the 'mental' order in the pericarp of which is the sacred monosyllable OM, this center being so named because here the command (*ājñā*) of the inner Guru, who is *Paramashiva*, with whom the 'Self' is in reality identical, is received from above (that is to say from the supra-individual domain).[20] The 'localization' of this *chakra* is in direct relation with the 'third eye', the 'eye of Knowledge' (*jñāna-chakshus*), the corresponding cerebral center being the pineal gland, which is definitely not the 'seat of the soul'—following the truly absurd conception of Descartes—but which nonetheless plays a particularly important role as a connecting organ with the extra-corporeal modalities of the human being. As we have explained elsewhere, the function of the 'third eye' refers essentially to the 'sense of eternity' and the restoration of the 'primordial state' (we have repeatedly noted its relationship with *Hamsa*, under whose form *Paramashiva* is said be manifested at this center); the stage of 'realization' corresponding to the *ājñā chakra* thus implies the perfection of the human state, the point of contact with the superior states to which everything that lies beyond this stage is related.[21]

---

of *Purusha*: this latter is 'located' in the heart itself, considered as the 'vital center' of the individuality.

20. This command corresponds to the 'celestial mandate' of the Far-Eastern tradition; moreover, the term *ājñā chakra* could be rendered exactly in Arabic by *maqām al-amr*, indicating that here is the direct reflection in the human being, of the 'world' called *'ālam al-amr*, just as, from the 'macrocosmic' point of view, this reflection in our state of existence is located in the central place of the 'Terrestrial Paradise'; from this one could even deduce precise considerations on the modality of 'angelic' manifestations in relation to man, but this would lead us away from our subject entirely.

21. The vision of the 'third eye', by which the being is set free from the temporal condition (and which has nothing in common with the 'clairvoyance' of occultists and Theosophists), is intimately linked to the 'prophetic' function; this is what the Sanskrit word *rishi* alludes to, which word properly signifies 'seer', and has its exact equivalent in the Hebrew *roeh*, the ancient designation of the prophets, later replaced by the word *nābi* (that is, 'he who speaks by inspiration'). And let us add,

Above *ājñā* are two secondary *chakras* called *manas* and *soma*;[22] and in the pericarp of *sahasrāra* itself is yet another 'lotus' of twelve petals, containing the supreme triangle *Kāmakalā*, which is the abode of the *Shakti*.[23] *Shabdabrahma*, that is to say the 'causal' and non-manifested state of sound (*shabda*), is represented by *Kāma-kalā*, the 'root' (*mūla*) of all the *mantras*, of which the lower correspondence (which can be considered as its reflection with respect to gross manifestation) is found in the triangle *Tripura* of *mūlādhāra*. We cannot think of entering into the details of the very complex descriptions that are given of these various centers of meditation, and which relate for the most part to the *mantravidyā*, nor of the enumeration of the various *shaktis* that have their 'seats' between *ājnā* and *sahasrāra*. Finally, *sahasrāra* is called *Shivasthāna* because it is the abode of *Paramashiva* in union with the supreme *Nirvāna Shakti*, the 'Mother of the three worlds'; it is the 'abode of beatitude', where the 'Self' (*Ātmā*) is realized. He who truly and fully knows *sahasrāra* is liberated from 'transmigration' (*samsāra*), for by this very knowledge he has broken all the bonds that tied him to it, and from that moment has attained the state of *jīvanmukta*.

We shall conclude with an observation that we believe has never before been made anywhere, which concerns the concordance of the centers here in question with the *Sephiroth* of the Kabbalah, for like all things these latter must have their correspondence in the human being. One could object that the *Sephiroth* are ten in number, whereas the six *chakras* and *sahasrāra* make a total of only seven; but this objection falls when one observes that in the disposition of the 'sephirothic tree' there are three pairs placed symmetrically on the right and left 'columns', so that all the *Sephiroth* together are distributed on only seven different levels; viewing their projections on the central axis or 'middle column', which corresponds to the *sushumnā*

---

without however dwelling upon it, that what we are pointing out in this as in the preceding note, is related to the esoteric interpretation of the *Sūrat Al Qadr*, concerning the 'descent of the Koran'.

22. These two *chakras* are represented as 'lotuses' of six and sixteen petals respectively.

23. One of the reasons why the *Shakti* is symbolized by a triangle is the triplicity of its manifestation as Will (*Ichchhā*), Action (*Kriyā*), and Knowledge (*Jñāna*).

(the two lateral 'columns' being related to *iḍā* and *piṇgalā*), we find ourselves indeed brought back to the septenary.[24]

By beginning at the top, there is at first no difficulty as concerns the assimilation of *sahasrāra*, 'located' at the crown of the head, to the supreme *Sephirah—Kether—*whose name means precisely 'crown'. Then comes the pair *Hokmah* and *Binah*, which must correspond to *ājñā* and whose duality could even be represented by the two petals of that 'lotus'; moreover, they have as 'resultant' *Da'ath*, that is, 'knowledge', and we have seen that the 'localization' of *ājñā* also refers to the 'eye of knowledge'.[25] As regards man, the following pair, that is, *Hesed* and *Geburah*, can be linked to the two arms,[26] according to a very general symbolism concerning the attributes of 'Mercy' and 'Justice'; these two *Sephiroth* will thus be placed at the two shoulders, and consequently on a level with the region of the throat, and so correspond to *vishuddha*.[27] As for *Tifereth*, its central position obviously refers to the heart, which immediately shows its correspondence to *anāhata*. The pair *Netsah* and *Hod* will be placed at the hips, the points at which the lower limbs are attached, as are *Hesed* and *Geburah*, at the shoulders, the points where the upper limbs are attached; now the hips are on a level with the umbilical region, thus of *manipūra*. Finally, as regards the last two *Sephiroth*, it seems there is cause to envisage an inversion, for *Yesod*, according to

24. One will note the similarity of the symbolism of the 'sephirothic tree' with that of the caduceus, following what we have noted above; moreover, the different 'channels' linking the *Sephiroth* among themselves are not without analogy with the *nāḍīs* (this, of course, as concerns the particular application that can be made of it to the human being).

25. The pair *Hokmah* and *Binah* can moreover be placed in a symbolic relationship with the two eyes, right and left—a 'microcosmic' correspondence of sun and moon.

26. See what we have said in *The King of the World* concerning the symbolism of the two hands, in relation precisely with the *Shekinah* (whose relation with the Hindu *Shakti* we mention in passing) and the 'sephirothic tree'.

27. The two shoulders are also where in Islamic tradition stand the two angels charged with recording, respectively, man's good and bad actions, and who also represent the divine attributes of 'Mercy' and 'Justice'. And on this subject let us note further that one could analogously 'situate' in the human being the symbolic figure of the 'scales' spoken of in the *Siphra Di-Tzeniutha* [See *Traditional Forms and Cosmic Cycles*, pt. 3, chap. 5, and *The King of the World*, chap. 10. ED.]

the very significance of its name, is the 'foundation', which exactly corresponds to *mūlādhāra*. It would then be necessary to assimilate *Malkuth* to *svādhishthāna*, which moreover the meaning of the names seems to justify, for *Malkuth* is the 'kingdom' and *svā-dhistāna* literally means 'the proper abode' of the *Shakti*.

Despite the length of this account, we have only sketched some aspects of a subject that is truly inexhaustible, thereby hoping only to have been able to offer some useful clarifications to those who would wish to carry its study further.

4

THE HINDU THEORY
OF THE FIVE ELEMENTS

In Hindu doctrine the 'cosmological' point of view is represented principally by *Vaisheshika*, and also, under a different
aspect, by the *Sānkhya*, the latter being characterizable as 'synthetic'
and the former as 'analytic'. The name *Vaisheshika* is derived from
vishesa, meaning 'distinctive character' and hence 'individual thing';
it therefore properly designates the branch of doctrine that applies
to the knowledge of things in distinct and individual mode. This
point of view corresponds most exactly to what the Greeks, especially during the 'pre-Socratic' period, called 'natural philosophy',
although one must not forget the unavoidable differences in the
respective modes of thought of the two peoples. We however prefer
to use the term 'cosmology' in order to avoid all ambiguity, and to
better indicate the profound difference that exists between what is
here in question and modern physics—it being in just this way
moreover that 'cosmology' was understood in the Middle Ages of
the West.

Including in its subject matter what pertains to sensible or corporeal things, which are of an eminently individual order, the
Vaisheshika applied itself to the theory of the elements—which are
the constitutive principles of bodies—in more detail than have
other branches of Hindu doctrine; it is to be noted however that one
is obliged to have recourse to these latter, and especially to the
Sānkhya, when it is a question of determining which among them
are the most universal principles, those from which the elements
proceed. According to Hindu doctrine there are five elements, called
in Sanskrit *bhūtas*, a word derived from the verbal root *bhū*, which
means 'to be', but more particularly in the sense of 'to subsist', that is

to say designating the manifested being envisaged in its 'substantial' aspect (the 'essential' aspect being expressed by the root *as*); consequently a certain suggestion of 'becoming' also attaches to this word, for it is the aspect of 'substance' that is the root of all 'becoming', as opposed to the immutability of 'essence'; and it is in this sense that *Prakriti*, or 'universal substance', can be properly designated as 'Nature', a word that, precisely by its etymological derivation, above all implies this same idea of 'becoming'—as does its Greek equivalent *physis*. The elements are thus regarded as substantial determinations, or in other words as modifications of *Prakriti*, modifications moreover that have only a purely accidental character with respect to the latter, just as corporeal existence itself, insofar as it is a modality defined by a certain ensemble of determined conditions, is nothing more than a simple accident in relation to universal Existence envisaged in its fullness.

If in respect of the being we now consider the 'essence' correlatively to the 'substance', these two aspects being complementary to one another and corresponding to what we can call the two poles of universal manifestation (which amounts to saying that they are the respective expressions of *Purusha* and *Prakriti* in this manifestation), it is necessary that these substantial determinations, which are the five elements, should correspond to an equal number of essential determinations or 'elementary essences', which one could say are their 'archetypes', their ideal or 'formal' principles in the Aristotelian sense, belonging no longer to the corporeal domain but to the domain of subtle manifestation. And indeed this is how the *Sānkhya* considers the five elementary essences, which are given the name *tanmātras*, the name signifying literally a 'measure' or an 'assignment' delimiting the proper domain of a certain quality or 'quiddity' in universal Existence. It goes without saying that these *tanmātras*, by the very fact that they are of the subtle order, are in no way perceptible to the senses, unlike the corporeal elements and their combinations; they are only 'conceivable' ideally, and cannot receive particular designations except by analogy with the different orders of sensible qualities that correspond to them, since here it is the quality that is the contingent expression of the essence. In fact, they are habitually designated by the very names of these qualities:

auditive or sonorous (*shabda*), tangible (*sparsha*), visible (*rūpa*, with the double meaning of form and color), sapid (*rasa*), and olfactive (*gandha*); but we say that these designations must not be taken as analogical, for here these qualities can only be envisaged in the principial state—and as it were 'non-developed'—since, as we shall see, it is only through the *bhūtas* that they will be effectively manifested in the sensible order. The idea of *tanmātras* is necessary when one wants to link the notion of elements to the principles of universal Existence, to which moreover they still do relate, but this time from the 'substantial' side through another order of considerations which we shall discuss in due course; but on the other hand this idea clearly has no place when we confine ourselves to the study of individual existences and of sensible qualities as such, and that is why there is no question of this in the *Vaisheshika*, which by very definition places itself precisely at this last point of view.

We will recall that the five elements recognized by Hindu doctrine are the following: *ākāsha*, ether; *vāyu*, air; *tejas*, fire; *ap*, water; *prithivī*, earth. This is the order of their development or of their differentiation starting from ether, which is the primordial element; this is always the order of their enumeration in any text of the *Veda* in which they are mentioned, notably in the passages from the *Chāndogya Upanishad* and the *Taittirīya Upanishad* where their genesis is described, and their order of resorption or of return to the undifferentiated state is naturally inverse to the former. Moreover, to each element there corresponds a sensible quality that is regarded as its proper quality, that which manifests its essential nature and by which the latter is made known to us; and the correspondence thus established between the five elements and the five senses is as follows: to ether corresponds hearing (*shrotra*); to air, touch (*vāch*); to fire, sight (*chakshus*); to water, taste (*rasana*); and to earth, smell (*ghrāna*)—the order of development of the senses also being that of the elements to which they are linked and on which they directly depend. And this order of course conforms to the order already enumerated above for the sensible qualities by relating them principially to the *tanmātras*. In addition, every quality manifested in one element is manifested equally in those following it, no longer as belonging to them in their own right, but insofar as they proceed from the preceding elements—after all, it would be contradictory to suppose that the very process of development of manifestation, effectuated thus by degrees, could, for what has already been developed in the stages of lesser differentiation, bring about at a later stage a return to the non-manifested state.

Before proceeding further we should point to certain important differences with the theories of those Greek 'natural philosophers' to whom we alluded at the beginning concerning the number of the elements and their order of derivation as well as their correspondence with the sensible qualities. First of all, most of these latter admitted only four elements, not recognizing ether as a distinct element, and in this—a rather curious fact—they agree with the Jains and the Buddhists, who on this point as well as on many others stand opposed to orthodox Hindu doctrine. There are some exceptions however, notably Empedocles, who admitted the five elements but set forth in the following order: ether, fire, earth, water, and air, which seems scarcely justifiable; and yet according to some[1] this philosopher too would not have admitted more than four elements, which are then enumerated in a different order: earth, water, air, and fire. This latter order is exactly the inverse of that found in Plato, so that here one must no longer see the order of production of the elements but, on the contrary, the order of their resorption into each other. According to diverse testimonies, the Orphics and the Pythagoreans recognized the five elements, which is perfectly normal given the properly traditional character of their doctrines, and later on, Aristotle admitted them as well. However that may be, the role of ether has never been as important or as sharply defined among the Greeks, at least in their exoteric schools, as among the Hindus. In spite of certain passages from the *Phaedo* and the *Timaeus*, which are undoubtedly of Pythagorean inspiration, Plato generally envisages only four elements: for him, fire and earth are the extreme elements, air and water the middle elements, which differs from the traditional order of the Hindus in that air and fire are inverted. We may wonder if here we do not see a confusion between the order of production (if indeed this is really how Plato himself

---

1. Struve, *De Elementis Empedoclis.*

meant it) and distribution according to what could be called degrees of subtlety, a subject moreover to which we shall presently return. Plato agrees with the Hindu doctrine in attributing visibility to fire as its proper quality, but he diverges from it in attributing tangibility to earth instead of air; besides, it seems quite difficult to find among the Greeks a correspondence rigorously established between the elements and the sensible qualities, which is easy enough to understand since if one considers only four elements one must immediately notice the gap in that correspondence, the number five being in other respects everywhere uniformly admitted as concerns the senses.

In Aristotle one finds considerations of a very different kind, for although he was also concerned with qualities, these for him were not sensible qualities properly speaking. His views were in fact based on the combinations of hot and cold, which are respectively the principles of expansion and condensation, with dry and moist: fire is hot and dry, air is hot and moist; water is cold and moist, earth cold and dry. The groupings of these four qualities in opposing pairs therefore concern only the four ordinary elements, ether being excluded—which moreover is justified by the observation that the latter, as a primordial element, must comprise in itself the groups of opposing or complementary qualities thus coexisting in a neutral state insofar as they are perfectly balanced by one another prior to their differentiation, which may be regarded as resulting precisely from a rupture in that original equilibrium.

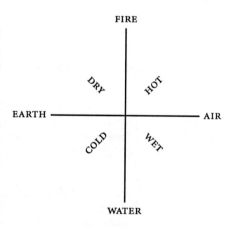

Ether must therefore be represented as situated at the point where oppositions do not yet exist, but from which these latter arise, that is to say at the center of the figure of the cross, whose branches correspond to the other four elements; and this representation is indeed what was adopted by the Hermeticists of the Middle Ages, by whom the ether was expressly recognized under the name 'quintessence' (*quinta essentia*), which moreover implies an enumeration of the elements in an ascending or 'regressive' order, that is, an order inverse to that of their production—for otherwise ether would be the first element and not the fifth. One may also note that in reality we have here a question of a 'substance' and not of an 'essence', and in this respect the expression illustrates a confusion frequent in medieval Latin terminology, where this distinction between 'essence' and 'substance', in the sense indicated, seems never to have been made very clearly, as can be observed only too easily in scholastic philosophy.[2]

While on the subject of comparisons we would also do well to be on guard against a false assimilation which Chinese doctrine sometimes occasions, for one also finds therein something customarily designated as the 'five elements', which are enumerated thus: water, wood, fire, earth, and metal, the order here again being envisaged as that of their production. What can be misleading is that the number is the same in both cases, and that, of five terms, three bear equivalent names. But to what might the other two correspond, and how can one make the order here indicated coincide with that of Hindu doctrine?[3] The truth is that in spite of the apparent similarities it is really a question of an entirely different point of view which, moreover, it would be irrelevant to examine at present; and to avoid all confusion it would certainly be very much preferable to

---

2. In the diagram placed at the head of Leibnitz' treatise *De Arte Combinatoria*, which reflects the Hermeticists' conception, the 'quintessence' is figured at the center of the cross of elements—or, if one prefers, of the double cross of elements and qualities—by a rose of five petals, in this way forming the Rosicrucian symbol. The expression *quinta essentia* can also be related to the 'quintuple nature of ether', which must be understood not as five different 'ethers', as certain moderns have imagined (which is in contradiction with the indifferentiation of the primordial element), but as ether envisaged in itself and as principle of the four other elements, this moreover being the alchemical interpretation of the five-petaled rose under discussion.

3. These 'five elements' are arranged according to the figure of a cross formed by the double opposition of water and fire, wood and metal; but the center is occupied by earth.

translate the Chinese term *hing* by something other than 'elements', by 'agents' for example, as has been suggested,[4] which at the same time is closer to its real meaning.

Having made these remarks, if we now wish to make the notion of the elements more precise, we must first rule out several erroneous opinions widespread in our day—although without stressing the point unduly. In the first place, it need hardly be said that if the elements are the constitutive principles of bodies, this is in a very different sense from that envisaged by chemists when they consider these bodies as resulting from the combination of certain 'simple substances' or some such thing: on the one hand, the multiplicity of substances called 'simple' is manifestly opposed to such an assimilation, and on the other it is not at all proven that there are any truly simple substances, this name in fact being given only to those substances that chemists cannot break down further. In any case, the elements are not material substances, even simple ones, but rather the substantial principles from which such substances are formed; and one must not be deceived by the fact that they are designated analogously by names that can be used simultaneously of certain material substances, to which they are in no way identical for all that, since each of the latter, whichever it may be, in reality proceeds from the group of five elements, although there may be in its nature a certain predominance of one or another element.

More recently, some have also wished to assimilate the elements to the different physical states of matter as understood by modern physicists, that is, to the different degrees of its condensation from the homogeneous, primordial ether that fills all space, thus uniting all the parts of the corporeal world. From this point of view, and proceeding from the denser to the more subtle (that is, in an order inverse to that accepted for their differentiation) they draw correspondences between earth and the solid state, water and the liquid state, air and the gaseous state, and fire and a still more rarefied state rather similar to what certain physicists have called the 'radiant state', and which should then be distinguished from the etheric state. Here again one finds the vain preoccupation so common

4. Marcel Granet, *La Pensée chinoise* [Paris: A. Michel, 1988], p313.

today of trying to reconcile traditional ideas with profane scientific conceptions, which is not to say however that such a point of view may not contain some degree of truth in the sense that one may concede that each of these physical states has certain more particular ties to a specific element; but this is at most only a correspondence and not an assimilation, which would moreover be incompatible with the persistent coexistence of all the elements in a given body, in whatever state it appears; and it would be even less legitimate to want to go further than to attempt to identify the elements with the sensible qualities that, from another point of view, are related to them much more directly. On the other hand, the order of increasing condensation thus established among the elements is the same as that found in Plato: he places fire before air and immediately after ether, as if it were the first element to differentiate itself at the heart of that original cosmic milieu; and so it is not in this way that we can find the justification for the traditional order affirmed by Hindu doctrine. Moreover one must always take the greatest care to avoid holding exclusively to one point of view that is overly systematic, that is, too narrowly limited and particularized; and we would assuredly misunderstand Aristotle's theory, and that of the Hermeticists to whom we have alluded, if, under the pretext that it invokes the principle of condensation and expansion, we sought to interpret it in favor of an identification of the elements with the various physical states just now in question.

If one absolutely insists on looking for a point of comparison with physical theories, in the current meaning of the word, it would undoubtedly be more correct to consider the elements—in referring to their correspondence with the sensible qualities—as representing different vibratory modalities of matter, modalities under which matter becomes perceptible to each of our senses successively; and when we say 'successively' it must be clearly understood that here we mean only a purely logical succession.[5] But when one speaks of the

5. It goes without saying that by positing a chronological succession in the exercise of the different senses one cannot in any way hope to realize a conception such as that of the ideal statue Condillac imagined in his too famous *Traité des Sensations*.

vibratory modalities of matter, as well as when one speaks of physical states, it must be carefully observed that at least among the Hindus (and for the most part among the Greeks) one does not find the notion of matter in the sense used by modern physicists, the proof being that, as we have already pointed out elsewhere, Sanskrit has no word that may even approximately be translated as 'matter'. If then there is some justification in using this notion of matter to interpret the conceptions of the ancients in an effort to make them better understood, one must always do so with certain precautions. Still, it is possible to envisage vibratory states, for example, without necessarily appealing to the special properties that the moderns attribute essentially to matter. Nonetheless, such a conception seems to us still more appropriate to indicate by analogy what the elements are (aided in this by a manner of speaking that makes use of a certain imagery so to speak) than to truly define them; and this perhaps is all that it is possible to do in the language presently at our disposal, owing to the oblivion into which traditional ideas have fallen in the Western world.

However, we should add that in relation to our human individuality, sensible qualities express the conditions characterizing and determining corporeal existence as a particular mode of universal Existence, since it is by these qualities that we know a body to the exclusion of every other thing; we can therefore see in the elements the expression of those same conditions of corporeal existence, no longer from the human, but from the cosmic point of view. It is not possible for us to develop this question adequately here, but this can at least lead to an understanding of how the sensible qualities proceed from the elements as a translation or 'microcosmic' reflection of corresponding 'macrocosmic' realities, and also how bodies, being specifically defined by the totality of the conditions in question, are thereby constituted as such by the elements in which they 'substantialize' themselves. And this, it seems, is at once the most exact and most general notion one may give of these same elements.

We now move on to other considerations that will show better still how the conception of the elements relates not only to the special conditions of corporeal existence, but also to conditions of existence of a more universal order, and, more precisely, to the very conditions of all manifestation. We know what importance Hindu doctrine accords the consideration of the three *gunas*: this term designates the qualities, or constitutive and primordial attributes, of beings envisaged in their different states of manifestation, which they hold from the 'substantial' principle of their existence—for from the universal point of view these qualities are inherent to *Prakriti*, in which they exist in perfect equilibrium in the 'indistinction' of pure undifferentiated potentiality. All manifestation or modification of 'substance' represents a rupture of that equilibrium. Manifested beings therefore participate in the three *gunas* to various degrees, and these are not states but general conditions to which they are subject in their state—by which they are in a way bound—and which determine the present tendency of their 'becoming'. We need not enter into a full exposition of the *gunas* here, but only to envisage their application to the distinction of the elements. We will not even repeat the definition of each *guna*, which we have already given on several occasions, but merely recall—for this is what is most important here—that *sattva* is represented as an ascending tendency, *tamas* as a descending tendency, and *rajas*, which is intermediate between the two, as horizontal expansion.

The three *gunas* must be found in each of the elements, as in all things that belong to the domain of universal manifestation, but they occur in them in different proportions, establishing among these elements a sort of hierarchy that may be regarded as analogous to that hierarchy which from another and incomparably more extensive point of view is similarly established among the multiple states of universal Existence, although here it is a case only of simple modalities comprised in the interior of one and the same state. In water and earth, but especially in earth, it is *tamas* that predominates; physically, gravity or weight corresponds to this descending and compressive force. *Rajas* predominates in air, which is why this element is regarded as endowed essentially with a transverse movement. In fire it is *sattva* that predominates, for fire is the luminous element, the ascending force being symbolized by the tendency of the flame to rise, and it is represented physically by the dilating power of heat insofar as this power opposes the condensation of bodies.

To give a more precise interpretation of this, we can represent the distinctions among the elements as being operative inside a sphere: within this sphere the two tendencies we have mentioned—the ascending and the descending—will be exerted according to the two opposite directions taken on the same vertical axis, each contrary to the other and proceeding respectively to the two poles; as for horizontal expansion, which marks an equilibrium between these two tendencies, it will naturally occur on the perpendicular plane at the middle of this vertical axis, that is, the equatorial plane. If we now consider the elements as being distributed in this sphere according to the tendencies that predominate in them, earth, by virtue of the descending tendency of gravitation, must occupy the lowest point, which is regarded as the region of darkness and is at the same time the depths of the waters, whereas the equator marks their surface, according to a symbolism common to all cosmogonic doctrines, to whatever traditional form they may belong. Water therefore occupies the lower hemisphere, and although the descending tendency is still affirmed in the nature of this element, we cannot say that its action operates in an exclusive fashion therein (or even a nearly exclusive fashion, since the necessary coexistence of the three *gunas* in all things prevents the extreme limit from ever being effectively reached in any mode of manifestation whatsoever), for if we consider any given point of the lower hemisphere other than the pole, the radius corresponding to this point has an oblique direction, intermediate between the descending vertical and the horizontal. We can thus regard the tendency marked by such a direction as being resolved into two others, of which it is the resultant, and these will be respectively

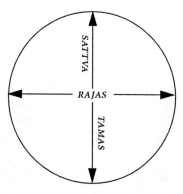

the action of *tamas* and of *rajas*; if we relate these two actions to the qualities of water, the vertical component, as a function of *tamas*, will correspond to density, and the horizontal aspect, as a function of *rajas*, to fluidity. The equator marks the intermediate region, which is that of air, the neutral element that maintains equilibrium between the two opposing tendencies (as does *rajas* between *tamas* and *sattva*) at the place where these two tendencies neutralize one another, and which, extending transversely on the surface of the waters, separates and delimits the respective zones of water and fire. Indeed, the upper hemisphere is occupied by fire, in which the action of *sattva* predominates, although that of *rajas* still operates, for the tendency at every point of this hemisphere is intermediate, as indicated previously of the lower hemisphere, but in this instance between the horizontal and the ascendant vertical. As a function of *rajas*, the horizontal component will here correspond to heat, and the vertical component, as a function of *sattva*, to light, inasmuch as heat and light are envisaged as complementary terms united in the nature of the igneous element.

But we have not yet spoken of ether. Since it is the highest and most subtle of all the elements, it must be placed at the highest point, that is, at the superior pole, which is the region of pure light, as contrasted to the lower pole, which as we have said is the region of darkness. Ether thus dominates the sphere of the other elements but at the same time is to be regarded as enveloping and penetrating all those elements, whose principle it is by reason of the state of indifferentiation that characterizes it, and which allows it to realize a true 'omnipresence' in the corporeal world. As Shaṇkarāchārya says in *Ātmā-Bodha*: 'ether prevails everywhere, and it penetrates both the outside and the inside of things.' We can thus say that of the elements ether alone attains the point where the action of *sattva* operates at the highest degree, although we must not localize it

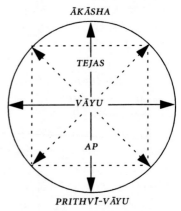

there exclusively as we did for earth at the opposite point, but consider it rather as occupying at the same time the totality of the elementary domain, whatever the geometric representation used to symbolize the entirety of this domain may be. If we have opted to represent it with a spherical figure this is not only because it is the one that allows the easiest and clearest interpretation but also, and even primarily, because it agrees better than any other with the general principles of cosmogonic symbolism such as can be found in all traditions; there would be some very interesting comparisons to make in this regard, but we cannot broach them here, as this would lead us too far from the subject of the present study.

Before leaving this part of our account it should be noted that if we take the elements in the order in which we have distributed them in the first spherical figure, that is, proceeding top to bottom from the most subtle to the most dense, we once again meet precisely the order indicated by Plato; but this order, which we may call hierarchical, is not to be confused with the order of production of the elements, and must be carefully distinguished therefrom. Indeed, in the first case air occupies a rank intermediate between fire and water, but it is nonetheless produced before fire, and in truth the reason for these two locations is basically the same: air is as it were a neutral element and thus corresponds to a state of less differentiation than fire and water, for the ascending and descending tendencies are in perfect balance. Conversely, in fire this equilibrium is broken to the advantage of the ascending tendency, and in water to the advantage of the descending tendency; and the obvious opposition between the respective qualities of these two elements clearly marks the state of greatest differentiation to which they correspond. If one adopts the point of view of the production of the elements, their differentiation must be regarded as being effected from the center of the sphere, the primordial point where ether insofar as it is their principle must then be placed; from thence we have in the first place the horizontal expansion corresponding to air, then the manifestation of the ascending tendency corresponding to fire, and that of the descending tendency corresponding first to water and then to earth, which is the stopping-point and final end of differentiation of all the elements.

We must now enter into some detail as to the properties of each of the five elements, and shall immediately begin by establishing that the first of them, *ākāsha* or ether, is indeed a real element distinct from the others. Indeed, as we have already pointed out above, some, notably the Buddhists, do not recognize it as such, and under the pretext that it is *nirūpa* or 'without form' by reason of its homogeneity, regard it as a 'nonentity' and identify it with the void, for to them the homogenous can only be a pure void. Moreover, the theory of the 'universal void' (*sarva-sūnya*) is here presented as a direct and logical consequence of atomism, for if in the corporeal world only atoms have a positive existence, and if those atoms must move in order to join together and so form all bodies, that movement can only occur in a void. However, this consequence is not accepted by the school of Kanāda, which is representative of *Vaisheshika*, but heterodox precisely in that it admits atomism, with which the 'cosmological' point of view in itself is in no way inextricably linked; conversely, the 'natural philosophers' of Greece, who do not count ether among the elements, are far from all being atomists, a position they seem moreover to overlook rather than to expressly reject. However that may be, the opinion of the Buddhists is easily refuted by pointing out that there cannot be an empty space since such a conception is contradictory. In the whole domain of universal manifestation, of which space is part, there can be no void because such a thing, which can only be conceived negatively, is not a possibility of manifestation. Furthermore, a conception of an empty space would be that of a container without a content, which is obviously without meaning. Ether is therefore that which occupies all space, but for all that it is not to be confused with space itself, which, being only a container, that is to say a condition of existence and not an independent entity, cannot as such be the substantial principle of bodies, or give birth to other elements. Ether is thus not space, but actually the contents of space envisaged prior to all differentiation. In this state of primordial indifferentiation, which is a sort of image of the 'indistinction' of *Prakriti* relative to this special domain of manifestation that is the corporeal world, ether already contains potentially not only all the elements, but also all bodies, and its very homogeneity renders it suitable to receive all forms in its modifications. Being the principle of corporeal things, it possesses quantity, which is a fundamental attribute common to all bodies; moreover, it is regarded as essentially simple, always by reason of its homogeneity, and as impenetrable, because it itself penetrates all.

Put this way, the existence of ether presents itself quite otherwise than as a simple hypothesis, and this shows clearly the profound difference separating traditional doctrine from all modern scientific theories. Nevertheless, we must consider yet another objection: ether is a real element, but this is not sufficient to prove that it is a distinct element; in other words, it could be that the element that is extended throughout all corporeal space (by which we mean the space capable of containing bodies) is not other than air, which in reality would then be the primordial element. The answer to this objection is that each one of our senses allows us to know as its proper object a quality distinct from those known by the others. Now, a quality can only exist in something to which it is related as is an attribute to its subject, and as each sensible quality is thus attributed to an element of which it is the characteristic property, it follows necessarily that to the five senses there correspond five distinct elements.

The sensible quality related to ether is sound. This requires some explanation, which will be easily understood if one considers the mode of production of sound as vibratory movement, which is a far from recent discovery as some people believe, for Kanāda expressly declares that 'sound is propagated by undulations, by wave after wave, or ripple after ripple, radiating in all directions, starting from a determined center.' Such a movement spreads out from its point of origin in concentric waves, uniformly distributed in all directions of space, giving rise to the figure of a non-defined and non-closed spheroid. This is the least differentiated movement of all because of what we can call its 'isotropism', and this is why it can give birth to all other movements, which differ from it in that they do not proceed uniformly in all directions; and likewise, all more particularized forms will proceed from the original spherical form. Thus, the differentiation of primitively homogeneous ether—a differentiation that engenders the other elements—has as its origin an elementary movement produced in the way just described, starting from any initial point in the indefinite cosmic milieu; but this elementary movement is nothing other than the prototype of a sound wave. Auditory sensation is moreover the only sensation that allows us to perceive a vibratory movement directly. Even if we admit, with the most modern physicists, that the other sensations result from a transformation of similar movements, it remains no less true that they differ from it qualitatively as sensations, which is the essential consideration here. On the other hand, after what has just been said it must be clearly understood that although the cause of sound lies in ether, this cause must be distinguished from the various media that may serve secondarily for the propagation of sound, and contribute to making it perceptible to us by amplifying the elementary etheric vibrations, the more so as the surroundings are the more dense. Finally, let us add in this connection that the sonorous quality is equally perceptible in the other four elements inasmuch as the latter all proceed from ether. Aside from these considerations, the attribution of the sonorous quality to ether—that is, to the first of the elements—has yet another profound reason, related to the doctrine of the primordiality and the perpetuity of sound; but at present this is a point to which we can only allude in passing.

The second element, that which is the first to be differentiated from ether, is *vāyu* or air. The word *vāyu*, which is derived from the verbal root *vā*, meaning 'to go' or 'to move', properly designates breath or wind, so that mobility is considered the essential characteristic of this element. More precisely, air, as we have already said, is regarded as endowed with a transverse movement, that is, a movement in which all the directions of space no longer play an equal role, as was the case with the spheroidal movement considered earlier, but one that follows a particular direction; ultimately, therefore, the determination of this direction gives rise to a rectilinear movement. This propagation of movement along certain determined directions implies a rupture of the homogeneity of the cosmic environment, giving rise to a complex movement which, as it is no longer 'isotropic', must result from a combination or coordination of elementary vibratory movements. Such a movement produces equally complex forms, and since the form is what first affects touch the tangible quality can be related to air as belonging properly to it insofar as by its mobility air is the principle of the differentiation of forms. It is therefore by the effect of mobility that air is made perceptible to us; by analogy, moreover, atmospheric air becomes perceptible to touch only by its displacement; however, recalling the general remark made above, one must be careful not to identify the element air with this atmospheric air—which is a body—as some have not failed to do by proposing certain comparisons of this kind. Thus Kanāda declares air to be colorless, but it is easy to see that this must be so without needing to refer to the properties of atmospheric air, for color is a quality of fire, and since fire is logically posterior to air in the order of the development of the elements, this quality is not yet manifested at the stage represented by air.

The third element is *tejas*, or fire, which manifests itself to our senses under two principal aspects, as light and as heat. The quality belonging to it in its own right is visibility, and in this respect fire must be envisaged in its luminous aspect—something too clear to need further explanation, for it is obviously by light alone that bodies are made visible. According to Kanāda 'light is colored, and it is the principle of the coloration of bodies.' Color is therefore a property characteristic of light. In light itself it is white and resplendent; in the diverse bodies it is variable, and simple colors and mixed or blended colors can be distinguished among its modifications. Note that the Pythagoreans, as reported by Plutarch, also affirmed that 'colors are nothing else than a reflection of light, modified in different ways,' and one would thus be greatly mistaken to see herein yet another discovery of modern science. On the other hand, in its caloric aspect fire is sensible to touch, producing the impression of temperature, while air is neutral in this connection since it is anterior to fire, of which heat is an aspect; and as for cold, it is regarded as a property characteristic of water. Thus, with respect to temperature as well as in what concerns the action of the ascending and descending tendencies defined previously, fire and water oppose each other, with air in a state of equilibrium between them. Moreover, if one considers that cold augments the density of bodies by contracting them whereas heat dilates and makes them subtle, it will be easily recognized that the correlation of heat and cold with fire and water respectively is included as a particular application and simple consequence in the general theory of the three *gunas* and of their distribution throughout the elementary domain.

The fourth element, *ap* or water, has as its characteristic properties (besides the cold we just mentioned) density or gravity (which it has in common with earth) and fluidity or viscosity, which is the quality that distinguishes it essentially from all the other elements. We have already pointed out the correlation of these two properties with the respective actions of *tamas* and *rajas*. On the other hand, the sensible quality that corresponds to water is taste, and although there is no reason to attach too great an importance to considerations of this sort, we note incidentally that this is in agreement with the opinion of modern physiologists, who think that a body is 'sapid' only to the degree that it dissolves in saliva, in other words that in any body taste is a consequence of fluidity.

Finally, the fifth and last element is *prithivī* or earth, which, no longer possessing fluidity as does water, corresponds to the most condensed corporeal modality of all. Thus it is in this element that we find gravity, which manifests itself in the descent or fall of bodies, at its highest degree. The sensible quality proper to earth is odor, which is why this quality is regarded as inhering in solid particles that, detaching themselves from bodies, enter into contact with the organ of smell. On this point too there seems to be no disagreement with current physiological theories, although even if there were some disagreement it would really matter little, for in every case the error would of necessity be on the side of profane science and not on that of traditional doctrine.

To conclude, we will say a few words on the way Hindu doctrine envisages the organs of the senses in their relation to the elements. Since each sensible quality proceeds from an element in which it essentially inheres, the organ by which this quality is perceived must conform to it, that is, must itself be of the nature of the corresponding element; it is thus that the true organs of the senses are constituted, and, contrary to the opinion held by Buddhists, one must distinguish them from external organs, that is to say from the parts of the human body that are only their centers and their instruments. Thus, the true organ of hearing is not the auricle of the ear, but the portion of ether contained in the inner ear that vibrates under the influence of a sound wave; and Kanāda points out that neither the initial nor the intermediate waves cause the sound to be heard, but the last wave that comes into contact with the organ of hearing. Similarly, the true organ of sight is not the eye, or the pupil, or even the retina, but a luminous principle residing in the eye that enters into communication with the light emanating from external objects or reflected by them. This luminosity of the eye is not ordinarily visible, but it can become so under certain circumstances, particularly among animals that see in the dark of night. It must be noted also that the luminous ray by which the visual perception operates, and which extends between the eye and the perceived object, may be considered in both ways: on the one hand as going from the eye to the object, and on the other, reciprocally, as coming from the object to the pupil of the eye. One finds a similar theory of vision among the Pythagoreans, and this agrees also with the definition that Aristotle gives of sensation, conceived as 'the common act of the perceiver and the perceived.' One could consider the organs of each of the other senses in the same way, but we think we have given ample indications in this respect with these examples.

Such, in broad outline and interpreted as exactly as possible, is the Hindu theory of the elements, which, over and above its intrinsic interest, is capable of offering in a more general way an explanation of the 'cosmological' point of view in traditional doctrines.

5

DHARMA

THE word *Dharma* seems to be one of the Sanskrit terms
that give the most difficulty to translators, and not without reason,
since its many meanings certainly cannot always be rendered by a
single word in another language; it might often perhaps even be
preferable simply to keep it untranslated, on condition that it be
explained in a comment. Gualtherus H. Mees, who has devoted a
recently published book to this subject,[1] and who, though restricting himself almost exclusively to the social point of view, displays
more understanding than one usually encounters among Westerners, very correctly notes that if there is a certain indeterminateness
in the term, it is in no way synonymous with vagueness and in no
way proves that the conceptions of the ancients lacked clarity, or
that they were unable to differentiate among the various aspects of
the matter in question. This so-called vagueness, of which one could
find many examples, shows rather that the thought of the ancients
was much less narrowly limited than that of the moderns, and that,
instead of being analytic, as is the latter, was essentially synthetic.
Something of this indetermination still survives moreover in such a
term as 'law', which also embraces many different meanings; and
along with the word 'order', this word 'law' is precisely one that in
many cases may least imperfectly render the idea of *dharma*.

We know that *dharma* is derived from the root *dhri*, meaning 'to
carry', 'to support', 'to sustain', 'to maintain';[2] it is therefore properly

---

1. *Dharma and Society* (London: Luzac & Co., 1935). The greatest part of this
book concerns more especially the question of *varnas* or castes, but such a point of
view merits being made the exclusive subject of another article.

2. Whatever the author may say, a connection of this root with the word 'form'
hardly seems likely, and in any case we do not see clearly what consequences can be
drawn from it.

a question of a principle of conservation of beings and thus of stability inasmuch as this latter is at least compatible with the conditions of manifestation, for all the applications of *dharma* relate to the manifested world. And so is it not possible to allow, as the author seems disposed to do, that this expression may more or less be a substitute for *Ātmā* if one adds the proviso that it is 'dynamic' rather than 'static', for *Ātmā* is non-manifested and therefore immutable. *Dharma* is one of its expressions, as it were, in the sense that it reflects principial immutability in the order of manifestation, and it is 'dynamic' only in the measure that manifestation necessarily implies 'becoming'; but it is also that which makes of this 'becoming' something other than pure mutability, something that always maintains a certain relative stability through change itself. In this regard moreover it is important to note that the root *dhri* is almost identical in form and meaning to another root, *dhru*, derived from the word *dhruva*, which designates 'pole'. In fact, if one really wishes to understand the notion of *dharma*, one ought to refer to this idea of a 'pole' or 'axis' of the manifested world, for the pole is what remains invariable at the center of the revolutions of all things and regulates the course of change by the very fact that it does not participate therein. We must not forget that by the synthetic character of the thought it expresses, language is here much more closely bound to symbolism than it is in modern languages, and that it is from symbolism that it receives the multiplicity of meanings of which we spoke earlier; and perhaps one could even show that the conception of *dharma* is connected quite directly to the symbolic representation of the 'axis' through the figure of the 'World Tree'.

On the other hand, Mees correctly points out the relationship of the notion of *dharma* to that of *rita*, which has etymologically the sense of 'rectitude' (in the same way as does the *Te* of the Far-Eastern tradition, which is also very closely related to *dharma*), obviously recalling again the idea of the 'axis', which is that of a constant and invariable direction. At the same time, this term *rita* is identical to the word 'rite', and one could indeed say that at least in its original sense the latter designates all that is accomplished in conformity with order. It only comes to assume a more restricted meaning in consequence of the degeneration that gives rise to a 'profane' activity, whatever the domain. It must be clearly understood that the rite always preserves the same character and that it is non-ritual activity that is in some way a deviation. No 'convention' or 'custom' lacking any profound reason existed originally, and traditional rites have no relationship with such things, which can never be anything but a counterfeit or parody thereof. But there is something more: when we speak here of conformity to order, this does not mean the human order alone, but also—and even above all—the cosmic order. In every traditional conception there is in fact always a strict correspondence between the two, and it is precisely the rite that maintains the relationship in a conscious way, implying as it were a collaboration of man in the sphere of his own activity with the cosmic order itself.

Similarly, the notion of *dharma* is not limited to man, but extends to all beings and to all their states of manifestation, which is why an exclusively social conception is not sufficient for a profound understanding thereof, for it is nothing more than a particular application that should never be separated from the 'law' or the primordial and universal 'norm' of which it is only the translation in specifically human mode. One can doubtless speak of the *dharma* proper to each being (*svadharma*) or proper to each group of beings, such as a human collectivity for example, but this is really only a particularization of the *dharma* with respect to the special conditions of that being or that group, whose nature and constitution are necessarily analogous to those of the whole of which it is a part, whether this whole be a certain state of existence or even total manifestation, for the analogy always applies to all levels and all degrees. In this we are clearly far from any 'moral' conception, for if an idea such as 'justice' is sometimes suitable to render the meaning of *dharma*, it is so only insofar as it is a human expression of equilibrium or harmony, that is to say as one of the aspects of the preservation of cosmic stability. With all the more reason is the notion of 'virtue' inapplicable here except in the measure that it indicates that the actions of an individual are in conformity with its own nature and thereby with the total order that has its reflection or image in the nature of each one. Similarly again, if one considers a human collectivity and no longer an isolated individuality, the idea of 'legislation' only enters into that of *dharma* because such legislation must normally be an adaptation of the cosmic order to the social milieu; and this characteristic is particularly visible as concerns the institution of the castes, as we shall see in chapter six. All the secondary meanings of the word *dharma* can be accounted for in this way, a difficulty arising only when one wishes to consider them separately and without seeing how they are derived from a common principle, which one could say is a sort of fundamental unity in which their multiplicity is resolved.[3]

In order to situate the notion of *dharma* more exactly before concluding this survey, we must still point out the place it occupies among the goals that the traditional Hindu scriptures assign to human life. These goals are four in number, enumerated as follows in hierarchically ascending order: *artha, kāma, dharma, moksha.* The last, that is to say 'Deliverance', is the one supreme goal, and since it lies beyond the domain of manifestation it is of an order totally different from that of the other three, and has no common measure with them, just as the absolute is without common measure with the relative. As for the first three goals, all are related to manifestation: *artha* comprises the entirety of goods of the corporeal order; *kāma* is desire, whose satisfaction constitutes the good of the psychic order; and *dharma*, being superior to *kāma*, must be considered as having a realization deriving properly from the spiritual order, which indeed accords with the universal character we have realized in it. It is obvious however that since these goals, including *dharma* itself, are always contingent—as is the manifestation outside of which they cannot be envisaged—they could only be subordinate in relation to the supreme goal, toward which they tend as no more than simple means. Moreover, each of these goals is subordinated to those superior to it, even while still remaining relative; but when *moksha* is excluded, and they alone enumerated, this is because the point of view adopted is limited to a consideration of

---

3. It is easy to understand also that the social application of *dharma* always translates, to use modern language, as 'duty' and not as 'law'; the proper *dharma* of a being can obviously only be expressed by what it itself must do, and not by what others must do in its regard, and which naturally arises from the *dharma* of those other beings.

what is manifested; and only thus can *dharma* at times appear as the highest goal proposed for man. In due course we shall see that these goals stand more particularly in respective correspondence with the different *varnas*,[4] and we can say here and now that this correspondence rests essentially on the theory of the three *gunas*, which clearly shows that here too the human order appears as indissolubly linked to the cosmic order in its entirety.

4. Cf. the following chapter.

6

*V*ARNA

In his book *Dharma and Society*, which we have already mentioned, Gualtherus H. Mees pays particular attention to the question of caste. Moreover he does not accept this word in the sense in which we understand it but prefers to retain the Sanskrit term *varna* untranslated, or to render it by an expression such as 'natural classes', which indeed well defines the matter in question since it is truly a question of the hierarchical distribution of human beings in conformity with the nature proper to each. However, it is to be feared that the word 'classes', even if qualified, may evoke the idea of something more or less comparable to the social classes of the West, which in reality are purely artificial, and have nothing in common with a traditional hierarchy of which they represent at most a sort of parody or caricature. For our part then we find it better to use the word 'castes', which, while it assuredly has only an altogether conventional value, was at least coined expressly to designate the Hindu mode of organization. Mees, however, reserves it for the multiple castes that in fact exist in present-day India and in which he claims to see something altogether different from the original *varnas*. We cannot share this way of viewing things, for these present-day castes are really only secondary subdivisions due to complexity or a greater differentiation of the social organization, and whatever may be their multiplicity, they nonetheless always fall within the framework of the four *varnas*, which alone constitute the fundamental hierarchy and necessarily remain invariable as an expression of traditional principles and a reflection of the cosmic order in the human social order.

Although no reference is made to them, it seems to us that the idea underlying the distinction that Mees wishes to make between *varna* and 'caste' is inspired in great part by Bergsonian theories on 'open societies' and 'closed societies', for he tries to distinguish two aspects of *dharma*, one of which more or less corresponds to *varna* and the other to 'caste', the predominance of each being affirmed alternately in what he calls 'periods of life' and 'periods of form', to which he attributes respectively 'dynamic' and 'static' characteristics. We have no intention of discussing these philosophico-historic conceptions, which obviously do not rest on any traditional evidence. For us, it is of more interest to note a misunderstanding of the word *jāti*, which the author believes designates what he calls 'caste', whereas in reality it is quite simply employed as an equivalent or synonym of *varna*. The word *jāti* means literally 'birth', but this must not be understood in the sense of 'heredity', at least not exclusively or in principle. It designates the individual nature of the being insofar as it is necessarily determined from the very moment of birth as a totality of the possibilities that it will develop in the course of its existence, this nature resulting above all from what the being is in itself and only secondarily from the influences of the environment—of which heredity properly speaking is a part. And it is fitting to add that normally this environment is itself determined by a certain law of 'affinity' so as to be as consonant as possible with the tendencies proper to the being that is born into it; we say 'normally' because there may be more or less numerous exceptions to it, at least in a period of confusion like the *Kali-Yuga*. This being so, we in no way see what an 'open' caste could be if by this is meant—and what else could be meant?—that an individual would have the possibility of changing castes at a given moment, implying a change in his nature that would be quite as inconceivable as would be a sudden change of species on the part of an animal or plant (and one might remark that the word *jāti* also has the sense of 'species', rendering this comparison the more complete). An apparent change of caste could only be the correcting of an error in a case where an individual had initially been assigned a caste that was not really his; but the fact that such an error can sometimes occur (and again precisely as a result of the obscuration that characterizes the *Kali-Yuga*) in no way precludes the general possibility of determining true caste from birth. If Mees seems to think that only heredity can be considered in such a case, it is because he is doubtless unaware that the means for this determination can be furnished by certain traditional sciences, even if only by astrology, which of course is here something completely different from the so-called 'scientific astrology' of certain modern Westerners, and has nothing to do with a 'conjectural' or 'divinatory' art, any more than with empirical statistics or the calculation of probabilities.

Having settled this, let us return to the notion of *varna* itself, a word properly signifying 'color', but also by extension 'quality' in general, which is why it can be taken to mean individual nature. Mees rightly rejects the bizarre interpretation proposed by those who wish to see in the meaning of 'color' proof that the distinction of the *varnas* would originally have been based upon differences of race, something of which it is altogether impossible to find the slightest confirmation anywhere. The truth is that if colors are in fact attributed to the *varnas* it is in a purely symbolic way, the 'key' to that symbolism being given by the correspondence with the *gunas*, a correspondence indicated most explicitly in this text from the *Vishnu Purana*: 'When *Brahmā*, in conformity with his plan, wished to create the world, beings in whom *sattva* prevailed issued from his mouth; others, in whom *rajas* was predominant, issued from his chest; yet others, in whom *rajas* and *tamas* were both strong, issued from his thighs; and finally, others issued from his feet, having *tamas* as their principal characteristic. From these beings were composed the four *varnas*, the Brahmins, the Kshatriyas, the Vaishyas, and the Shūdras, who

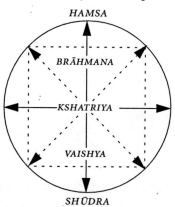

issued respectively from his mouth, his chest, his thighs, and his feet.' *Sattva*, being represented by the color white, is naturally attributed to the Brahmins; similarly, red, the color representative of *rajas*, is attributed to the Kshatriyas; the Vaishyas, characterized by a mixture of the two inferior *gunas*, have yellow as their symbolic color; and finally, black, the color of *tamas*, is the one befitting the Shūdras.

This hierarchization of the *varnas* as determined by the respective *gunas* predominating in them is exactly superimposed on that of the elements, such as we have described them in our study on the subject,[1] which is immediately evident if one compares the diagram on the preceding page with that below. Only, in order that the similarity be complete it must be noted that the place of ether must be taken here by *Hamsa*, that is to say the single primordial caste that existed in the *Krita-Yuga* and that contained the four subsequent *varnas* in principle and in the undifferentiated state in the same way as the ether contains the other four elements.

On the other hand, although Mees resists pressing the analogies too far, he attempts to show a correspondence between the four *varnas* and the four *āshramas*, or regular stages of existence (which we shall not examine here), and also with the four goals of human life of which we spoke previously in respect of *dharma*. But in this last instance the very fact that it is once again a quaternary division has led him to an obvious inaccuracy, for it is clearly inadmissible to propose as goal, be it the most inferior, the acquisition of something that corresponds purely and simply to *tamas*. The distribution, if effectuated from bottom to top, must then really begin at the degree immediately above the bottom, as our second diagram shows; and it is easy to see that *dharma* quite effectively corresponds to *sattva*, *kāma* to *rajas*, and *artha* to a mixture of *rajas* and *tamas*. At the same time, the relationships of these

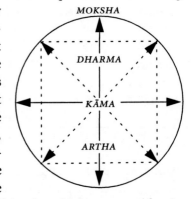

goals with the character and role of the three higher *varnas* (that is, of those whose members possess the qualities of *ārya* and *dvija*) then appear of themselves: the function of the Vaishya clearly relates

1. See chap. 4.

to the acquisition of *artha* or the goods of the corporeal order, *kāma* or desire represents the motive for the activity that specifically befits the Kshatriyas; and the Brāhmins are the true representatives and natural guardians of *dharma*. As for *moksha*, as we have already said, this supreme goal is of an altogether different order from the other three and shares no common measure with them. It is thus situated beyond all that corresponds to the particular functions of the *varnas* and unlike transitory and contingent goals cannot be contained in the sphere that represents the domain of conditioned existence since it is precisely liberation from that very existence. It is of course also beyond the three *gunas*, which concern only the states of universal manifestation.

These few considerations show clearly enough that when traditional institutions are involved, a merely 'sociological' point of view proves insufficient to get to plumb the depths of things since the true foundation of these institutions is properly of a 'cosmological' order; but it goes without saying that certain lacunae in this respect must nonetheless not prevent our recognizing the merit of Mees's work, which is certainly far superior to most of the works that other Westerners have devoted to the same questions.

7

Tantrism
& Magic

It is the custom in the West to attribute to Tantrism a 'magical' character, or at least to believe that magic plays a predominant role in it. This is an error of interpretation as concerns Tantrism, and perhaps also as concerns magic, on which subject our contemporaries have in general only vague and confused ideas, as we showed in a recent article. We shall not return at present to this last point, but, taking magic strictly in its proper sense—and supposing that it is really thus that one understands it—will ask only what, in Tantrism itself, could serve as a pretext for this false interpretation, for it is always more interesting to explain an error than to simply point it out.

Recall first that magic, no matter to how inferior an order it may pertain, is nevertheless an authentic traditional science, and as such can legitimately take its place among the applications of an orthodox doctrine, providing that it be only the subordinate and very secondary place that befits its essentially contingent character. On the other hand, given that the effective development of the particular traditional sciences is in fact determined by conditions proper to one or another epoch, it is natural and in a sense normal that the most contingent among these sciences should develop above all in the period when humanity is the furthest from pure intellectuality, that is, in the *Kali-Yuga*, and that they should, while remaining within the limits assigned to them by their very nature, at that time assume an importance they never could have had in earlier periods. The traditional sciences, whatever they may be, can always serve as 'supports' for ascending to knowledge of a superior order, and it is this more than what they are in themselves that confers on them a properly doctrinal value; but as we have said elsewhere, in order to remain adapted to the human possibilities of each age, such 'supports' must in general become more and more contingent to the degree that the cyclical 'descent' is accomplished. The development of the inferior traditional sciences is then in fact only a particular case of that necessary 'materialization' of which we have spoken; but at the same time it goes without saying that the dangers of deviation become all the greater as one goes further in this direction, which is why a science like magic is obviously among those that most readily give rise to all sorts of deformations and illegitimate usages, deviations that are in all cases attributable to the very conditions of that period of 'obscuration' we call the *Kali-Yuga*.

It is easy to understand the direct connection that all these considerations have with Tantrism, a doctrinal form especially adapted to the *Kali-Yuga*; and if we add that, as has already been pointed out elsewhere, Tantrism lays stress especially on 'power' as a means and even as a possible 'foundation' for 'realization', it is no cause for surprise that it must by that very fact accord a rather considerable importance—one could even say the maximum importance compatible with their relativity—to the sciences that are in one way or another capable of contributing to the development of that 'power' in any given domain. Magic obviously being one of these sciences, there is no denying that it finds a place here, but it must be clearly stated that it could not in any way constitute what is essential in Tantrism. To cultivate magic for itself, or to take as one's goal the study or the production of 'phenomena' of any kind, is to imprison oneself in illusion rather than to strive to break free of it. This can only be a deviation and consequently it is no longer Tantrism, which is an aspect of orthodox tradition and a 'way' destined to lead the being to true 'realization'.

It is generally admitted quite freely that there is a Tantric initiation, but most often no account is taken of what this really implies. We hardly need stress this point again in view of our many previous expositions on the subject of the spiritual ends which are those of all orthodox traditions without exception. Magic as such, referring exclusively to the 'psychic' domain by very definition, certainly contains nothing initiatic, so that even if it happens that an initiatic ritual brings into play certain apparently 'magical' elements, it necessarily follows from the goal it assigns them and the use it makes of them in conformity with that goal, that it 'transforms' them into something of another order altogether, in which the 'psychic' becomes no more than a mere 'support' for the spiritual; and thus in reality it is no longer a question of magic any more than it is, say, of geometry in the ritual laying out of a *yantra*. The 'support' in its 'materiality', if we may put it so, must never be confused with the superior nature that is conferred on it essentially by its end. This confusion can only occur in superficial observers incapable of seeing anything whatever beyond the most external formal appearances, which is indeed the case with almost all those in the modern West who have occupied themselves with these matters, always approaching them with the incomprehension inherent in the profane mentality. Let us also note in passing that this same confusion is the point of departure for the 'naturalistic' interpretations they have tried to apply to all traditional symbolism.

To these few observations we will add yet another of a somewhat different character. One knows the importance of Tantric elements that have penetrated into those forms of Buddhism that are included under the general designation of *Mahāyāna*, but far from being only a 'corrupt' Buddhism, as it seems fashionable to call it in the West, these forms on the contrary represent the result of an altogether traditional adaptation of Buddhism. That in certain cases we can no longer easily uncover the proper character of original Buddhism is of little importance, or rather merely testifies to the extent of the transformation that has taken place.[1] How then, one might ask, could such a thing really have been the doing of Tantrism, if the latter were truly nothing more nor other than magic? We have here an impossibility perfectly evident to anyone with the least knowledge of traditional realities, an impossibility that is fundamentally

1. This passage has been arranged to agree with the modification that René Guénon himself brought to the question of Buddhism in the fourth edition of *Introduction to the Study of the Hindu Doctrines* (1952).

none other than that the inferior should produce the superior, or that a 'greater' should derive from a 'lesser'. But is not this precisely the absurdity that is implied in all the 'evolutionist' thought of modern Westerners and that thereby contributes in great part to the irremediable falsity of all their conceptions?

8

THE FIFTH *VEDA*

AMONG the specifically modern errors we have frequently had occasion to denounce, one of those most directly opposed to any true comprehension of traditional doctrines is what can be called 'historicism', which moreover is basically simply a consequence of the 'evolutionist' mentality that consists of supposing all things to have originated in the most rudimentary and crude fashion and subsequently to have undergone a progressive elaboration such that this or that conception then appears at a determined moment. What appears later in time is considered to be of a higher order, with the implication that it could only be 'the product of an already advanced civilization' according to an expression that has become so pervasive as to be repeated almost mechanically even by those who try to react against such a mentality, but whose 'traditionalist' intentions lack any basis in traditional knowledge. Against this way of looking at things we must on the contrary flatly affirm that all that pertains to the spiritual and intellectual domains is found in a state of perfection at the beginning, from which it only afterward falls away gradually in the course of the 'obscuration' necessarily accompanying every cyclical process of manifestation. This fundamental law, which we must be content to recall here without entering into a more ample development of it, obviously suffices to reduce to nothing all the results of the so-called 'historical criticism'. It is noteworthy that the latter implies a fixed bias to deny every supra-human element and to treat the traditional doctrines themselves as purely human 'thought', which in this respect is altogether comparable to profane philosophy and the profane sciences. From this point of view no compromise is possible either, and in reality it is this profane 'thought' itself that is of very recent date, its appearance having become possible only as 'the product of an already advanced degeneration', if we may invert in an 'anti-evolutionist' sense the phrase just cited.

Applying these general considerations to the Hindu tradition, we can say that, contrary to the opinions of orientalists, nothing of the sort called 'Vedism', 'Brāhmanism', and 'Hinduism' ever existed if by these terms are meant doctrines that came to light and replaced one another in successive ages, each one characterized by conceptions essentially different from, if not contradictory to, those of the others, conceptions that would thus have been formed successively in consequence of a 'thinking' modeled after simple philosophical speculation. Should one insist on retaining them, these various terms must be regarded as designating one sole and identical tradition, to which in fact they may all refer; and the most that can be said is that each relates more directly to a certain aspect of this tradition, the different aspects moreover being linked closely together and unable to be isolated from each other in any way. This results directly from the fact that in principle the tradition in question is contained integrally in the *Veda*, so that all that is contrary to the *Veda* or that is not legitimately derived from it is thereby excluded from that tradition, no matter from what point of view it is considered. The essential unity and invariability of the doctrine is thus assured, whatever may otherwise be the developments and adaptations to which it gives rise in response to the particular needs and aptitudes of the men of one age or another.

It must be clearly understood that the doctrine's immutability is in itself no obstacle to development or adaptation, as long as these developments strictly conform to the principles and never constitute 'novelties', since in any case it could not be a question of anything but an 'explanation' of what that doctrine always and for all time implies, or else of a formulation of the same truths in different terms in order to render them more accessible to the mentality of a 'darker' age. What in the principle itself was grasped immediately and without difficulty at the outset, men of later ages—apart from exceptional cases—are no longer able to see, and it is then necessary to compensate for this general lack of comprehension by providing detailed explanations and commentaries previously unnecessary. Moreover, since the aptitudes for arriving directly at pure knowledge become ever more rare, it is necessary to open other 'ways' providing more and more contingent means to remedy to the degree possible the 'descent' taking place from age to age in the course of the cycle of terrestrial humanity. Thus one could say that for the purpose of attaining its transcendent ends humanity has received facilities all the broader as its spiritual and intellectual level has fallen, facilities that take into account conditions inevitably determined by the law of the cycle in order that all who can might still be saved.

It is in the light of these considerations that one can truly understand the place occupied in Hindu tradition by what is customarily called 'Tantrism' insofar as this latter represents the body of teachings and means of 'realization' more especially appropriate to the conditions of the *Kali-Yuga*. It would thus be completely erroneous to see herein a separate doctrine, still less a 'system' of any kind, as Westerners are all too willing to do. To tell the truth, it is more a question of a 'spirit', if one may so express it, which in a more or less diffuse way penetrates the entire Hindu tradition in its present form, so that it would be almost impossible to assign it precise and well-defined limits within the latter; and if we recall that the beginning of the *Kali-Yuga* extends back well before 'historical' times, it must be acknowledged that the very origin of Tantrism, far from being as 'late' as some claim, necessarily eludes the limited means at the disposal of profane investigation. Again, when we speak here of the origin, making it coincide with that of the *Kali-Yuga* itself, this is only a half truth, for more precisely this is only true on condition that we specify that here it is a question of Tantrism as such, by which we mean Tantrism insofar as it is the external expression or manifestation of something that, like all the rest of the tradition, existed in principle in the *Veda* itself, although it was not more explicitly formulated and its applications developed except until circumstance demanded. We see then that there are two points of view to be considered: on the one hand, we can find Tantrism even in the *Veda* since it is comprised therein principially, but on the other it can only properly be named as a distinct aspect of the doctrine from the moment it is made 'explicit' for the reasons indicated, and it is in that sense alone that we must consider it peculiar to the *Kali-Yuga*.

The designation of what is here in question derives from the fact that the teachings on which it is based are expressed in works that bear the generic name *Tantras*, a name that relates directly to the symbolism of weaving, which we have discussed on other occasions, for *tantra* is properly the 'warp' of a fabric; and we have pointed out elsewhere too that words with the same significance are found applied to the sacred books. These *Tantras* are often regarded as forming a 'fifth Veda' especially destined for men of the *Kali-Yuga*, which would be completely unjustified if they were not, as we have just explained, derived from the *Veda* understood in its most rigorous sense as an adaptation to the conditions of a definite age. Moreover, it is important to bear in mind that in reality the *Veda* is one principially and as it were 'intemporally' before becoming threefold and then fourfold in its formation; if it can also be fivefold in the present age owing to the supplementary developments required by faculties of comprehension that are less 'open' and no longer able to function as directly in the order of pure intellectuality, it is obvious that this will not in the least affect its original unity, which is essentially its 'perpetual' (*sanātana*) aspect, and therefore independent of the particular conditions of any age whatsoever.

In the final analysis therefore the doctrine of the *Tantras* is not and cannot be anything but a normal development following certain points of view, of what is already contained in the *Veda*, since it is in this way and in this way only that it can be, as it is in fact, an integral part of Hindu tradition. And as concerns the means of 'realization' (*sādhana*) prescribed by the *Tantras*, one can say that by this very fact they are also legitimately derived from the *Veda* since they are really nothing but the application and effective implementation of that same doctrine. If these means, by which we must naturally understand rites of every kind, whether principal or merely accessory, seem nevertheless to display a certain character of 'novelty' with respect to those that preceded them, it is because there was no reason to consider them in previous times, except perhaps as pure possibilities, since men of those times had no need of them, able as they were to make use of other means better suited to their nature. There is in this something altogether comparable to the special development of a traditional science in one age or another, a development likewise constituting no spontaneous 'apparition' or 'innovation' since in this case also there can really never be a question of anything but an application of principles, and therefore of something preexisting at least implicitly in the latter, which in consequence could always be made explicit at any moment supposing there were reason to do so—such a reason being found in fact only in the contingent circumstances that condition a definite age.

Now, that the strictly 'Vedic' rites—that is, such as they were 'in the beginning'—are no longer practicable in our day, is only too clearly the result of the single fact that *soma*, which plays a key role in them, has been lost since a time impossible to evaluate 'historically'; and it should be understood that when we speak here of *soma*, this latter must be considered as representing a whole collection of things of which the knowledge—at first manifest and accessible to all—has become hidden during the course of the cycle, at least for ordinary humanity. It was therefore necessary that since that time there should be 'substitutes' for these things which could only be found in an order inferior to their own, which amounts to saying that the 'supports' by virtue of which 'realization' remained possible became more and more 'materialized' from one period to another in conformity with the descending course of cyclical development. A relationship such as that of wine to *soma* in ritual usage could serve as a symbolic example. This 'materialization' must not be understood simply in the most limited and ordinary sense of the word; indeed, in our view it begins to emerge the moment one begins to leave behind that pure knowledge which alone is also pure spirituality. And the appeal of sentimental and volitional elements is not the least of the signs of such a 'materialization', even if these elements are employed legitimately as means subordinated to an end that remains always knowledge. If it were otherwise, one could no longer speak in any way of 'realization' but only of a deviation, of a semblance or a parody, all of which, needless to say, are strictly excluded by traditional orthodoxy under whatever form and at whatever level we may envisage it.

What we have just pointed out applies exactly to Tantrism, of which the 'way' appears in general as more 'active' than 'contemplative', or in other words as situated more on the side of 'power' than of knowledge; and in this connection the importance it gives to what is designated the 'way of the hero' (*vīramārga*) is particularly significant. It is obvious that *vīrya*, a term equivalent to the Latin *virtus*—at least according to the sense it had before it was diverted in a 'moral' direction by the Stoics—properly expresses the essential and in a way 'typical' quality, not of the Brahmin, but of the Kshatriya. And the *vīra* is distinguished from the *pashu*, that is, from the being subject to the bonds of common existence, less by an effective knowledge than by a voluntary affirmation of 'autonomy', which at this stage can still lead as easily away from its goal as toward it, according to the use made of it. The danger is that 'power' may be sought for its own sake and thus become an obstacle instead of a support, the individual mistakenly taking it for his proper end; but it goes without saying that this is only a deviation and an abuse that never need result except through incomprehension, something for which the doctrine can in no way be held responsible. Moreover, what we have just said concerns only the 'way' as such and not the goal, which in reality—we insist yet again—is always the same and cannot in any case be other than knowledge, since it is in and through the latter that the being truly 'realizes' itself in all its possibilities, although it is no less true that the means offered to attain this goal are marked, as they must inevitably be, by the special characteristics of the *Kali-Yuga*. Let us recall in this connection that the proper role of the 'hero' is everywhere and always represented as a 'quest', which, if it may sometimes be crowned with success, also risks ending in failure; and the 'quest' itself presupposes that by the time the 'hero' appears something has already been lost, which he must recover. This task, during which the *vīra* will become *divya*, can if one so desires be defined as the search for the *soma* or the 'drink of immortality' (*amrita*), which, from the symbolic point of view, is the exact equivalent of what in the West was called the 'Grail Quest'. And when the *soma* is again found the end of the cycle rejoins its beginning in the 'intemporal'.

9

ṄĀMA-ṚŪPA

IT is known that in the Hindu tradition individuality is
considered to be constituted by the union of two elements (or, more
exactly, of two sets of elements) designated respectively by the terms
nāma and *rūpa*, signifying literally 'name' and 'form' and generally
united in the composite expression *nāma-rūpa*, which thus covers
the whole individuality. *Nāma* corresponds to the 'essential' aspect
of this individuality and *rūpa* to its 'substantial' aspect, so that the
two are nearly the equivalent of the εἶδος [*eidos*] and the ὕλη [*hyle*]
of Aristotle, or of what the scholastics called 'form' and 'matter'. But
here we must be wary of a rather unfortunate imperfection of Western terminology. In the latter, 'form' is indeed equivalent to *nāma*,
whereas if one takes the same word 'form' in its usual sense it is
rather *rūpa* that must be translated by it.[1] Since for reasons we have
explained on other occasions and cannot repeat here,[2] the word
'matter' is also not without in drawbacks, we find it preferable to use
the terms 'essence' and 'substance', these taken naturally in the relative sense in which they are able to be applied to an individuality.

From a somewhat different point of view *nāma* also corresponds
to the subtle part of the individuality and *rūpa* to its corporeal or
sensible part, but in the final analysis this distinction coincides
essentially with the previous one, for it is precisely these two

---

1. In English one could up to a certain point evade the ambiguity by agreeing to
render the scholastic 'forme' by the word *form* and 'form' in the ordinary sense by
shape; but in French it is impossible to find two words allowing of such a distinction.

2. See *The Reign of Quantity and the Signs of the Times*, chaps. 1–3. ED.

aspects, the subtle and the corporeal, that play the role of 'essence' and 'substance' in the totality of the individuality. In all cases we can say that when the being is liberated from the individual condition it is thereby 'beyond name and form' since these two complementary terms are properly constitutive of individuality as such. Here, of course, we are concerned with the being that has passed to a supra-individual state, for in another individual state—one still 'formal' therefore—it would necessarily reacquire the equivalents of *nāma* and *rūpa*, although the 'form' might no longer be corporeal, as it is in the human state.

It must also be said however that *nāma* is subject to a certain transposition in which it is no longer the correlative of *rūpa*, this being especially apparent when it is said that when man dies what subsists is *nāma*.[3] It is true that at first one could think that this was only a matter of extra-corporeal prolongations of the human individuality, and this way of seeing things is moreover acceptable in a certain sense insofar as *rūpa* is identified with the body. There would then be no true transposition properly speaking, but the subtle part of the individuality would simply continue to be designated as *nāma* after the disappearance of the corporeal part, and it could still be so designated when *nāma* is said to be 'without end', for this can only be understood to refer to cyclical perpetuity (any cycle can be said to be 'without end' in the sense that its end analogically rejoins its beginning, as one sees clearly in the annual cycle, *samvatsara*).[4] The case is obviously no longer the same however when it is specified that the being subsisting as *nāma* has passed into the world of the *devas*,[5] that is to say into an 'angelic' or supra-individual state. Since such a state is 'non-formal', one can no longer speak of *rūpa*, whereas *nāma* is transposed in a superior sense made possible by virtue of the suprasensible character attached to it even in its ordinary and individual acceptation. In such a case the being is still 'beyond form', but it would not also be 'beyond name' unless it had attained the unconditioned state and

3. *Brihadāraṇyaka Upanishad*, III.2.12.
4. *Jaiminīya Brāhmaṇa Upanishad*, I.35.
5. Ibid., III.9.

not merely a state that, however elevated it might be, still belongs to the domain of manifested existence. It is worth noting that this is no doubt what is meant in Western theological doctrines by the idea that the angelic nature (*devatva*) is a pure 'form' (what can be rendered in Sanskrit by *shuddha-nāma*), that is to say form not united with a 'matter', which, if we take into account the particularities of scholastic terminology alluded to above, amounts precisely to saying that it is a question of what we have called a 'non-formal' state.[6]

In this transposition *nāma* is still equivalent to the Greek εἶδος, but this time understood in the Platonic rather than in the Aristotelian sense. It is the 'idea', not in the psychological and 'subjective' sense of the moderns, but in the transcendental sense of 'archetype', that is to say a reality of the 'intelligible world' of which the 'sensible world' offers but a reflection or a shadow.[7] In this respect moreover one may take the 'sensible world' as representing symbolically the whole domain of formal manifestation, the 'intelligible world' being that of non-formal manifestation, or the world of the *devas*. It is also in this way that one must understand the application of the term *nāma* to the 'ideal' model that the artist must first contemplate inwardly, and from which he then realizes his finished work in a sensible form (or *rūpa*, properly speaking). This is done in such a way that when the 'idea' is thus 'incorporated', the work of art, just as the individual being, can be regarded as a combination of *nāma* and *rūpa*.[8] There is thus a kind of 'descent' (*avatarana*) of the 'idea' into the formal domain—not of course that the 'idea' in itself is

6. It is no less true that the angelic nature, like everything that is manifested, necessarily comprises a mingling of 'act' and 'potency'; apparently some people have simply assimilated these two terms to 'form' and 'matter', which indeed do correspond to them although these latter normally have more limited acceptance. Such terminological differences have not failed to give rise to certain confusions.

7. Here one will recall the symbolism of Plato's allegory of the cave.

8. On this point, and also for a good part of the other considerations set forth in this article, see Ananda K. Coomaraswamy, 'The Part of Art in Indian Life,' in the commemorative collection of the centenary of Srī Ramakrishna, *The Cultural Heritage of India*, vol. III, pp 485–513 [now in *Coomaraswamy, Volume 1: Selected Papers, Traditional Art and Symbolism*, ed. Roger Lipsey (Princeton: Princeton University Press, 1977) Ed.].

affected in any way, but rather that it is reflected in a certain sensible form that proceeds from it and to which it gives a certain life. In this connection one could say further that the 'idea' in itself corresponds to the 'spirit', and that its 'incorporated' aspect corresponds to the 'soul'. This similitude with the work of art allows us to understand in a more precise way the true nature of the relationship between the 'archetype' and the individual, and consequently that between the two meanings of the term *nāma*, according to whether it is applied in the 'angelic' or in the human domain, that is, designating, the informal or 'spiritual' principle of being on the one hand— which can also be called its pure 'essence'—and on the other the subtle part of the individuality, which is 'essence' only in a very relative sense and only in relation to its corporeal part, but which by that token represents 'essence' in the individual domain and may therefore be considered as a reflection therein of the veritable transcendent 'essence'.

It remains to explain the symbolism inherent in the very terms *nāma* and *rūpa*, which will allow us to pass from their literal sense (that is, as designating 'name' and 'form') to the applications we have just considered. At first sight the relationship may appear more evident for 'form' than for 'name', perhaps because in the case of 'form' we do not altogether leave the sensible order, to which the ordinary sense of the words is directly related, at least to the extent that we are concerned with human existence; and if another individual state were in question it would suffice to consider that there must necessarily be a certain correspondence between the constitution of the being manifested in that state and that of the human individual by the very fact that it is always a 'formal' state that is involved. On the other hand, in order to understand the true meaning of *nāma* we must appeal to notions less widely known, and above all remember that the 'name' of a being, even taken literally, is effectively an expression of its 'essence', as we have already explained elsewhere. Moreover this 'name' is also a 'number' in the Pythagorean and Kabbalistic sense, and we know that even from the simple point of view of historical filiation the concept of the Platonic 'idea', which we have just been discussing, is closely connected to that of Pythagorean 'number'.

But there is more, for it is important to note that strictly speaking the 'name' in the literal sense is a sound and hence belongs to the auditive order, whereas 'form' belongs to the visual order, the 'eye' (or sight) being thus taken here as a symbol of sensible experience, and the 'ear' (or hearing) as a symbol of the 'angelic' or intuitive intellect;[9] similarly, 'revelation', or the direct intuition of intelligible truth, can be taken as an 'audition', and hence the traditional meaning of the word *shruti*.[10] It goes without saying that in themselves hearing and sight are also dependent on the sensible domain, but for their symbolic transposition when thus placed in relation to one another we must envisage between them a certain hierarchy resulting from the order of development of the elements, and consequently of the sensible qualities respectively related to them. The auditive quality, referring to the ether, which is the first of the elements, is more 'primordial' than the visual quality, which is related to fire, from which we can see that the meaning of the term *nāma* is bound up in a direct way with certain traditional ideas which have a truly fundamental character in Hindu doctrine, that is, those concerning the 'primordiality of sound' and the 'perpetuity of the Veda'.

9. *Brihadāraṇyaka Upanishad*, 1.4.17.

10. It is nevertheless worth adding that in certain cases sight and its organ may also symbolize intellectual intuition (the 'eye of knowledge' in the Hindu tradition and 'the eye of the heart' in the Islamic), but then it is a matter of another aspect of the symbolism of light, and consequently of 'visibility', different from that which is presently under consideration, for in this case it is above all the relationships of sight and hearing, or the corresponding sensible qualities, that is operative, it being always necessary to remember that traditional symbolism is never 'systematic'.

10

$M\bar{A}Y\bar{A}$

A. K. COOMARASWAMY recently observed that it is preferable to translate *Māyā* as 'art' rather than 'illusion', as is commonly
done, and this translation does indeed correspond to a point of view
that might be called more principial:

> He who produces manifestation by means of his 'art' is the Divine
> Architect, and the world is his 'art'; as such the world is neither
> more nor less unreal than are our own works of art, which,
> because of their relative impermanence, are also unreal if com-
> pared to the art that 'resides' in the artist.[1]

The chief danger in using the word 'illusion' is indeed that one too
often risks making it synonymous with 'unreality' understood in an
absolute fashion, that is, in considering things that are called illusory as nothingness pure and simple, whereas it is only a question of
different degrees of reality—but we shall return to this point later.
For the moment we shall add in this connection that the fairly frequent translation of *Māyā* as 'magic', which is based on a verbal similarity that is wholly external and in fact rests on no etymological
kinship, seems to have been strongly influenced by the Western
prejudice that magic has only purely imaginary effects with no basis
in reality, which again amounts to the same error. In any case, even
for those who recognize the reality of the phenomena produced by
magic in their relative order, there is obviously no reason to
attribute to the productions of divine 'art' an especially 'magical'

---

1. From review of the posthumous book by Heinrich Zimmer, *Myths and Symbols in Indian Art and Civilization*, in *The Review of Religion*, March, 1947 issue,
p 286.

character, any more than to restrict in any other way the scope of the symbolism that assimilates them to 'artifacts' understood in the most general sense.[2]

'*Māyā* is the maternal "power" (*Shakti*) by which the Divine Understanding acts.'[3] More precisely yet it is *Kriyā-Shakti*, that is, 'Divine Activity' (which is *Ichchhā-Shakti*). As such, it inheres in *Brahmā* himself, or in the supreme Principle; it is therefore situated at an incomparably higher level than *Prakriti*, and, if the latter is also called *Māyā*, notably in the *Sānkhya*, this is because it is in reality only the reflection of this *Shakti* in the 'cosmological' order.[4] Moreover, here one can observe the application of the inverse sense of the analogy, the Supreme Activity being reflected in pure passivity, and the principial 'omnipotence' in the potentiality of *materia prima*. Furthermore, by the very fact that it is the divine 'art' residing in the Principle, *Māyā* is also identified with 'Wisdom' or *Sophia*, understood in exactly the same sense as in the Judeo-Christian tradition, and as such it is the mother of the *Avatāra*. This is so primarily in view of its eternal generation as the *Shakti* of the Principle, which moreover is one with the Principle itself of which it is but the 'maternal' aspect,[5] and also in view of its birth in the manifested world as *Prakriti*; this illustrates yet more clearly the connection that exists between the superior and inferior aspects of *Māyā*.[6]

2. It is understood that this meaning must conform to the traditional conception of art, and not to the 'aesthetic' theories of the moderns.

3. A.K. Coomaraswamy, idem.

4. In Western terminology, one could say that *Natura naturans* must not be confused with *Natura naturata*, although both may of course be called by the same name *Natura*.

5. Krishna says: 'Although without birth... I am born of my own *Māyā*.' *Bhagavad-Gītā*, IV.6.

6. Cf. *The Great Triad*, chap. 1, final part. In this connection it must be strictly understood that as regards its conception of the Theotokos [God-bearer or Mother of God, an appellation of Mary], the Christian tradition, not distinctly envisaging the 'maternal' aspect in the Principle itself, can only place itself, at least explicitly, at the second of the two points of view we just indicated. As Coomaraswamy says [idem], 'nor is it any accident that the Buddha's mother's name was *Māyā*' (and similarly, among the Greeks *Maïa* is the mother of Hermes; the comparison that some prople have wished to draw between the name *Māyā* and that of *Maria* also rests upon this.

In connection with what has just been said concerning divine 'art', we can add that the meaning of the 'veil of *Māyā*' is primarily that of the 'fabric' which, as it is woven, gives rise to manifestation (we have spoken of this elsewhere),[7] and although it seems to escape the attention of most, this meaning is quite clearly indicated in certain representations where the various beings belonging to the manifested world are represented upon this veil. It is therefore only secondarily that the veil appears at the same time to hide or somehow envelop the Principle, and this is because the deployment of manifestation in effect conceals the latter from our sight. This point of view, which is that of manifested beings, is moreover the inverse of the principial point of view, for it causes the manifestation to appear 'exterior' with respect to the Principle, whereas in reality it can only be 'interior' since nothing can in any way exist outside of the Principle, which by the very fact that it is infinite necessarily contains all things in itself.

This brings us back to the question of illusion. What is properly illusory is the point of view that leads us to consider manifestation as exterior to the Principle, and it is in this sense that illusion is also 'ignorance' (*avidyā*), that is to say precisely the opposite, or inverse, of the 'Wisdom' mentioned above. One could say that this is the other face of *Māyā*, but with the stipulation that this face exists only in consequence of the erroneous way in which we envisage its productions. These latter are not really what they seem to be, for as every work of art expresses something of its author so do they all express something of the Principle, in which all their reality consists. Their reality is therefore only a dependent and 'participated' reality that can be called null in regard to the absolute reality of the Principle,[8] but which is no less real in itself for that. Illusion can then be understood in two different senses: either as a false appearance that things assume with respect to us, or as a lesser reality of those same things with respect to the Principle; but in both cases a real basis is necessarily implied, so that illusion could never in any way be assimilated with pure nothingness.

7. *The Symbolism of the Cross*, chap. 14.
8. In this connection Coomaraswamy recalls a remark made by St Augustine: *Quo comparato nec pulchra sunt nec bona sunt nec sunt* [Compared with God they are not beautiful nor are they good nor do they exist] (*Confessions* XI, 4).

11

SANĀTANA DHARMA

THE notion of *Sanātana Dharma* has no equivalent in the West, to the point that it seems impossible to find a term or an expression that could convey its meaning entirely and in all its aspects, any translation one might propose for it being, if not altogether false, at least quite inadequate. A.K. Coomaraswamy thought that the expression best approximating it would be *Philosophia Perennis*, taken in the sense in which this was understood in the Middle Ages, and this is indeed true in certain respects although there are nevertheless considerable differences, which it will be all the more useful to examine here because there are those who too easily believe in the possibility of simply assimilating these two notions.

We should note at the outset that the difficulty does not hinge on the translation of the word *sanātana*, for which the Latin *perennis* is really a true equivalent; it is properly a question here of 'perenniality' or perpetuity, and not of eternity, as is sometimes claimed. Indeed, this term *sanātana* implies a notion of duration, whereas eternity on the contrary is essentially 'non-duration', the duration in question being indefinite so to speak, or, more precisely, 'cyclical'—as in the Greek *aiōnios*, which likewise lacks the meaning of 'eternal', which, through a regrettable confusion the moderns too often attribute to it. What is perpetual in this sense is what subsists continuously from the beginning to the end of a cycle, and according to Hindu tradition the cycle that must be considered in the case of the *Sanātana Dharma* is a *Manvantara*, that is to say the duration of manifestation of a terrestrial humanity. We must immediately add— for its full importance will become evident later—that *sanātana* also has the sense of 'primordial', and it is moreover easy to understand its very direct link with what we have just noted because what is truly perpetual can only be what goes back to the very beginning of the cycle. Finally, it must be clearly understood that this perpetuity and the stability it necessarily implies, while it must not in any way be confused with eternity, with which it has no common measure, is a sort of reflection in the conditions of our world, of the eternity and the immutability belonging to those principles of which *Sanā-tana Dharma* is likewise the expression with respect to our world.

The word *perennis* can itself also include all we have just explained, but it would be quite difficult to say to what degree the scholastics of the Middle Ages, to whose language the term *Philo-sophia Perennis* more particularly belongs, were clearly aware of it, for although obviously traditional their point of view nonetheless only extended to an exterior domain and was in many respects limited. However that may be, and admitting that, independently of all historical considerations, one could restore to this word the pleni-tude of its meaning, what remains nonetheless a cause for more serious reservations as concerns the assimilation just discussed is the use of the term *Philosophia*, which in a certain way corresponds precisely to the very limitations of the scholastic point of view. In the first place, this word too easily gives rise to ambiguities, espe-cially as the moderns habitually use it. One could of course resolve them by making it clear that the *Philosophia Perennis* is by no means 'a' philosophy, that is to say one particular conception more or less limited and systematic and having this or that individual as its author, but is rather the common foundation from which proceeds whatever is truly valid in all philosophies; and such a way of envis-aging it would certainly correspond to the thought of the Scholas-tics. But there is still an impropriety here, for if it is considered, as it must be, as an authentic expression of truth, it would much more likely be a question *Sophia* than *Philosophia*: 'wisdom' must not be confused with the aspiration that leads to it, or that seeks it and may lead to it, which is all the word 'philosophy' properly designates according to its etymology. It can perhaps be said that the word is subject to a certain transposition, and although in our view this term does not seem indispensable (as it would be if we really had none better at our disposal), we do not intend to contest such a possibility; but even in the most favorable case it would still be very far from a legitimate equivalent of *Dharma*, for it can never designate more than one doctrine, which, whatever may be the extent of its domain, will in any event remain merely theoretical, and consequently can in no way correspond to all that the traditional point of view comprehends in its integrality. From the traditional point of view, doctrine is in fact never seen as a simple theory sufficient in itself but as knowledge that must be realized effectively, and it comprises applications moreover that extend to all modes of human life without exception.

This extension results from the very meaning of the word *dharma*, which in any case is impossible to render by a single term in Western languages; by its root *dhri*, which has the meaning of carrying, supporting, sustaining, and maintaining, it designates above all a principle of conservation of beings, and consequently of stability, at least to the extent that the latter is compatible with the conditions of manifestation. It is important to note that the root *dhri* is almost identical in form and meaning with another root *dhru*, from which is derived the word *dhruva*, which designates 'pole'. One must actually turn to this idea of 'pole' or 'axis' of the manifested world if one wishes to understand the notion of *dharma* in its most profound sense, for it is what remains invariable at the center of the revolutions of all things, ruling the course of change by the very fact that it does not participate in it. It must not be forgotten in this connection that such language, by virtue of the synthetic character of the thought it expresses, is much more closely linked to symbolism than are modern languages, where such a link no longer subsists to any extent except by virtue of a distant derivation. And if it did not lead us too far from our subject, one could even demonstrate that this notion of *dharma* is connected quite directly to the symbolic representation of the 'axis' through the figure of the 'World Tree'. [1]

One could say that if thus envisaged only in principle, *dharma* is necessarily *sanātana*, and is so in an even broader sense than indicated above since instead of being limited to a certain cycle and to

---

1. The following passage often repeats verbatim a corresponding passage from the study on *Dharma*, chap. 8.

the beings manifested therein, it applies equally to all beings and to all their states of manifestation. Indeed, here again we meet the idea of permanence and stability, but it goes without saying that this latter, outside of which there could be no question at all of *dharma*, can nevertheless be applied in a relative way to different levels and in more or less restricted domains, and this justifies all the secondary or 'specialized' meanings of this term. By the very fact that it must be conceived as the principle of conservation of beings, *dharma* consists for these beings in the conformity of each to its own essential nature. In this sense one can therefore speak in this sense of the *dharma* proper to each being—designated more precisely as *svadharma*—or of each category of beings, as well as of a world or state of existence, or again of only a definite portion of the latter, that of a certain people or a certain period; and when one speaks of *Sanātana Dharma*, it is then as we have said a question of the totality of a humanity throughout the duration of its manifestation, which constitutes a *Manvantara*. It can also be said that in this case it is the 'law' or the 'norm' proper to that cycle, formulated from its very beginning by the *Manu* governing it, that is to say by the cosmic intelligence that reflects the divine Will and expresses universal Order therein. In principle this is the true sense of the *Mānava Dharma*, considered apart from all the particular adaptations that can be derived from it, although these latter may legitimately receive the same designation in that in the final analysis they will only be translations required by varying circumstances of time and place. We must add however that in such cases it may happen that the very idea of 'law' in fact entails a certain restriction, for although it can be applied by extension to the contents of the whole body of sacred scriptures, as is true of its Hebrew equivalent *Torah*, it makes us think most immediately and naturally of the 'legislative' aspect properly speaking, which is assuredly very far from constituting the entire tradition, although it is an integral part of every civilization that can be qualified as normal. This legislative aspect, although in reality only an application to the social order, necessarily presupposes (as do all other such applications) the purely metaphysical doctrine constituting the essential and fundamental part of the tradition, the principial knowledge upon which all the rest wholly depends and without which nothing really traditional, in whatever domain it may be, could in any way exist.

We have spoken of the universal order, which is the expression of the divine Will in manifestation and which in each state of existence assumes particular modalities determined by the conditions proper to that state. Now in certain respects at least, *dharma* may be defined as conformity to order, which explains the close relationship between it and *rita*, which is also order and has the etymologically sense of 'rectitude', as does the *Te* of the Far-Eastern traditions, with which Hindu *dharma* has much in common— and this clearly calls to mind once again the notion of 'axis', of a constant and invariable direction. At the same time this term *rita* is obviously identical with the word 'rite', which in its original meaning also effectively designated everything accomplished in conformity with order, all integrally traditional civilizations, especially at their inception, being characterized by a properly ritual character. Rites only began to take on a more restricted meaning in consequence of the degeneration that gave rise to 'profane' activity in all domains, the distinction between 'sacred' and 'profane' implying of course that certain things were thenceforth envisaged as outside the traditional point of view rather than the latter applying equally to all—and these things, by the very fact that they are considered 'profane', have truly become *adharma* or *anrita*. By contrast it must be understood that rites, which then correspond to the 'sacred', always conserve the same 'dharmic' character as it were and represent what still remains of what preceded that degeneration. In reality, it is non-ritual activity that is deviant or abnormal, in particular all mere 'conventions' or 'customs', which, lacking any profound reason and being of purely human invention, did not exist originally but only arose through deviation. Whatever some may think, rites envisaged from the traditional point of view (as they must be to be worthy of the name) can have absolutely no relation with such counterfeits or parodies. Furthermore—and this point is essential—when conformity to order is spoken of this must not be understood in respect of the human order alone, but also and even above all of the cosmic order. In every traditional conception there is in fact always a strict correspondence between the one and the other, and it is precisely the rite that consciously preserves the relationships, implying in a way a collaboration of man in that sphere where his activity takes place—the cosmic order itself.

From this it follows that if the *Sanātana Dharma* is considered as an integral tradition, it includes principially all branches of human activity, which moreover are 'transformed' thereby, since by virtue of this integration they participate in the 'nonhuman' character inherent in every tradition, or, better yet, constitute the very essence of tradition as such. It is therefore the exact opposite of 'humanism', that is to say of the point of view that would like to reduce everything to the purely human level, which basically is one with the profane point of view itself. It is especially in this that the traditional conception of the sciences and of the arts and sciences differs most profoundly from their profane conception, to such a point that one could say without exaggeration that the two are separated by a veritable abyss. From the traditional point of view the sciences and arts are really only valid and legitimate insofar as they adhere to universal principles in such a way that they in fact appear as applications of the fundamental doctrine in a certain contingent order, just as social legislation and organization are such in another domain. Through this participation in the essence of the tradition, science and art, in all their modes of operation, also have that ritual character of which we have just spoken, and of which no activity is deprived so long as it remains what it must normally be. And we might add that from this point of view there is no distinction to be made between arts and crafts, which traditionally are but one and the same thing. We cannot dwell further on all these considerations, which have in any case already been elucidated on previous occasions, but we think that we have at least said enough to show how in every respect all this goes beyond 'philosophy', no matter how this latter may be understood.

It should now be easy to understand what the *Sanātana Dharma* really is: it is nothing other than the primordial tradition, which alone subsists continuously and without change across the entire *Manvantara* and thus possesses cyclical perpetuity because its very primordiality removes it from the vicissitudes of successive ages, and it is this tradition alone that can in all strictness be regarded as

truly and fully integral. Moreover, owing to the descending course
of the cycle and the resulting spiritual obscuration, the primordial
tradition has become hidden and inaccessible to ordinary humanity. It is the primary source and the common foundation of all particular traditional forms which proceed from it by adaptation to the
particular conditions of peoples and times, but none of these can be
identified with the *Sanātana Dharma* itself or be considered an adequate expression of it, although they are nevertheless always more
or less veiled images of it. Every orthodox tradition is a reflection of
and, one could say, a 'substitute' for the primordial tradition in the
measure permitted by contingent circumstances, so that if it is not
the *Sanātana Dharma* it nevertheless truly represents it for those
who effectively adhere to it and participate in it, since they can only
reach it in this way and since it expresses, if not the fullness thereof,
at least everything that concerns them directly, and under the form
most suited to their individual nature. In a certain sense, all these
diverse traditional forms are contained principially in the *Sanātana
Dharma*, for they are just so many regular and legitimate adaptations of it, and not one of the developments to which they are subject in the course of time could ultimately ever be anything else.
And in another inverse and complementary sense they all contain
the *Sanātana Dharma* as that in them which is most inner and 'central'. In their different degrees of exteriority they are like so many
veils concealing the *Sanātana Dharma*, permitting it to show
through only in an attenuated and more or less partial fashion.

This being true for all traditional forms, it would be an error to
wish to assimilate the *Sanātana Dharma* purely and simply to one
among them, whichever one that might be, even the Hindu tradition such as we find it at present. And if this error is in fact sometimes made, it can only be by those whose horizon, by reason of the
circumstances in which they find themselves, is limited to that tradition alone. If however that assimilation is in a certain measure
legitimate according to what we have just explained, the adherents
of other traditions could in the same sense and by the same right
also say that their own tradition is the *Sanātana Dharma*, such an
affirmation always remaining true in a relative sense although obviously false in the absolute sense. There is however a reason why the

notion of the *Sanātana Dharma* appears to be linked more particularly with the Hindu tradition, for of all the traditional forms existing today, the latter derives most directly from the primordial tradition. It prolongs it outwardly, as it were, although always of course conforming to the conditions in which the human cycle unfolds (of which moreover it gives a more complete description than is to be found elsewhere), and hence participating in its perpetuity to a higher degree than all the others. It is also interesting to note that the Hindu and the Islamic traditions explicitly affirm the validity of all the other orthodox traditions, and if this is so it is because as the temporally first and the last in the course of the *Manvantara* they must to the same extent integrate—although in different modes—all the diverse forms that have arisen in the interval, so as to render possible the 'return to origins' by which the end of the cycle will rejoin its beginning, whence, at the starting-point of another *Manvantara*, the true *Sanātana Dharma* will again be outwardly manifest.

We must still point out two erroneous conceptions only too prevalent in our time, bearing witness to a lack of understanding that is far more serious and more complete than is the assimilation of the *Sanātana Dharma* to a particular traditional form. One of these misconceptions is that of the so-called 'reformers'—met with today even in India—who think themselves capable of recovering the *Sanātana Dharma* by proceeding with a sort of simplification of the tradition that is more or less arbitrary, something that in reality merely corresponds to their own individual tendencies and most often betrays prejudices stemming from the influence of the modern Western spirit. What these 'reformers' generally have in mind in the first instance is the elimination of precisely what has the most profound significance, either because it eludes them entirely or because it runs counter to their preconceived ideas, and this attitude is quite comparable to that of the 'critics' who reject as 'interpolations' everything in a text that does not agree with the idea they have of it or with the meaning they wish to discover there. When we speak of a 'return to origins', as we did a moment ago, it is assuredly a matter of something else entirely, something that in no way depends on the initiative of individuals as such; besides, we do not at all see why the primordial tradition should be as simple as these people claim, if it is not that an intellectual infirmity or weakness wishes it were so. And why should truth be obliged to accommodate itself to the mediocrity of the faculties of comprehension of the average individual today? To realize that this is not at all the case it suffices to understand on the one hand that the *Sanātana Dharma* contains everything without exception, and more besides, that has been expressed through all traditional forms, and on the other that it necessarily involves truths of the highest and most profound order, such as have become most inaccessible through the spiritual and intellectual obscuration inherent in the cyclical descent. Under these conditions the simplicity dear to modernists of every ilk is obviously as far as may be from constituting a mark of the antiquity of a traditional doctrine, and with even greater reason of its primordiality.

The other erroneous conception to which we want to draw attention belongs above all to the various contemporary schools that are connected to what is fitly designated 'occultism'. As a rule these schools proceed 'syncretically', that is, by bringing together various traditions, to the extent that they are acquainted with them, in a wholly exterior and superficial manner without even trying to draw out what they have in common, but only to juxtapose as well as they can elements borrowed from one or another of them. The results, as incongruous as they are fanciful, are nonetheless presented as the expression of an 'ancient wisdom' or of an 'archaic doctrine' from which all traditions would have issued, and which they identify with the primordial tradition, or with the *Sanātana Dharma*, although these terms themselves seem not to be understood by the schools concerned. It goes without saying that all of this, whatever be the pretensions, cannot have the least value and only corresponds to a purely profane point of view, the more so as these conceptions are almost invariably accompanied by a total failure to grasp the necessity of adhering above all to a given tradition for whomever wishes to penetrate the spiritual domain to any degree whatever. And in this connection it should be understood that we speak of an affective adherence with all the consequences that this implies, including the practice of the rites of that tradition, and not of a vague 'ideal' feeling of connectedness such as leads some Westerners to declare themselves Hindus or Buddhists without much knowledge of what these are, and at all events without ever thinking of establishing a real and regular attachment to these traditions, although such an attachment is the indispensable point of departure from which each according to his capacity may seek to go further. In effect, what is required are not speculations in the void, but knowledge which must be essentially ordained with a view to spiritual realization. It is only in this way that from within the traditions—and one can speak with more exactitude of their very center, should it be successfully reached—one can truly realize that which constitutes their essential and fundamental unity, and thereby truly attain full knowledge of the *Sanātana Dharma*.

12

Eastern Metaphysics

I have taken Eastern metaphysics as the subject of this essay. It would perhaps have been better simply to say metaphysics unqualified, for in truth pure metaphysics is neither Eastern nor Western, but universal, being in essence above and beyond all forms and all contingencies. It is only the exterior forms in which it is clothed in order to serve the necessities of exposition, so as to express whatever is expressible, that can be either Eastern or Western; but beneath their diversity there is always and everywhere a selfsame basis, at least wherever true metaphysics exists, and this for the simple reason that truth is one.

If this be so, what need is there to speak specifically of Eastern metaphysics? The reason is that in the present intellectual state of the Western world metaphysics is a thing forgotten, generally unknown and more or less entirely lost, whereas in the East it still remains the object of an effective knowledge. If one wishes to know metaphysics, therefore, one must turn to the East; and even if one's wish is to recover some of the metaphysical traditions that may once have existed in the West, a West that was in many respects much closer to the East than it is today, it is above all with the help of Eastern doctrines and by comparison with them that one may succeed, because these are the only teachings in the domain of metaphysics that can still be studied directly. But in order to do so, it is quite clear that they must be studied as the Easterners themselves study them, and not in giving oneself over to more or less hypothetical and occasionally wholly fantastical interpretations. It is also too often forgotten that the Eastern civilizations still exist and that they still have qualified representatives to whom one need only apply in order to learn the true nature of the subject.

I have said 'Eastern metaphysics' and not exclusively Hindu metaphysics, for doctrines of this order, with all they imply, are not to be found only in India, contrary to what some people believe, who in any case have but a poor understanding of their true nature. The case of India is by no means exceptional in this respect—it is precisely that of all civilizations that possess what might be called a traditional foundation. What is exceptional and abnormal, rather, are those civilizations which lack such a foundation; and in all truth, the only one known to us is that of the modern West. To take only the principal Eastern civilizations, in China the equivalent of Hindu metaphysics can be found in Taoism; elsewhere it can be found in certain esoteric schools of Islam (it should be understood, furthermore, that this Islamic esoterism has nothing in common with the overt philosophy of the Arabs, which is for the most part of Greek inspiration). The only difference is that everywhere but in India these doctrines are reserved for a relatively restricted and insular elite. This was also the case in the West during the Middle Ages, for an esoterism similar in many respects to that of Islam, and just as purely metaphysical, but of which the moderns for the most part do not even suspect the existence. In India it is not possible to speak of esoterism in the strict sense of the word because there one does not find doctrine with the two aspects, exoteric and esoteric. One can only speak of a natural esoterism, in the sense that each individual will reach just those depths or go just so far into the doctrine as his own intellectual capacities allow, because for certain human individuals there are limitations inherent in their very nature that are impossible for them to overcome.

Naturally, forms differ from one civilization to another since they must adapt to different conditions. Although more familiar myself with the Hindu forms, I have no qualms in employing others as need arises if they can further the understanding of certain points. There is nothing problematic in this, since they are only different expressions of the same thing. Once again, truth is one, and it is the same for all who, by whatever way, come to know it.

This being said, it should now be made clear just what is meant by the word 'metaphysics', and all the more so since I have frequently had occasion to note that everyone does not understand it in quite the same way. I think the best course to take in dealing with words that might give rise to ambiguity is to restore to them as much as possible their primal and etymological meaning. Now, according to its composition, the word 'metaphysics' means literally 'beyond physics', taking the word 'physics' in the accepted sense it always had for the ancients, that is to say as 'knowledge of nature' in its widest sense. Physics is the study of all that pertains to the domain of nature; metaphysics, on the other hand, is the study of what lies beyond nature. How, then, can some people claim that metaphysical knowledge is natural knowledge, either in respect of its object or with regard to the faculties by which it is obtained? Here we have a complete misconception, a contradiction in terms; and yet what is more amazing is that this confusion affects even those who should preserve some idea of true metaphysics and know how to distinguish it clearly from the pseudo-metaphysics of modern philosophers.

But perhaps one might say that if the word 'metaphysics' gives rise to such confusion, would it not be better to abandon it and replace it with something more suitable? In reality this would cause problems, since by its formation this word is perfectly suited for that to which it refers; moreover, it would hardly be possible, seeing that Western languages posses no other word equally well adapted to this usage. It is out of the question to use the word 'knowledge' pure and simple, as is done in India, although this is indeed knowledge par excellence, the only kind truly worthy of the name, because it would only make things more confusing for Westerners who habitually associate knowledge with nothing outside the scientific and rational domain. And in any event, is it necessary to be so concerned over the abuse made of one word? If all such words had to be rejected, how many would remain at our disposal? Is it not sufficient to take precautions to avoid misunderstandings and misrepresentations? We are no more attached to the word 'metaphysics' than to any other, but until a better term is suggested to take its place, we will continue to use it as before.

Unfortunately, there are people who think they can 'judge' that of which they are ignorant, and who, because they apply the name 'metaphysics' to a purely human and rational knowledge (which for us is merely science or philosophy), imagine that Eastern metaphysics is nothing more nor other than that, whence they draw the logical conclusion that this metaphysics cannot truly lead to any particular results. Yet it does indeed lead to such results, but only because it is something quite other than they supposed. Now what they envisage really has nothing to do with metaphysics, since it is only knowledge of a natural order, a knowledge that is profane and superficial; this is definitely not what we wish to discuss. Do we then make 'metaphysical' synonymous with 'supernatural'? We would willingly accept such an assimilation, since, as long as we do not go beyond nature, that is to say the manifest world in all its extension (and not only the perceptible world, which is but one infinitesimal element of it), we remain in the realm of the physical. What is metaphysical, as we have already said, is that which lies beyond and above nature, and is thus properly speaking 'supernatural'.

But here an objection will undoubtedly be raised: is it possible, then, to go beyond nature? We do not hesitate to answer plainly: not only is it possible, but it is done. But those are just words, it will be said; what proofs can you give us? It is truly strange that people ask for proof concerning the possibility of a kind of knowledge instead of searching for it and verifying it for themselves by undertaking the work necessary to acquire it. For those who possess this knowledge, what interest can there be in all this discussion? Substituting a 'theory of knowledge' for knowledge itself is perhaps the greatest admission of impotence in modern philosophy.

Moreover, all certitude contains something incommunicable; no one can truly attain to any knowledge other than through a strictly personal effort, and all that one can do for another is to provide an opportunity and indicate the means by which to attain it. That is why it would be vain to attempt to impose any belief in the purely intellectual realm; in this respect the best argument in the world cannot replace direct and effective knowledge.

Now, can metaphysics as we understand it be defined? No, for to define is always to limit, and what is under consideration is, in and of itself, truly and absolutely limitless and thus cannot be confined to any formula or any system whatsoever. Metaphysics might be partially characterized, for example, by saying that it is the knowledge of universal principles, but this is not a definition in the proper sense and in any case only conveys a fairly vague notion. Something can be added by saying that the scope of these principles is far greater than was thought by some Westerners, who, although really studying metaphysics, did so in a partial and incomplete way. Thus, when Aristotle considered metaphysics as a knowledge of being as being, he identified it with ontology, which is to say that he took the part for the whole. For Eastern metaphysics, pure being is neither the first nor the most universal of principles, for it is already a determination. It is thus necessary to go beyond being, and it is this that is of the greatest importance. This is why in all truly metaphysical conceptions, allowance must always be made for the inexpressible; and just as everything that can be expressed is literally nothing in comparison with that which surpasses expression, so the finite, whatever its magnitude, is as nothing to the infinite. One can intimate much more than one can express, and ultimately, this is the part played by exterior forms; all such forms, whether words or symbols, merely constitute supports, footholds from which to rise to possibilities of conception that transcend them immeasurably. We will return to this point later.

We speak of metaphysical conceptions for lack of any other term whereby to make ourselves understood, but this should not be taken to mean that here is something comparable to scientific or philosophic conceptions; it is not a question of effecting some sort of 'abstraction', but of attaining direct knowledge of reality as it is. Science is rational, discursive knowledge, always indirect, a knowledge by reflection; metaphysics is a supra-rational, intuitive and unmediated knowledge. Moreover, this pure intellectual intuition, without which there is no true metaphysics, has no connection with the intuition spoken of by certain contemporary philosophers, which is, on the contrary, infra-rational. There is an intellectual intuition and a sensible intuition; the one is beyond reason, but the other is within it; the latter can know only the world of change and becoming, that is to say of nature, or rather of a minute part of nature. The realm of intuition, on the contrary, is that of eternal and immutable principles—the metaphysical realm.

To comprehend universal principles directly, the transcendent intellect must itself be of a universal order; it is no longer an individual faculty, and to consider it as such would be contradictory, because it is not within the power of the individual to go beyond its own limits or to step outside the conditions that limit it as an individual. Reason is wholly and specifically a human faculty, but what lies beyond reason is truly 'non-human'; it is what makes metaphysical knowledge possible, and this knowledge, it must be reaffirmed, is not a human knowledge. In other words, it is not as man that man can attain it, but as that being which is human in one of its aspects and at the same time is something other, more than a human being; and it is the attainment of effective awareness of supra-individual states that is the real object of metaphysics, or better still, of metaphysical knowledge itself. Thus, we arrive at one of the most essential points, which it is necessary to stress: if the individual were a complete being, if it constituted a closed system in the manner of Leibnitz's monad, metaphysics would not be possible; irremediably closed in on itself, such a being would have no means of becoming aware of anything outside its own order of existence. But such is not the case: in reality, the individual represents but one transitory and contingent manifestation of the true being; it is but one specific state among an indefinite multitude of states of the same being, and that being is in itself absolutely independent of all its manifestations, just as, to use an analogy that appears frequently in Hindu texts, the sun is absolutely independent of the many images in which it is reflected. Such is the fundamental distinction between 'Self' and 'ego', the personality and the individuality; and, just as the images are connected by the luminous rays to the solar source without which they would have neither existence nor reality, so the individuality, either of the human individual or of any analogous state of manifestation, is bound by the personality to the principial center of being by this transcendent intellect of which we have just spoken. Within the limits of this exposition it is impossible to develop such considerations more fully, or to give a more exact idea of the theory of the multiple states of being, but I think I have said enough to give at least a sense of the paramount importance of any truly metaphysical doctrine.

I said 'theory', but it is not only a question of theory, and this is yet another point that requires clarification. Theoretical knowledge, which is still only indirect and in some way symbolic, is merely a preparation—although indispensable—for true knowledge. It is, moreover, the only knowledge that is in any way communicable, and this is why all exposition is but a means of approaching knowledge, which, being only virtual in the beginning, must later be effectively realized. Here we find another difference from the more limited metaphysics to which we referred earlier, that of Aristotle for instance, which remains theoretically inadequate in that it limits itself to being, and in which, moreover, theory seems to be presented as self-sufficient rather than expressly bound up with a corresponding realization, as is the case in all Eastern doctrines. And yet, even in this imperfect metaphysics—we might be tempted to call it a demi-metaphysics—statements sometimes are encountered which, had they been properly understood, should have led to entirely different conclusions. Thus, did not Aristotle specifically state that a being is all that it knows? This affirmation of identification through knowledge is the very principle of metaphysical realization; but here the principle remains isolated, its value merely that of a wholly theoretical statement; it carries no weight, and it seems that, after having been propounded, it is no longer even thought of. How was it that Aristotle himself and his followers failed to see all that was implied therein? Admittedly, the same holds true in many other cases, where they seem to have forgotten other equally essential things, such as the distinction between pure intellect and reason, even after having defined them no less explicitly. Such lapses are strange indeed. Should one see in this the effect of certain limitations inherent in the Western mind, apart from some rare but always possible exceptions? This might be true to a certain extent, yet it is not necessary to believe that Western intellectuality has always been as narrowly limited as it is in the present age. However, such doctrines are only outward, after all, although certainly superior to many others since in spite of everything they incorporate a part of true metaphysics, even if always in conjunction with considerations of another order that have nothing to do with metaphysics... For our part, we are certain that there was in antiquity and in the Middle Ages more than this in the West, that there were available to the elite doctrines of a purely metaphysical nature that could be called complete, including that realization which for most moderns is certainly a thing barely conceivable. If the West has lost its memory of such teachings so completely, it is because it has broken with its own tradition, and this is why modern civilization is an abnormal and deviant one.

If purely theoretical knowledge were itself its own end, and if metaphysics went no further, it would still assuredly be worth something, but it would be altogether insufficient. In spite of conferring the genuine certainty, even greater than mathematical certainty, that belongs to such knowledge, it would remain analogous to that certainty which at an inferior level constitutes terrestrial and human, scientific and philosophical, speculation, although in an incomparably superior order. That is not what metaphysics should be. Let others dabble in 'mental sport', or in what passes for such; that is their affair. But such things as these are of no interest to us, and we think moreover that the inquisitiveness of the psychologist must remain entirely alien to the metaphysician. For the latter, what matters is to know what is, and to know it in such a manner that one is truly and effectively the sum-total of what one knows.

As for the means of metaphysical realization, we are well aware of such objections as can be made by those who believe it their duty to contest the possibility of such realization. These means, indeed, must be within man's reach; they must, in the first stages at least, be adapted to the conditions of the human state, since this is the state in which the being actually finds itself and from which it must subsequently take possession of the higher states. Thus it is the forms belonging to the world in which its current manifestation is situated that the being will use as a support to raise itself above this very world. Words, symbolic signs, rites, or preparatory methods of various kinds, have no other raison d'être or function; as we have already said, they are supports and nothing else. But, some will ask, how is it possible that merely contingent means produce effects that immeasurably surpasses them, effects of a wholly different order than that to which they themselves belong? We should first point out that in reality these are only accidental means, and that the results they help to obtain are in no way effected by them; they place the being in the desired frame of mind to achieve these results more easily, and that is all. If this objection were valid in the present case, it would be equally valid for religious rites, the sacraments for example, in which the disparity between means and end is no less disproportionate. Perhaps some of those who raise such objections have not considered them sufficiently. As for us, we do not confuse a simple means with a cause in the true sense of the word, and we do not regard metaphysical realization as an effect of anything at all, because it is not the production of something that does not yet exist, but the awareness of that which is, permanently and immutably, beyond all succession, temporal or otherwise, since all states of the being considered in their principle exist in perfect simultaneity in the eternal present.

Thus we see no difficulty in recognizing that there is no common measure between metaphysical realization and the means leading to it, or, if one prefers, that prepare for it. Furthermore, that is why none of these means are strictly or absolutely necessary, or at least there is only one truly indispensable preparation, and that is theoretical knowledge. On the other hand, the latter could not go very far without a means that should thus be considered as playing the most important and constant part, which means is concentration, something completely foreign, even contrary, to the mental habits of the modern West, where everything tends toward dispersion and incessant change. All other means are secondary in relation to this one; they serve above all to promote concentration and to harmonize the diverse elements of human individuality in order to facilitate effective communication between this individuality and the higher states of the being.

From the very start, moreover, these means can be almost indefinitely varied, for they have to be adapted to the temperament of each individual and to his particular aptitudes and dispositions. Thereafter, the differences diminish, for it is a case of multiple paths all leading to the same end. At a certain stage all multiplicity disappears, but at that stage the individual and contingent means will have played their part. This part, which it is unnecessary to enlarge upon, is compared in certain Hindu writings to a horse that helps a man to reach the end of his journey more quickly and easily, but without which he could still reach it. Rites and various methods point the way to metaphysical realization, but one could nevertheless set them aside, and by unswervingly setting the mind and all powers of the being on the aim of this realization, could finally attain the supreme goal. But if there are means that make the effort less laborious, why choose to neglect them? Is it confusing the contingent and the absolute to take into account the conditions of our human state, since it is from this state, itself contingent, that we are at present obliged to set forth in conquest of the higher states, and finally of the supreme and unconditioned state?

Having considered the teachings common to all traditional doctrines, let us now turn to the principal stages of metaphysical realization. The first, which to a certain extent is merely preliminary, operates in the human domain and does not extend beyond the limits of the individuality. It consists of an indefinite extension of that individuality of which the corporeal modality, the only modality developed in the ordinary man, represents but the smallest portion. In fact one must start from the corporeal modality, whence the use in the beginning of means borrowed from the sensible order, which means must have repercussions throughout the other modalities of the human being. In short, the phase in question is the realization or development of all the potentialities contained virtually within the human individuality, constituting multiple prolongations thereof that reach out in diverse directions beyond the corporeal and sensible realm; and it is by means of these prolongations that it is possible to establish communication with the other states.

This realization of the integral individuality is described by all traditions as the restoration of what is called the 'primordial state', which is regarded as the state of true man and which already escapes some of the limitations characteristic of the ordinary state, notably those due to the temporal condition. The being that has attained this 'primordial state' is still only a human individual and is without effective possession of any supra-individual states. Nevertheless he is henceforth liberated from time, the apparent succession of things having been transmuted for him into simultaneity; he is in conscious possession of a faculty unknown to the ordinary man, which might be called the 'sense of eternity'. This is of extreme importance, for he who cannot rise above the vantage-point of temporal succession and envisage all things in simultaneous mode is incapable of the least conception of the metaphysical order. The first thing to be done by those who wish to achieve true metaphysical understanding is to step outside time—we would willingly say into 'non-time', if such an expression did not seem too peculiar and unusual. This knowledge of the intemporal can, moreover, be achieved in some real measure, if incompletely, before one has attained the fullness of the 'primordial state' of which we have just spoken.

Perhaps it will be asked why this designation 'primordial state'? It is because all traditions, including that of the West (for the Bible itself says nothing different), are in accord in teaching that this was originally the normal state for humanity, while the present state is merely the result of a decline, the effect of a kind of progressive materialization occurring down the ages and throughout the duration of a particular cycle. We do not believe in 'evolution' in the sense the moderns have given the word; the so-called scientific hypotheses they have devised in no way correspond to reality. In any case, it is not possible here to make more than a passing mention of the theory of cosmic cycles,[1] which is particularly expounded in the Hindu doctrines; to do so would be to go beyond our subject, for cosmology is not metaphysics, although it depends closely upon it. Cosmology is no more than an application of metaphysics to the physical order, while the true natural laws are only the consequences, in a relative and contingent domain, of universal and necessary principles.

But let us return to metaphysical realization. Its second phase corresponds to supra-individual states which are still conditioned, although their conditions are completely different from those of the human state. Here the human world in which we remained in the preceding stages has been entirely and definitively left behind. It must also be added that what has been left behind is the world of forms in its most general sense, comprising all possible individual

1. See *Traditional Forms and Cosmic Cycles*, chap 1. ED.

states, for form is the condition common to all such states, by which individuality is defined as such. The being, which can no longer be called human, is henceforth free from the 'current of forms', to use a Far Eastern expression. There are moreover further distinctions to be made, for this stage can be subdivided: in reality it includes several stages, from the acquisition of states which, though non-formal, still belong to manifested existence, to the stage of universality which is that of pure being.

Nevertheless, as elevated as these states are when compared to the human state, and as remote as they may be from it, they are still only relative, and this is true even of the highest among them, which corresponds to the principle of all manifestation. The possession thereof is thus only a transitory result that should not be confused with the ultimate goal of metaphysical realization, which lies beyond being, and in comparison with which all the rest is but a journey and preparation. This supreme goal is the absolutely unconditioned state, set free from all limitation. For this very reason it is completely inexpressible, and anything we might say about it must be put in the form of a negation, the negation of all limits that determine and define all existence in its relativity. The attainment of this state is what the Hindu doctrine calls 'Deliverance' when considering it in relation to conditioned states, and 'Union' when envisaged in relation to the supreme Principle.

Moreover, all other states of the being can in principle be found in this unconditioned state, but transformed, disengaged from the particular conditions that determined them as special states. What subsists is everything that has a positive reality, since it is there that everything has its principle; the 'delivered' being is truly in possession of the fullness of its own potentialities. What have disappeared are merely the limiting conditions, of which the reality is negative, since they represent no more than a 'privation' in the Aristotelian sense of the word. Thus, far from being a kind of annihilation, as some Westerners believe, this final state is on the contrary absolute plenitude, the supreme reality compared to which all else is but illusion.

Let us add too that every result, even partial, obtained by the being in the course of metaphysical realization, is obtained definitively. For this being, the result is a permanent acquisition that nothing can ever take from it; the work accomplished in this order, even if interrupted before it is completed, is achieved once and for all by the very fact that it is outside of time. This is true even of simple theoretical knowledge, for all knowledge carries its benefit within it, in this way quite different from action, which is but a momentary modification of the being and is always distinct from its own effects. Furthermore, these effects are of the same domain and the same order of existence as that which has produced them; action cannot effectively liberate from action, and its consequences cannot reach beyond the limits of individuality, even when this is considered in its fullest possible extension. Action of any sort, not being opposed to the ignorance that is the root of all limitation, cannot dispel that ignorance; only knowledge can dispel ignorance, as sunlight disperses shadow, and it is at this point that the 'Self', the immutable and eternal principle of all manifested and unmanifested states, appears in its supreme reality.

After this brief and very imperfect sketch, which provides only the weakest notion of what metaphysical realization might be, it is absolutely essential to stress one point in order to avoid grave errors of interpretation: nothing referred to here has any connection whatsoever with phenomena of any kind, however extraordinary they may be. All phenomena are of the physical order; metaphysics is beyond phenomena, even taking the word in its widest sense. Among other consequences, it follows from this that the states to which we are referring are in no way 'psychological'; this must be stated plainly, since strange confusions sometimes arise in this connection. By very definition psychology can be concerned only with human states, and even then, as it is understood today, it reaches to only a very limited part of the individual's potentialities, which include far more than practitioners of this science could ever suspect. Indeed, the human individual is both much more and much less than is generally supposed in the West: much more, by reason of his possibilities of indefinite extension beyond the corporeal modality, to which, in short, everything belongs that is commonly studied; but he is also much less, since far from constituting a complete and self-sufficient being, he is but an outward manifestation, a fleeting appearance assumed by the true being, which in no way affects the essence of the latter in its immutability.

It must be emphasized that the metaphysical domain lies entirely outside the phenomenal world, for by dint of habit the moderns hardly ever recognize or investigate anything but phenomena, in which their interests lie almost exclusively, as the attention they have given to the experimental sciences bears witness; and their metaphysical inaptitude stems from the same tendency. Undoubtedly, it may happen that certain particular phenomena may occur during the labor of metaphysical realization, but in a wholly accidental manner. This is a rather unfortunate result, as occurrences of this sort can only be an impediment to those who might be tempted to attach some importance to them. Those who allow themselves to be stopped or turned aside by phenomena, and above all those who indulge in the search for extraordinary 'powers', have very little chance of pressing their realization any further than the degree already achieved before this deviation occurred.

This observation leads naturally to the correction of some erroneous interpretations on the subject of the term 'Yoga'; indeed, has it not been claimed that what the Hindus indicate by this word is the development of certain powers latent in the human being? What we have just said suffices to demonstrate that such a definition is to be rejected. In reality, the word 'Yoga' is the same as that which we have translated as literally as possible by the word 'Union'. What it properly defines is thus the supreme goal of metaphysical realization; and the 'Yogi', in the strictest sense of the term, is solely the person who attains this end. However, it is true that in some cases the same terms may be applied by extension to stages preparatory to 'Union' or even to simple preliminary techniques, as well as to the being that has reached the states corresponding to such stages or that uses those teachings to reach them. But how can it be maintained that a word having the primary meaning of 'Union' designates in its proper and original application breathing exercises or other things of that sort? Such exercises, and others generally based on what we might call the science of rhythm, do indeed figure among the means most widely practiced in promoting realization, but one must not mistake as an end that which amounts to no more than a contingent and accidental means, nor must one confuse the original meaning of a word with a secondary acceptation that is more or less distorted.

In referring to the original 'Yoga', and in saying that this word has always meant essentially the same thing, we might be prompted to pose a question regarding which we have as yet said nothing: what is the origin of these traditional metaphysical doctrines from which we have borrowed all our fundamental ideas? The answer is very simple, although it risks raising objections from those who would prefer to consider everything from an historical point of view, and the answer is that there is no origin—by which we mean no human origin—that can be determined in time. In other words, the origin of tradition, if indeed the word 'origin' has any place at all in such a case, is as 'non-human' as is metaphysics itself. Doctrines of this order did not appear at any particular moment in the history of humanity; the allusion we have made to the 'primordial state', and also what we have said of the timeless nature of all that concerns metaphysics, should enable us to grasp this point without too much difficulty, on condition that we concede, contrary to certain prejudices, that there are some things to which the historical point of view does not apply. Metaphysical truth is eternal, and by that very fact there have always existed beings able to know it truly and completely. What changes is only external forms and contingent means, and the change has nothing to do with what people today call 'evolution', it is simply an adaptation to such and such particular circumstances, to special conditions of some given race or age. From this springs the multiplicity of forms; but the foundation of the doctrine is no more modified and affected by it than the essential unity and identity of the being is altered by the multiplicity of its states of manifestation.

Thus metaphysical knowledge, as well as the realization it implies in order to truly be what it ought to be, are possible everywhere and always, at least in principle, and when this possibility is regarded in a quasi-absolute sense; but in fact, in practice so to speak, and in a relative sense, are they equally possible in just any environment and without making the least allowance for contingencies? On this score we shall be much less affirmative, at least as concerns realization, and this can be explained by the fact that in its beginning such a realization must take its support in the realm of contingencies. The conditions may be particularly unfavorable, such as those offered by the contemporary West, so much so that such a labor is almost impossible and can even be dangerous in the absence of any support offered by one's environment and in an ambiance that can only impede or even destroy the efforts of one who undertakes such a task. On the other hand, those civilizations that we call traditional are organized in a way that can actually prove an effective help, which no doubt is not strictly indispensable, any more than is anything else external, but without which it is however quite difficult to obtain effective results. Here is something that exceeds the strength of an isolated human individual, even if that individual happens to possess the requisite qualifications in other respects; hence we would not wish to encourage anyone in the present conditions to embark heedlessly upon such an undertaking, and this brings us to our conclusion.

For us, the great difference between the East and West (meaning here exclusively the modern West), the only difference that is truly essential, since all the other differences are derivative, is this: on the one hand, preservation of tradition and all that it implies, and on the other hand the neglect and loss of that same tradition; on the one side, the safeguarding of metaphysical knowledge, on the other, utter ignorance of all that relates to that realm. Between civilizations that open to their elite such possibilities as we have tried to intimate, which give the most appropriate means to realize these possibilities effectively, and in the case of at least a few, to realize them fully— between those traditional civilizations and a civilization that has developed along purely material lines, how could a common measure be found? And who, unless he were blinded by I know not what prejudice, would dare claim that material superiority compensates for intellectual inferiority? When we say intellectual, we mean true intellectuality, that which is limited neither to the human nor to the natural order, that which makes pure metaphysical knowledge possible in its absolute transcendence. A moment's reflection on these questions seems to me sufficient to leave no doubt or hesitation as to the appropriate answer in response.

The material superiority of the West is beyond dispute; nobody denies it, but it is hardly grounds for envy. But one must go further: sooner or later this excessive material development threatens to destroy the West if it does not recover itself in time and if it does not seriously consider a 'return to the source', as goes a saying current in certain schools of Islamic esoterism. Today one hears from many quarters of the 'defence of the West', but unfortunately it does not seem to be understood that it is chiefly against itself that the West needs to be defended, that the greatest and most formidable of the dangers that threaten it stem from its own present tendencies. It would be wise to meditate deeply on this, and one cannot urge this too strongly on all who are still capable of reflection. So it is with this that I will end my account, glad if I have succeeded in giving a sense, if not a full understanding, of that Eastern intellectuality that no longer has any equivalent in the West, and if I have been able to provide a glimpse, imperfect though it may be, of what true metaphysics is—knowledge par excellence, which alone, as the sacred texts of India say, is completely true, absolute, infinite, and supreme.

REVIEWS OF BOOKS & ARTICLES:
ANANDA K. COOMARASWAMY

REVIEWS OF BOOKS:
A. K. COOMARASWAMY

The Darker Side of Dawn (Washington, DC: *Smithsonian Miscellaneous Collections*, XCIV, 1935). This booklet contains some very interesting remarks on cosmogonic dualities, principally insofar as they are represented by an opposition between 'light' and 'darkness', and by certain connected questions, the symbolism of the serpent, among others. Let us also note a curious link between the subject-matter of the *Mahābhārata* and the Vedic conflict between the *Devas* and the *Asuras*, which also recall similarities with what is found in other traditional forms; and the same holds true of the color black as symbol of the unmanifest. We only regret that the author limited himself to noting all these observations a little too succinctly, in scarcely twenty pages, and can only hope that he will have occasion to return to these ideas and develop them further.

The Ṛg-Veda as Land-Náma-Bók (Luzac and Co., London [New Delhi: Bharatiya Publishing House, 1980]), also included in *The Vedas: Essays in Translation and Exegesis* (Kent: Prologos Books, 1976 [first ed., 1935]). The title of this book refers to an ancient Icelandic text, literally the 'Book of the taking of the land', considered here as comparable in certain respects to the *Ṛg-Veda*. The author's thesis, which seems perfectly correct to us, is that in all traditional writings of this sort, what is actually described is not a conqueror's appropriation of land, but the manifestation of beings at the very beginning and their establishment in a world designated symbolically as a 'land', so that any geographical and historical allusions have value only as symbol and analogy, as indeed any event can effectively have by reason of macrocosmic and microcosmic correspondences. These views are supported by an examination of the significance of a number of characteristic and frequently used terms, which gives rise to very interesting reflections touching many points of doctrine. Here we are far removed from the grossly materialist interpretation of orientalists; will the latter consent at least to reflect upon them a little?

'Angel and Titan: An Essay in Vedic Ontology' (*Journal of the American Oriental Society*, LV, no. 4, 1935). This important study is a sequel to *The Darker Side of Dawn*, which we reviewed previously. The principal idea here is that although opposed in their action, the *Devas* or 'Angels' and the *Asuras* or 'Titans', powers respectively of Light and Darkness in the *Ṛg-Veda*, are nonetheless one in essence, their distinction in reality bearing on their orientation or state. The *Asura* is potentially a *Deva*, the *Deva* is still an *Asura* by its original nature, the two designations can be applied to one and the same entity according to its mode of operation, as we see for example in the case of *Varuna*. On the other hand, while the *Devas* are usually represented in the forms of men and birds, the *Asuras* are shown in the shape of animals, especially serpents. This leads to a series of reflections of the greatest interest on various aspects of the symbolism of the serpent, principally from the cosmogonic point of view. Many other questions are addressed in the course of this work, and we cannot enumerate them all in detail, but let us at least mention that they include the nature of *Agni* and his relation with *Indra*, the significance of sacrifice and of *Soma*, the symbolism of the Sun and its rays and of the spider and its web, etc. The whole is envisaged in a clearly traditional spirit as shown by these few phrases taken from the conclusion:

> What must appear outwardly and logically as a double operation of alternate sleep and wakening, of potentiality and act, is inwardly and in reality the pure and simple nature of the Supreme Identity. Neither Vedic ontology nor the formulas by which it is expressed are specific only to the *Rig-Veda*, but can be recognized in the extra-Indian forms of the universal and unanimous tradition.

Elements of Buddhist Iconography (Harvard Univ. Press, Cambridge, Massachusetts [New Delhi: Munshiram Manoharlal, 1979, first ed., 1935]). This important work interprets the principal Buddhist symbols, which symbols, however, greatly precede it, being in fact of Vedic origin, for as the author quite rightly says, 'Buddhism in India represents a heterodox development, all that is metaphysically correct in its ontology and its symbolism being derived from the primordial tradition.'

The symbols which have been applied to the Buddha are principally those of the Vedic *Agni*, and that not at a late date, but on the contrary even at the beginning, when he was not yet represented in human form. The symbols given special attention here (and of which the plates reproduce a series of significant examples) are: the tree, which, as in all traditions, is the 'Tree of Life' or the 'Tree of the World'; the *vajra*, with its double meaning of 'thunderbolt' and 'diamond', the latter corresponding to the ideas of indivisibility and of immutability; the lotus, representing the 'ground' or 'support' of manifestation; and the wheel, which, both as 'wheel of the Law' and 'cosmic wheel', represents the operation of principles in manifestation. The author emphasizes the close link between these symbols and the idea of the 'World Axis', whence it follows that in the Buddhist legend geographical localizations themselves are fundamentally purely analogical. In addition, the author addresses a great number of other interesting points, such as the similarity of the symbol of the *vajra* with the *trishūla*, the significance of footprints representing 'traces' of the principle in the manifested world, the pillar of fire as an 'axial' symbol equivalent to that of the tree, the symbolism of the chariot and that of the throne, etc. This simple survey should suffice to show that the scope of this work goes far beyond a study of Buddhism. The particular consideration of the latter is, as the author says, really only an 'accident', for the subject is traditional symbolism in its truly universal sense. Let us add that these considerations are of a nature to singularly modify the 'rationalistic' idea Westerners have of 'primitive Buddhism', which was on the contrary perhaps less completely heterodox than certain of its later derivatives. If there has been a 'degeneration', would it not be precisely in the inverse sense of that presupposed by the orientalists' prejudices and their natural sympathy as 'moderns' for everything that proclaims itself anti-traditional?

The Mirror of Gesture, being the Abinaya Darpana of Nandikeshvara, tr. with intro. and illustrations by AKC and Duggirala Gopalakrishnayya (E. Weyhe, New York, first ed., 1917, second ed., 1936 [New Delhi: Munshiram Manoharlal, 1977]). This book is the translation of an ancient Hindu treatise on the art of theater and dance (both designated in Sanskrit by the same word *nātya*). It is, of course, a matter of a strictly traditional art ascribed to *Brahmā* himself and to the beginning of the *Treta-Yuga*, in which everything has a precise meaning, and consequently nothing is left to individual fancy; the gestures (especially the *mudrās* or signs formed by the position of the hands) constitute a true hieratic language which can be found moreover in the whole of Hindu iconography. The translators' intention must be considered above all as 'an illustration of the general principles of an art of communication through gestures, and of all traditional and normal art.' Moreover, 'the modern division of life into watertight and independent compartments is a real aberration, and the traditional arts of a people are not a kind of outgrowth, but form an integral part of its life.' At the end of the volume are some very beautiful plates that reproduce examples taken from sculpture and painting, as well as illustrations of a number of poses and *mudrās* which greatly facilitate the understanding of the text.

The Nature of Buddhist Art (Boston: A. Townshend Johnson, 1938 [reprinted in *Coomaraswamy 1: Selected Papers, Traditional Art and Symbolism* ed. Roger Lipsey (Princeton: Bollingen Series, Princeton University Press, 1977), hereafter cited as *SP:1*]). This is the separately published introduction of the important work *The Wall-Paintings of India, Central Asia and Ceylon*, written in collaboration with Benjamin Rowland [Boston: Merrymount Press, 1938]. The author shows that to really understand Buddhist art, and in particular representations of the Buddha, one must refer to concepts that long precede Buddhism itself, since ultimately they relate to Vedic sources, and thereby to the universal symbolism common to all traditions. The more or less heterodox application that has been made of them does not in principle preclude the possibility that the Buddha's historical birth represents the cosmic manifestation of *Agni*, and that his life can in the same sense be called 'mythical'—which is not to deny its reality but on the contrary to emphasize its essential significance. The Buddha was at first represented only by footprints, or by symbols such as the tree or wheel (it is remarkable that for the first few centuries Christ, too, was represented by symbols). How and why was an anthropomorphic image of him later permitted? This must be seen as a concession to the needs of a less intellectual period, when doctrinal understanding was already weakened. In order to be as effective as possible, the 'supports of contemplation' must in fact be adapted to the conditions of each period. But it should be noted that here as also in the case of the Hindu 'deities' the human image itself is really only 'anthropomorphic' to a certain extent, for it is never 'naturalistic', and always retains, above all and even down to its details, an essentially symbolic character. However, this does not mean that it is a matter of a 'conventional' representation, as the moderns imagine, for a symbol is in no way the product of human invention.

> Symbolism is a hierarchical and metaphysical language, not a language determined by organic or psychological categories. Its foundation lies in the analogical correspondence of all orders of reality, states of being, or levels of reference.

The symbolic form is 'revealed' and 'seen' in the same sense that the Vedic incantations have been revealed and 'heard', and there can be no distinction in principle between vision and audition, for what matters is not the kind of perceptible support used but the significance which in some way is 'incorporated' in it. The properly 'supernatural' element is an integral part of the image, just as it is an integral part of narratives which have a 'mythical' value in the original sense of the word. In both cases, it is above all a question of means destined, not to communicate, which is impossible, but to permit the realization of the 'mystery', which obviously neither a simple portrait nor an historic fact as such could do. Thus the very nature of symbolic art in general inevitably escapes the 'rationalistic' point of view of the moderns, just as, for the same reason, the transcendent meaning of the 'miracles' and 'theophanic' character of the manifested world itself escapes them. Man can understand these things only if he is at the same time sensory and spiritual, and if he realizes that

> access to reality is not obtained by making a choice between matter and spirit supposed to be without relation between them, but rather by seeing in material and perceptible things a formal similitude with spiritual prototypes which the senses cannot reach directly.

It is a question of 'a reality viewed on different levels of reference or, if one prefers, different orders of reality which, however, do not mutually exclude each other.'

Asiatic Art (Chicago: New Orient Society of America, 1938). In this booklet intended to point out how the study of Asiatic art must be approached if it is really to be understood, the author once again emphasizes the notion of traditional and normal art, and on what distinguishes it from abnormal instances such as 'classical' decadence and European art since the Renaissance. On the other hand, a so-called 'objective' study, that is, in short, purely outward observation, can really lead to nothing, for there is no true knowledge where there is no conformity between the knower and the known. In the case of a work of art, one must therefore know above all for what use it was intended and also what meaning it should communicate to the understanding of those looking at it. In this respect, it is essential to realize that what is presented by traditional art is not the simple recall of visual perceptions, but the expression or perceptible realization of a 'contemplation' (*dhyāna*), which is that by which the artist works and without which the product of his work would not truly be a work of art. Finally, it is an error to think, as the moderns usually do, that the repetition of transmitted formulas hampers the distinctive gifts of the artist, for the latter must have really made those formulas his own by his understanding (this being the only sense in which one may speak of 'property' in respect to ideas), and he 'recreates' them, as it were, when, having assimilated them, he renders them in accordance with his own nature.

Hinduism and Buddhism (Philosophical Library, New York [New Delhi: Munshiram Manoharlal, 1996, first ed., 1943]). This work is divided in two parts which are so to speak parallel, the first relating to Hinduism and the second to Buddhism, although the author thinks it might have been better to treat the whole as one subject in order to emphasize even more the real agreement between the two. First of all, he rightly points out that to a certain extent a faithful account of Hinduism could be given by categorically denying most of what is said about it by Western scholars, and indeed, even by certain modern and Westernized Hindus. He then explains precisely what 'myth' is, understood in its true meaning and conceived as essentially valid outside all particular conditions of time and space: *agré*, 'at the beginning', signifies even more exactly 'at the summit', that is, 'in the first cause' or 'in the Principle' (like the Greek *en arché* and the Latin *in principio*); in every symbolic description of the cosmogonic process it is therefore an intemporal 'beginning' that is involved. The Sacrifice (*yajña*) is a ritual imitation of 'what was done by the Gods at the beginning'; it is therefore like a reflection of the 'myth', but, as any reflection, in reverse, in the sense that what had been a process of generation and division becomes now a process of regeneration and reintegration. To understand this operation, one must first of all ask oneself 'what is God' and 'what are we': God is an Essence without duality (*advaita*), but subsists in a double nature, whence the distinction between the 'Supreme' (*para*) and the 'Non-Supreme *(apara)*, to which correspond, from the various points of view, all the dualities in which one term, subordinate to the other, is 'eminently' contained in the other. We find these two terms also in ourselves, being then the 'Self' and the 'I'. The essential function of Sacrifice is to 'reunite what has been separated,' thus, as far as man is concerned, to lead the 'I' back to the 'Self'; this reunion is often represented symbolically as a marriage, the higher term of one such duality being masculine and the lower feminine in relation to each other. Moreover, it must not be forgotten that from the integrally traditional point of view every action must normally be considered 'sacred', that is, as having a 'sacrificial' character (*de sacra facere*), so that the notion of Sacrifice can thereby be extended to the whole of human life. This is precisely the 'path of works' (*karma mārga*) of the *Bhagavad-Gītā*, which, naturally, is opposed to the profane conceptions of the moderns. Moreover, since Sacrifice is accomplished *in divinis* by Vishva-karma, it demands the cooperation of all the arts (*vishvā karmāni*) for its ritual imitation in this world, whence it follows that in the traditional social order all functions, whatever they may be, also take on a sacred character. But at the same time the social organization can no more be considered an end in itself than can works, and it must be such that makes the realization of his own perfection possible for each of its members. In Hinduism, this corresponds to the institution of the four *āshramas*, through which all is prescribed in view of obtaining final Deliverance.

Passing on to Buddhism, AKC remarks that the more superficially it is studied, the more it seems to differ from Hinduism, and that if studied more profoundly, it becomes more and more difficult to specify the differences; and he adds that it could be said that in the West 'Buddhism has been admired above all for what it is not.' Moreover, the Buddha himself never claimed to teach a new doctrine or to preach 'social reform' with the precepts he gave to his 'lay' audience. In fact, the main part of his teaching was addressed to members of a 'monastic order' within which there could be no social distinction because the men concerned had already given up the world, like the *sannyāsīs* of Hinduism. Here the 'myth' is represented by the very 'life' of the Buddha, which offers all the features of an *Avatāra*; in the face of these features, the individual particularities have been entirely effaced. From this, the majority of moderns have supposed that he was a man who came to be 'deified' later, but this 'euhemeristic' conception runs counter to the truth. What emerges from all the authentic texts is that it was, on the contrary, a case of the 'descent' of a celestial Archetype that took on human form, and whose 'birth' and 'awakening' represent, one might say, intemporal events. With regard to doctrine, AKC particularly applies himself to demonstrating the falsity of the interpretation which would have it that the Buddha denied *Ātmā*: when speaking of the individual contingent and transitory modifications, he said, against those who identify their very being with those accidents (and among whom he would surely have included Descartes with his *Cogito ergo sum*), that 'this is not the Self', this is taken as if he had said that 'there is no Self'; and this is all the more absurd in that he himself in his state of Buddha cannot be conceived otherwise than as identical with the 'Self'. We cannot go into any more detail, but we should at least mention an excellent interpretation of the term *Nirvāna*. This is yet another question which, in view of all the confusion which has been introduced into it by the orientalists, stands in great need of clarification. Another very interesting point is that the names and epithets of the Buddha as well as his actions, are in general exactly those which Vedic tradition attributes especially to *Agni* and to *Indra*, to whom also the designation *Arnal* is often applied. Now, *Agni* and *Indra* are respectively Priesthood and Royalty *in divinis*; it is precisely with these two possibilities that the Buddha was born, and it can be said that in choosing the first, he realized them both, for this is one case where, as has been said before, one of the two terms is contained 'eminently' in the other.

Spiritual Authority and Temporal Power in the Indian Theory of Government (American Oriental Society, New Haven, Connecticut [New Delhi: Indira Gandhi National Centre for the Arts, 1993, first ed., 1942]). This book develops, clarifies, and supports with numerous references, some of the considerations already mentioned in the book reviewed above. But AKC also corrects an error held notably by J. Evola and A.M. Hocart, among others, on the subject of the relationship between Priesthood and Royalty. Hocart, in fact, claimed that the Priesthood played a feminine role with respect to Royalty, a statement which naturally tends to attribute supremacy to the latter. But this completely inverts the true hierarchic order. In fact, the relationships in question are ritually expressed by marriage formulas such as 'I am That, you are This: I am Heaven, You are the Earth,' etc. (*Aitareya Brāhmana*, VIII.27).

Now, it is the *Purohita* [priest] that is to say the *Brāhmana*, who addresses these words to the King on the occasion of his coronation (*rājasūya*) and not the other way round, as has been wrongly asserted. This is one of those pairs of which the two terms are in no way symmetrical, the first containing the second in principle, while the latter is subordinate to the former and, in short, exists only through it (which amounts to saying that they are *sat* and *asat* respectively). This is why the Priesthood is absolutely independent of Royalty, while Royalty could not validly exist without the Priesthood. This is confirmed by an examination of the relations between their divine types: *Agni* who is the Priesthood (*brāhmana*), and *Indra*, who is Royalty (*kshatra*,) or *Mitra* and *Varuna*, who are also similarly related. Likewise *Brihaspati* and *Vāch*, that is, in short, Intellect and Word, corresponding here to contemplation and action respectively. This last point calls for an important remark: if the Word is connected with Royalty, it is in fact because the King acts and 'works' by its decrees or its edicts, and in a traditional society things are normally accomplished as soon as they have been formulated by the one who has the power to do so (and one can compare this with the fact that in the Far-Eastern tradition, it is up to the sovereign to give things their 'correct denominations'), and therefore the King can never speak according to his fancy or his desires, but only in accordance with the order, that is, with the will of the Principle from which he holds his legitimacy and his 'divine right'. One sees how far is this essentially theocratic conception from that of an 'absolute monarchy' which has no rule of action other than the 'good pleasure' of the sovereign. In passing, the author studies many other pairs of the same kind, such as *Yama* and *Yamī*, the *Ashwins* (comparable in some respects to the Greek *Dioscuri*), and also pairs like Krishna and Arjuna, formed of an immortal and a mortal, corresponding naturally to *Paramātmā* and *jīvātmā*, or to the 'Self' and the 'I'. Another interesting case, in a somewhat different order, is that of Harmony (*sāma*) and Words (*rik*) in the science of *mantras*; but it is impossible to summarize all of this, or even to list all the questions of this kind treated in notes, of which some are so important that they really amount to special studies. To return to the main subject, the union of Priesthood and Royalty represents above all that of Heaven and Earth, on whose harmony depends the prosperity and the fertility of the entire Universe. This is why the prosperity of the kingdom also depends on the harmony of the two powers and on their union in the accomplishment of the rite; and the

King, whose essential function it is to assure it, can only do so on condition that he act in such a way as to maintain this harmony. Here again one finds the agreement between the cosmic and human orders unanimously confirmed by all traditions. Moreover, the feminine character of Royalty with respect to Priesthood explains what we have already pointed out, and as AKC recalls, that a feminine element, or one represented symbolically as such, often plays a leading part in the doctrines peculiar to the Kshatriyas. He also explains that a *bhaktic* path is more especially appropriate to the nature of the Kshatriyas, as is clearly seen in a case such as Western Chivalry. However, it must not be forgotten that since in all this it is only a matter of relationships, what is feminine in a certain respect can at the same time be masculine in another: thus, if the Priesthood is masculine in relation to Royalty, the King for his part is masculine in relation to his kingdom, just as every principle is masculine in relation to the domain over which its action is exercised, and especially *Agni*, *Vāyu*, and *Aditya* in relation to the 'three worlds' respectively, relations which, moreover, are only so many particularizations of the relationship of Light to the Cosmos. And we should also add that apart from its cosmic (*ādhidevata*) and political (*adhirājya*) aspects, the same doctrine has an application to the 'microcosmic' order (*adhyātma*), for man himself is the 'divine City', and one finds in him all the constitutive elements that correspond to those of the Cosmos and those of the social organization, so much so that between these elements similar relations will in all cases be observed. The two *ātmās*, that is to say the 'Self' and the 'I', correspond to the 'supreme' and 'non-supreme' double nature of *Brahma*, and consequently, on different levels, to *Mitra* and *Varuna*, *Deva* and *Asura*, *brāhmana* and *kshatra* [royalty], by whose marriage the kingdom is maintained.

> The outer, active, feminine and mortal aspect of our nature subsists more eminently in its inner, contemplative, masculine, and immortal side, to which it can and must be 'reduced', that is to say brought back or reunited.

For a king, autonomy (*swarāj*) consists in not letting himself be ruled by the multitude subordinate to him, and likewise for each person, in not letting himself be ruled by the inferior and contingent elements of his being. Hence the two meanings of the 'holy war', which we have discussed on various occasions, for the establishment and maintenance of order in both cases. Ultimately, in all spheres, everything depends essentially on 'self-control' *(ātmās imyama)*. That is why, according to the teaching of all traditions, man must first and foremost 'know himself'; and at the same time, the 'science of Self' *(ātmavidyā)* is also the final end of all doctrine, for 'what the Self is' and 'what Brahma is' are two questions that truly imply one and the same response.

The Religious Basis of the Forms of Indian Society; Indian Culture and English Influence; East and West (New York: Orientalia, 1946). In this booklet AKC has brought together three distinct studies. The first attempts to show by the example of India how 'in a traditional social order institutions represent an application of metaphysical doctrines to contingent circumstances,' in such a way that everything in them has a purpose that is not simply biological or psychological, but truly metaphysical. From this point of view the author examines, in succession, the fourfold aim of human life *(purushārtha)*, the institution of the four *āshramas*, the notion of *dharma* with all that it implies, and finally, in connection with *svadharma*, the institution of castes, with the character of 'vocation' that essentially clothes the practice of any profession whatsoever, as well as the sacred and ritual character that necessarily belongs to every activity when the castes themselves are considered as 'born of the Sacrifice', so much so that the profane point of view is not found there at all, and life as a whole appears as the accomplishment of a ritual in which nothing is devoid of significance.

In the second study, the author, having first cited various criticisms addressed to modern civilization both by Westerners themselves as well as Easterners, emphasizes the destructive effects which the European influence inevitably has in a country which, like India, still possesses a traditional civilization. These effects are felt not only in the intellectual sphere proper, but equally in the social order itself, where the influence in question tends above all to upset an organization in which, as has just been said, every profession is really a 'vocation', an organization that is in fact incompatible with the industrial system of the modern West, as A.M. Hocart has rightly pointed out. In the first place, one must react against the very concept of life implied by this system if one wants to avoid an irremediable catastrophe; and it is certainly not desirable to continue in the same direction, under the pretext of 'progress', when one is perched at the edge of a precipice.

Finally, in the last study, AKC explains that the antithesis of East and West as it currently appears must not be understood in a merely geographical sense, but that in reality it is the antithesis of the traditional spirit and modern spirit, so that fundamentally it is a question of time much more than of place, since as long as the West had a normal civilization comparable to all the others, such an opposition could never have existed. In order to make this opposition disappear, goodwill and 'philanthropy' are certainly not enough, especially in a state of affairs where what is considered as 'good' or 'bad' are equally lacking in any principle and are based only on an entirely quantitative conception of life. What is required above all is understanding, for only then can everything be resolved, including the political and economic questions that, in reality, are only the most outward and least important. Here the author returns to the concept of 'vocation', that is to the determination of occupations, not by arbitrary choice or considerations of gain or ambition, but by the proper nature of each man, thereby permitting him to work at his own perfection while at the same time perfecting the products of his craft. The problem of restoring this concept, which needs to be resolved first and foremost if we are to leave the present disorder behind, can only be resolved by understanding the principles upon which the traditional organization of the castes rests. It goes without saying, moreover, that a 'reconciliation' can only come from the side of the West, since it is the latter that has abandoned the once common norms, whereas the East still adheres to them for the most part; and it is only with this traditional East that the West could cooperate, whereas they could only be rivals to a modernized East. When the West has again found its 'Self', which is also the 'Self' of all other men, the problem of understanding the East will thereby be resolved, and there will remain only the task of putting into practice what one has understood. The alternative outcome is a reduction of the whole world to the present state of Europe; in the last resort, it is a choice between a movement deliberately directed toward a foreseen destiny, and a passive submission to an inexorable fatality.

Am I my Brother's Keeper? introduction by Robert Allerton Parker ("Asia Press", The John Day Company, New York [Freeport, NY: Books for Libraries Press, 1967, first ed., 1947, republished, with an additional essay, as *The Bugbear of Literacy* (Bedfont, Middlesex: Perennial Books, 1979)]). This book, the last which our late lamented colleague published before his sudden and untimely death, is a collection of articles chosen expressly to reach a wider public than most of his other works could hope to do, and is primarily concerned with various aspects of the problem of relations between East and West. Since we have already reviewed these articles, we simply list them here, as we did before with those in a previous collection, quoting the issues of *Études Traditionnelles* where we reviewed them: 'Am I my Brother's Keeper?' (June–July 1946); 'The Bugbear of Literacy' (June–July 1946); 'Paths that Lead to the Same Summit' (January–February, 1947); 'Eastern Wisdom and Western Knowledge' (June–July, 1946); 'East and West' (December 1946); '"Spiritual Paternity" and the "Puppet-Complex"' (October–November 1947); and finally, 'Gradation, Evolution and Reincarnation', a translation of which was published in this journal (October–November, 1947). In his introduction, R. A. Parker, having sketched the author's biography, applies himself to defining the traditional point of view adopted by AKC in the whole of his work, and more particularly in his studies on art. And in 'Eastern Wisdom and Western Knowledge' he concludes with a few lines directed to us and *Études Traditionnelles*, for which we must express to him our sincere thanks. [See later a second review of this work.]

Time and Eternity (Artibus Asiae, Ascona, Suisse [New Delhi: Indira Gandhi National Centre for the Arts, 1990, first ed., 1947]). In this posthumous work, our late lamented colleague has taken up and developed some points he had already partially explained in other articles, but which it is very interesting to find gathered together and coordinated in a continuous whole. He has above all undertaken to illustrate the unanimous agreement of the various traditional doctrines on the relationship between time and eternity, with the help of numerous references drawn, in as many successive chapters, from Hindu, Buddhist, Greek, Islamic, and Christian doctrines. It is obviously impossible to summarize all of this, and we must be content to mention some of the principal ideas that emerge. Time, which comprises past and future is, in its entirety, absolutely continuous, and it is only logically and not really, that it can be divided into parts. Through this continuity, which constitutes duration, it stands in contrast with eternity, which is on the contrary the intemporal 'instant' without duration, the true present of which no temporal experience is possible. Eternity is reflected or expressed in the 'now' which at any given time both separates and unites the past and the future. Even this 'now', inasmuch as it is really without duration and consequently invariable and immutable, in spite of an illusion of 'movement' due to a consciousness submitted to the conditions of time and space, is not really distinct from eternity itself, to which the whole of time is always present in the totality of its extension. The essential and absolute independence of eternity with regard to time and all duration, which most moderns seem to find so difficult to conceive, immediately resolves all the difficulties raised on the subject of Providence and divine omniscience. The latter do not refer to the past and the future as such, which represent only the contingent and relative point of view of the being conditioned by time, but they rather refer to a total simultaneity, without division or succession of any kind. In this respect, one can compare the relationship between eternity and time to that between the center and circumference; all points of the circumference and all the radii are simultaneously visible from the center, without this view interfering in any way with the movements taking place on the circumference or along the radii, which here represent respectively determination (succession of events in the ordered course of the circumference) and free will (centripetal or centrifugal movement), with which accordingly there could not be any conflict. Another consequence concerns creation: by the fact that he is not in time, God creates the world 'now' just as much as he has created it or will create it. The creative act is really intemporal, and it is only we who place it in a period that we relate to the past, or that we portray illusorily under the aspect of a succession of events when it is essentially simultaneous in principial reality. In time, all things incessantly move, appear, change, and disappear; in eternity, on the contrary, all things remain in a state of constant immutability. The difference between the two is properly that between 'becoming' and 'being'. Time itself, moreover, would be inconceivable without this intemporal 'instant' that is eternity, just as space would be inconceivable without the 'non-dimensional' point; and it is clear that the one of the two terms that gives the other all its meaning is also the most real in the true sense of the word.

The Living Thoughts of Gotama the Buddha, with I.B. Horner (Cassell and Co., London,1948 [New Delhi: Munshiram Manoharlal, 1982, first ed.,]). Although the contributions made to this book by the joint authors are not clearly attributed, it appears obvious to us that the late lamented AKC wrote the account of the life of the Buddha and of the

Buddhist doctrine which constitutes the first part of this volume, where we again find, in an abridged and somewhat simplified form, the interpretation he had given in earlier writings, particularly *Hinduism and Buddhism*. Since the main points are known to our readers, we shall merely recall that one of the most important is the refutation of the current error according to which Buddhism would deny the 'Self'; among other consequences this naturally rectifies the 'nihilistic' conception that some people have formed of *Nirvāna*. The alleged Buddhist 'atheism' is also dismissed by the remark that 'between the immutable will of God and the *Lex Aeterna* there is no real distinction,' and that in Buddhism itself '*Dharma*, which has always been a divine name, is still synonymous with *Brahma*.' Let us also point out that the author quite rightly insists on the fact that, contrary to another all too widespread error, neither the doctrine of causality nor that of the series of actions and their effects imply, the common idea of 'reincarnation', which no more exists in Buddhism than in any other traditional doctrine. The texts that follow, no doubt chosen by Miss Horner, comprise a series of extracts grouped under the questions to which they refer, some apparently retranslated from the Pāli, while others reproduce various English translations.

Hindouisme et Bouddhisme, tr. from the English by René Allar and Pierre Ponsoye (Paris: Gallimard, 1949). We must draw the attention of our readers to this excellent translation of the book of our late lamented colleague which has just been published in the collection *Tradition*. Since we have already reviewed (see August 1946 issue) the English edition of this important work rectifying a great number of errors and confusions committed by the orientalists, we will not enlarge on it again, repeating only that the two nearly parallel parts into which it is divided bring out clearly the true concordance between Hinduism and Buddhism. Of course, as far as the latter is concerned, it is not a matter of more or less belated and divergent schools such as those whose heterodox views Shankarāchārya refuted, but of true, original Buddhism, which resembles as little as can be what has been presented under that name in the West, where, as the author says, 'Buddhism has been admired above all for what it is not.'

REVIEWS OF ARTICLES:
A. K. COOMARASWAMY

'"Kha" and Other Words Signifying "Nought" in their Relation with the Metaphysics of Space' (London: *Bulletin of the School of Oriental Studies*, vol. VII, 1934 [reprinted in *Coomaraswamy 2: Selected Papers, Metaphysics*, ed. Roger Lipsey (Princeton: Bollingen Series. Princeton University Press, 1977), hereafter cited as *SP:2*]). In this very interesting study AKC shows clearly, contrary to all the modern 'empiricist' theories, that the Sanskrit terms in question first expressed conceptions of a metaphysical order, and that it was only by later derivation that they came to be applied by analogy to mathematical notions. He concludes with a quotation from our *East and West*, in which we have defined, in opposition to modern and profane science, the character of traditional sciences and their dependence on metaphysical doctrine.

'The Technique and Theory of Indian Painting', in *Technical Studies in the Field of the Fine Arts* (Boston: Harvard University Press, October 1934). From this study we observe, as more particularly interesting from our point of view, that the artist did not paint his picture from a model placed before him, but according to a mental image (which relates his art directly to a form of *dhyāna-yoga*), and that in this way it was less the perceptible details of things than their intellectual prototypes.

'The Intellectual Operation in Indian Art' (*Journal of the Indian Society of Oriental Art*, June 1935 [reprinted in *SP:1*]). In this interesting article AKC insists above all on the role played in Indian art by 'contemplative vision' (*dhyāna-yoga*), and not by direct observation of natural things, showing how much this conception, so close to that of the Western Middle Ages, is opposed to that of the moderns, for whom a work of art is intended only to provide pleasure of a sensible order.

'Chāyā' (*Journal of the American Oriental Society*, LV, no. 3, September 1935). AKC here studies the different meanings of the Sanskrit word

Chāyā, which means first 'shadow', then 'reflection' and 'resemblance'. On this occasion he points out similarities between the Vedic and the Christian tradition, 'not to demonstrate "influences", as the author quite rightly says, but to recall that there is nothing exceptional in the Vedic doctrine and that the voice of tradition is everywhere the same.'

'Vedic Exemplarism' (*Harvard Journal of Asiatic Studies*, April 1936 [republished in *SP*:2]). This important study focuses on the relationship between *nāma* and *rūpa*, considered as corresponding respectively to the ideas or eternal reasons of things and to the things themselves under their accidental and contingent aspects, for 'in the last analysis exemplarism is the traditional doctrine of the cognitive and causal relation between the one and the many.' This is remarkably illustrated by the symbolism of the wheel: 'all the spokes are represented *in principio* at their common center,' which is 'a unique point and yet, for each spoke, its own point of departure.' The Vedic texts that refer to this question give rise to numerous and very suggestive comparisons with the doctrines of medieval scholasticism, as well as with those of Neoplatonism. We recommend them to the attention especially of those who obstinately refuse to understand that truly traditional ideas are fundamentally the same everywhere.

'An Indian Crocodile' (Boston: *Bulletin of the Museum of Fine Art*, April 1936). In this is a note on the symbolism of the *makara* [the love god *Kāmadeva*], and we wish to mention especially some interesting reflections on the close relationship between the symbols of Love and Death, to which we have had occasion to refer in connection with the 'Fedeli d'Amore'.

'The Conqueror's Life of Jain painting' (*Journal of the Indian Society of Oriental Art*, December 1935). This important study on Jain Painting, conceived in the same spirit as the author's *Elements of Buddhist Iconography*, which we reviewed elsewhere, is a felicitous complement to the views set forth in the latter; and the sub-title '*Explicitur reductio haec artis ad theologiam*', inspired by an opuscule of Saint Bonaventure, expresses its intentions precisely. Like Buddhism, Jainism, although heterodox and even expressly rejecting the Vedic tradition, has nonetheless changed nothing essential of the primordial conception of an eternal *Avatāra*, so that in connection with the representations of the 'life of the Conqueror' (*Jina-charitra*) one can make observations parallel to those raised by the life of the Buddha. The author also points out that the revolt of the temporal power (*kshatra*) against the spiritual authority (*brāhmana*), which is reflected in Jainism as much as in Buddhism, is in some way prefigured as a possibility by a certain 'luciferian' aspect of the Vedic *Indra*. The heterodox doctrines presenting such a character could thus be considered the very realization of this possibility in the course of an historic cycle. The study concludes with some interesting observations on the method of 'continuous narrative' used in the paintings in question, through which 'a succession of events is represented in spatial simultaneity,' which in a way similarly reconstructs analogously the intemporal character of their metaphysical archetype. All this, of course, can equally well be applied to what one finds similarly in Christian art or in any other traditional art, which always proceeds through continuous derivation from the 'universal and unanimous tradition' (*sanātana dharma*) whose ultimate source is a 'revelation' (*shruti*) 'received at the beginning of the Light of Lights.'

'Vedic "Monotheism"', in *Dr. S. Krishnaswami Aiyangar Commemoration Volume* (Madras, 1936 [reprinted in *SP:2*]). In this article AKC shows that, from the origin, and not more or less belatedly as the moderns usually assert, the multiple divine names have never really described anything other than diverse aspects or attributes of the first and unique Principle. Moreover, this is why it has been rightly said that the *devas* are 'participants' (*bhakta*) of the divine essence, and that the original meaning of the word *bhakti* is in fact that of 'participation', whatever may be the other more or less derivative meanings it took later.

'Rebirth and Omniscience in Pāli Buddhism' (*Indian Culture*, vol. III, July 1936). This article contains a criticism of Mrs Rhys Davids' ideas, and is in total agreement with the criticism we formulated in this journal a short time ago when reviewing one of her works. The author rightly protests against a certain way of misrepresenting texts by brushing aside their metaphysical portions, from which only a complete distortion of their significance can result. Moreover, he points out that, having studied the doctrine of death and rebirth in the *Rig-Veda*, the *Brāhmanas*, the *Bhagavad-Gītā*, and Pāli Buddhism, he has found no 'development' of that doctrine through this series, nor any teaching of the return of the being to the same world which it has left at its death. Everywhere there is mention of 'transmigration', but never of 'reincarnation'.

'The Source of, and a Parallel to, Dionysius on the Beautiful' (Calcutta: *Journal of the Greater India Society,* vol. III, January 1936). Here AKC points out a 'source' of the passage of Saint Denys the Areopagite on the Beautiful (*De Divinis Nominibus,* IV.5) in Plato's *Phaedrus* (210-11), and a 'parallel' in the *Chāndogya Upanishad* (IV.15) which offers a striking similarity even in its wording.

'Two Passages in Dante's *Paradiso*' (*Speculum* [publ. by *Mediaeval Academy of America,* Cambridge, MA] July 1936 [reprinted in *SP:2*]). This is a study of two passages from Dante's *Paradise* (XXVII, 136–138, and XVIII, 110–111), whose meaning becomes remarkably clear and precise by a comparison with the modes of expression of the Hindu tradition. This constancy of certain symbolic terms and their 'technical' meaning in traditional forms so distant from each other in time and space can only be explained if one considers these 'diverse formulations of a common doctrine' (*dharma-paryāya*) to be as many 'dialects of one and the same language of the spirit,' or branches of one and the same 'universal and unanimous tradition' (*sanātana dharma*).

'A Note on the *Ashvamedha*' (Prague: *Archiv Orientalni,* vol. VII, August 1936). In this article AKC admirably brings out the error of those who introduce wholly modern ideas and sentiments into their interpretation of the Vedic texts, thus for example, attributing their own 'naturalistic' ways of thinking to the ancients, to whom they were so alien; this then leads to a complete misunderstanding of the true meaning of symbols such as the sexual symbols found in certain sacrificial rites. It must be well understood that 'in a traditional social order, what is correct or not is not determined by feeling as it is in our anti-traditional environment, but by knowledge,' and that 'there the rule is established metaphysically by what was made by the Gods at the beginning,' of which the rites are of an analogical image. Contrary to what various orientalists have maintained, the symbolism of the *Ashvamedha* is linked directly with the doctrines of the *Rig-Veda* and of the *Upanishads,* which moreover are in perfect accord with all the other orthodox traditions concerning the union *ab intra* of the complementary principles in the 'Supreme Identity', as well as on every other essential point.

'The Vedic Doctrine of the "Silence"' (*Indian Culture*, vol. III, April 1937 [reprinted in *SP:2*]). In this article AKC studies the Vedic doctrine of 'Silence', which he connects to what we have written concerning the 'initiatic secret', as well as to the 'myths' and to the 'mysteries' in their original meaning. It is thus essentially a matter of the inexpressible, which is the 'supreme' (*para*), whereas the expressed 'word' refers necessarily to the 'non-supreme' (*apara*). These two aspects, however, appear as inseparably associated in numerous texts, as well as in the ritual, in order to constitute together the total conception of the Principle.

'The Rape of a Nāgī: An Indian Gupta Seal' (*Boston Bulletin of the Museum of Fine Arts*, August 1937 [reprinted in *SP:1*]). In this article AKC emphasizes the insufficiency of all 'art history', which, confining itself to an exclusively aesthetic point of view, 'simply considers the decorative use of a given motif, and ignores the purpose of the elements of which it is formed and the logical relation of its parts.' This note constitutes an excellent reply to certain people who deny symbolism.

'*Janaka* and *Yājñavalkya*' (*Indian Historical Quarterly*, vol. XIII, June 1937). AKC shows in this article on *Janaka* and *Yājñavalkya* that these two interlocutors, engaged in conversation in the *Brihadāranyaka Upanishad*, are very far from being merely historical figures, for it could be said that above all they are eternal 'types'—something evident from the significance implied in their very names. *Yājñavalkya*, from *yajna-vaktri*, 'Promulgator of the sacrifice', which is a name belonging to *Agni*, represents in reality the 'eternal *Avatāra*'. *Janaka* is etymologically the 'Progenitor', which is identified with the *Asura pitri* or Vedic *janitri*; and the designation of *Janaka*'s realm as *Videha*, 'incorporeal', is equally significant. From this, the author is led to an explanation of numerous considerations that we cannot possibly summarize, all of which are very important for an understanding of the true symbolism of the Vedic 'personages', and also of rites as an image of 'what was done at the beginning', independent of any application that can be made to particular circumstances such as the events of human life, an application that on the contrary draws from this source all its worth and efficacy.

'The Pilgrim's Way' (*Journal of the Bihar and Orissa Research Society*, vol. XXIII, December 1937 [reprinted in *What is Civilisation?* (Great Barrington MA: Lindisfarne Press, 1989)]). Here AKC studies *The Pilgrim's*

Way in connection with a passage from the *Aitareya Brāhmana* (VII, 15), and develops very interesting ideas on the symbolism of the 'pilgrimage' or the 'journey', which is found in all traditions, and which, as he recalls, has been repeatedly mentioned here.

'Mediaeval Aesthetic' (*Art Bulletin of Chicago*, vol. xx, March 1938 [reprinted in *SP:1*]). This is the continuation of AKC's study of the same title, to the beginning of which we drew attention at the time of its appearance. This second part includes the annotated translation of the commentary by Saint Thomas Aquinas on the text of Saint Denys the Areopagite (*De divinis nominibus*, IV, 5), and a note on the relationship between Beauty and Truth. Let us mention especially what is said about the superiority of contemplation over action, 'which is the orthodox point of view constantly affirmed in universal tradition, and not only in the East, as is sometimes asserted, although it might have been obscured by the 'moralistic' tendencies of modern European religious philosophy'; the necessity to understand intellectually a work of art and not only to 'feel' it, contrary to present-day 'aesthetic' conceptions; and, finally, the unimportance of the individuality of the artist, which explains the characteristic anonymity of the works of the Middle Ages, for 'what matters is what is being said, and not who says it.' Therein lies a truth from which modern lovers of 'personality' ought to benefit!

'Symbolism of the Dome' (*Indian Historical Quarterly*, March 1938 [reprinted in *SP:1*]). This is an important article on the symbolism of the dome. However, since we devote a special article to this subject elsewhere,[1] we shall only add that AKC, in order to show that a 'cosmic' significance is attached not to architecture alone, points out in this respect the symbolism of the sword, which he has previously treated here, and that of archery, whose initiatic connections are equally remarkable.

'*Uṣṇīṣa* and *Chhatra*: Turban and Umbrella' (*Poona Orientalist*, April 1938). Here AKC examines the symbolism of the *chhatra*, that is, the umbrella, and of the *ushnīsha*, which, before being the cranial protuberance seen in depictions of the Buddha, was originally a turban. These two objects were among the attributes of royalty, and, as the reasons for

---

1. See *Symbols of Sacred Science*, chaps. 39 and 40 (*Études Traditionnelles*, October and November 1938). ED.

this are particularly interesting, we intend to return to this question in an upcoming article.

'Notes on the *Kaṭha Upaniṣad*' (*New Indian Antiquary*, April, May, and June 1938). In this study AKC examines various difficult and often badly interpreted passages from the *Katha Upanishad*. In the course of it he addresses numerous important questions, and we can do no more here than list briefly some of the principal ones: the real significance of 'Death' (*Mrityu* or *Yama*), under its higher aspect, and its identification with the Sun considered as keeper of the passage known as the 'solar gate', by which is reached the ultimate and 'extra-cosmic' state, the 'Empyrean', as distinguished from a sub-solar 'Elysium', which is still in the power of Death; the 'three deaths', represented by the three nights spent by *Nachiketas* (that is, according to the meaning of his name, 'he who does not yet have knowledge') on the threshold of the dwelling of *Mrityu*; the correspondence of the three favors asked by *Nachiketas* with the 'three steps' of *Vishnu*; the exact meaning of the word *srishti*, which could be rendered as 'expression' rather than as 'emanation', to indicate the production of the manifested world, and the application of the idea of 'measure' (*mātrā*) to the act of this production itself; the meaning of the word *rita*, meaning properly the cosmic order, to which the word 'order' (*ordo* in Latin) as well as that of 'rite' is directly related; the symbolism of the 'bridge' (*setu*), coinciding with that of *sūtrātmā*, which links between them all the states of the being; and the union of the manifested and the unmanifested (*vyaktāvyākta*), as 'one single essence and two-natures,' in the 'Supreme-Identity'. Let us also note some very accurate reflections on the way in which most orientalist interpretations of texts are affected by errors of points of view such as 'historicism' and 'naturalism', and the remark that 'thought' in the profane sense, and consequently 'science' and 'philosophy' in their modern meaning, do not really belong to the sphere of contemplative life, which relies exclusively on pure intellect, but only to the sphere of active life. This last remark is particularly useful in reducing to their true value the pretensions of a certain pseudo-intellectuality.

'Vedānta and Western Tradition' (*The American Scholar*, Spring 1939 [reprinted in *SP:2*]). This lecture was given before an audience of American students, who naturally had no knowledge of Eastern doctrines; which means that the task was certainly not without difficulties.

With remarkable clarity the author first of all explains the essential features of traditional metaphysics, what it is and also what it is not, with particular emphasis on the chief differences separating it from all that is usually called 'philosophy'. He then takes the principal points of the doctrine of the *Vedānta*, shedding light on them by means of parallels drawn with other traditional works, chiefly those of the Greeks and of Christianity—whose language must normally be more familiar to Westerners—thereby showing at the same time the universality of tradition. We wish to draw attention especially to the parts of the text concerning *Ātmā* and its relations with the manifested world, 'transmigration' as distinguished from 'metempsychosis' and the impossibility of 'reincarnation', and the process of spiritual realization. In the latter we again find the explanation of some of the symbols we have had occasion to mention recently, such as those of the 'solar ray', the treetop', and the 'narrow door', with the distinction between the 'Elysian' and 'Empyrean' states, and the passage from one to the other 'through the Sun'. In concluding, the author is careful to state that traditional doctrine never involves any 'research' but only an 'explanation', and that 'the ultimate Truth is not something to be discovered, but something to be understood by each, and everyone must accomplish the task for himself.'

'The Philosophy of Mediaeval and Oriental Art', in the first issue [1939] of the new Romanian journal *Zalmoxis*, a 'Journal of Religious Studies'. This important study, as AKC points out at the beginning, could quite as well have been titled 'the traditional doctrine of art', since it applies in reality to all art, with only two exceptions, that of the 'classical' decadence, and that of the modern period. In his exposition he employs the exact terms in use during the Middle Ages, for in order to express the concepts in question without deforming them, it is necessary to retain the precision of a 'technical' vocabulary that has no equivalent in our day, and that in addition corresponds with a 'way of thinking' very different from that of modern Westerners—although it is very close to those of Easterners—so much so that in this regard true equivalences cannot be found. Today, a work of art is no longer every object that is well made in accordance with its use, but only particular kinds of things, even if for the most part considered useless (that is to say 'without use'), whence the abnormal separation of art and industry. On the other hand, for moderns, the work of art is no longer something that must above all be understood intellectually but rather something addressing itself uniquely to feeling (whence the idea of the 'aesthetic'). It is to be pointed out in this connection that if traditional art can be called 'ideal' in that it is essentially an expression of ideas, this is in a way the opposite of the quite sentimental sense which the word 'ideal' has assumed in our day. The definition of art as 'the imitation of Nature in its mode of operation' must in no way be understood in a 'naturalistic' sense; it is not a matter of reproducing the appearance of natural things, but on the contrary of producing different things, although by a process similar to the production of natural things. And in this respect art in the human sphere is also a true imitation of divine activity, with the sole reservation that the human artisan is forced to use already existing materials, while the 'Divine Artisan' draws his materials from infinite Possibility. Art must start from an act of 'contemplating' (in Sanskrit *dhyāna*) the idea or the mental image that will later be realized outwardly in a way appropriate to the nature of the materials used, by means of tools which are as adequate as possible, and in view of a definite goal, which is in fact the use for which the produced object is intended. Here one recognizes the theory of the 'four causes' as applied to art, which we have already discussed on various occasions in connection with other studies on traditional art.

'Some Pāli Words' (*Harvard Journal of Asiatic Studies*, July 1939 [reprinted in *SP:2*]). In this article AKC studies the significance of various Pāli terms that have been incorrectly interpreted in recent publications. He points out that the terms can really be understood only by reference to their Sanskrit form and to the ideas implied by this form in the same milieu to which Buddhism was first addressed. This presupposes a knowledge of the *Vedas* and *Upanishads* which later Buddhist commentators too often lacked. The articles devoted to some of the terms in question constitute a true study of Buddhist rhetoric and dialectics; others touch more directly on points of doctrine and symbolism, and in these we recognize some of the observations that the author has set forth in this journal. There is also a note on the *pāsa*, which we discussed in our article on the 'eye of the needle'.[2]

---

2. See *Symbols of Sacred Science*, chap. 55 (*Études Traditionnelles*, January 1940). ED.

'The Nature of Mediaeval Art' (*Art News*, February 17, 1940 [reprinted in *Christian and Oriental Philosophy of Art* (New Delhi: Munshiram Manoharlal, 1994)]). In this issue, which is devoted to the 'Arts of the Middle Ages', AKC has published an article on 'the nature of mediaeval art', showing that the latter, like oriental art, cannot be understood by any of the ways in which the modern mentality views art, whether it be from the point of view of 'realism' or 'aestheticism'. In the Middle Ages, art 'was a kind of knowledge in accordance with which the artist imagined the form or design of the work to be done, and by which he reproduced this form in the required or available material.' In those times there was no distinction such as the moderns make between 'fine arts' and 'applied arts', between 'pure art' and 'decorative art'. Any work of art perfect of its kind, whatever its purpose, was thereby a work of art, and this perfection never implied the addition of 'ornaments' superfluous to the function which the object was to fulfill in meeting some spiritual or material need. To understand the art of the Middle Ages, one must first of all understand the spirit of that period, that is, the spirit of Christianity itself. 'If art has been properly called a universal language, it is not such because all men's sensory faculties enable them to recognize what they see . . . but because of the universality of the adequate symbolism in which its meanings have been expressed,' and of which Christian symbolism represents only a particular case, so that one is finally led thereby to the 'universal and unanimous Tradition', which Saint Augustine called 'a Wisdom that has not been made, but which is now what it has always been and always will be.'

'An Indian Enamel' (Boston: *Bulletin of the Museum of Fine Arts*, April 1940). AKC here presents a study of a sixteenth-century Indian enamel depicting the ten *Avatāras* of *Vishnu*, of which two show peculiarities which seem quite rare and are interesting from the symbolic point of view: the ninth *Avatāra* is represented by the figure of *Jagannātha*, and the tenth by a riderless horse, led by a someone carrying a parasol, perhaps *Indra*, which would recall ancient Buddhist depictions of the 'great departure'. However, could one not also think that this crowned person is he who, according to some traditions, must bring *Kalki* from the mysterious city of *Shambala*? In any case, it must be understood that the parallels one can find between Hindu and Buddhist iconography really only 're-establish a fundamental unity that has been obscured by the pseudo-historical form given to the legend of the

Buddha,' to the detriment of its original and truly profound signifi-cance. And in connection with another subject, the symbolism of the theater, let us further draw attention to the author's observation that the word *avatarana* is used to indicate the actor's entry onto the stage, 'which is an apparition from behind a curtain and a "manifestation" analogous to that of the *Avatāra* onto the world stage.' The explanation of the role of the *Avatāras* is, as we know, given by Krishna to Arjuna (*Bhagavad-Gītā*, IV.6–7), in the dialogue whose representation, perhaps for this very reason, occupies the central position in the enamel under consideration, as if Krishna, in order to 'illustrate' his words in some way, was thus showing to Arjuna all the other *Avatāras* gathered around him.

Zalmoxis, a 'review of religious studies' edited by Mircea Eliade, has produced two volumes, dated respectively 1938 and 1939, but which actually appeared somewhat later. The first volume contains AKC's study 'The Philosophy of Mediaeval and Oriental Arts', which we reviewed when it first appeared (June 1939 issue) and which was all that we then knew of this publication. — In the same volume, Raffaele Pet-tazzoni examines 'Le corps parsemé d'yeux', that is, the rather numer-ous cases belonging to very different traditions of divinities or mythic personages represented with multiple eyes. He rightly recognizes that this symbolism is connected to 'the idea of the omnipresence and omni-science of God'; nonetheless he seems in the final analysis to see here only a representation of the 'night sky', identifying the eyes with the stars; but even admitting this explanation one still has to wonder what the 'night sky' itself symbolizes... Let us add immediately, so that we need not return to the subject, that in the second volume a note by AKC puts things perfectly into perspective. He points out first that the divine forms in question are above all 'solar', which indicates that the eyes really correspond to rays of the Sun; 'From the point of view of our multiplicity, the Sun is at the center of a cosmic sphere, toward whose limits its innumerable rays spread in all directions,' and 'it is by means of these rays that he knows the forms expressed toward which they spread,' which allows them to be likened to as many eyes. And it should not be forgotten moreover that 'it is one being that has multiple eyes, the number depending on our point of view and not on the being itself.' Coomaraswamy also calls attention to a rather unusual error which, in connection with a passage of the Babylonian Talmud, takes the 'Angel of

Death' for Satan; these are two wholly distinct beings. — In his article 'Le Culte d'étendard chez les Scythes et dans l'Inde', J. Przyluski notes that certain columns which 'were probably connected to the cosmic axis' were sometimes given 'the name *dhwaja*, which generally designates a mobile banner'; but what is rather astonishing after making this statement, is that he does not seem to clearly realize that the pole of every banner is in fact an axial symbol just like the column (and more particularly the detached column). As to the question of 'fixed banners' and 'mobile banners', this seems to us quite clear: the fixed banner, generally erected close to a Temple and high enough to 'dominate it like a minaret', was a mast exactly comparable to that of a *stūpa* (and we could also say that of a chariot or ship, for the symbolism is the same in each case). The mobile banner (whose pole was most often a spear, another well-known axial symbol) was at root only a 'substitute' for the fixed banner, meant to accompany armies on campaign, which obviously did not make it any less symbolic of the 'cosmic axis', any more than the movement of an equally mobile sanctuary in the peregrinations of a nomadic people, as in the case of the Hebrews' Tabernacle, removed from this sanctuary its character as image of the 'Center of the World'. — We will merely mention Carl Hentze's article 'Le Culte de l'Ours et du Tigre et le T'ao-tie', without dwelling on it for the moment, for we intend to return soon to the symbolism of the *T'ao-tie* and other similar figurations. — 'Buddha and the Sun God' by Benjamin Rowland brings out in connection with a painting discovered in Afghanistan the 'solar' character of the Buddha, made particularly evident by the iconography, as Coomaraswamy has shown in various works. It is interesting to note that in certain series of scenes from the life of the Buddha, his birthplace is shown by a representation of *Sūrya* and his chariot, clearly referring to the idea of the *Avatāra*. — An article by Mircea Eliade entitled 'Metallurgy, Magic, and Alchemy', is hardly more than an account of facts of all kinds related to the subjects indicated by the title, from which no clear conclusion emerges. Some of these facts concerning blacksmiths could serve to 'illustrate' what we wrote about metallurgy in our recent book *The Reign of Quantity and the Signs of the Times* (chap. 22). And we must point out a truly extraordinary error, which is due, as it seems, to R. Eisler, and which is of a nature to throw suspicion on the value of his works: *Kaabah* is taken here to be the name of the 'black stone', but this can make no sense, for this stone is not a cube, it is the building in one of whose angles it is set that is called the '*Kaabah*' because its has the shape of a cube; and in addition this so-called 'Kaa-bah stone' then becomes a 'Kaabah goddess', something that has certainly never existed! Moreover, it is not very difficult to guess what is involved here, for a work by R. Eisler entitled *Kuba-Kybele* is cited in this connection; unfortunately, this comparison is just as fantastic as those that we have met elsewhere of the same Cybele with the 'Kabbalah' and with a 'mare' [*cavale* in French]. Etymologically, Cybele, like *Pārvatī* in India, is none other that the 'goddess of the mountain'; and we will add that the mountain is always represented symbolically in a conical and not a cubic shape, or perhaps in a vertical projection as triangular, and not as square. — Jen Coman devotes a long article to 'Orphée, civilisateur de l'humanité' (we would rather have said of a certain part of humanity), but he succeeds in giving only a very 'insipid' treatment of him and resolves no really important question; even the passages where there is reference to the Mysteries and to initiation (for they finally have to be mentioned despite everything) do not throw the least glimmer on the profound meaning of Orphism. Curiously, in speaking of the 'primitive men' civilized by Orpheus, the author does not seem to have the slightest doubt in the world that these more or less wild men (perhaps all the same it is a bit of an exaggeration to call them cannibals), far from being 'primitive', really belonged already to the 'iron age'. — We will not dwell on the 'folkloric' articles contained in this volume and in the following, which have only a purely documentary character and an interest above all local.

'*Svayamātṛṇṇā*: Janua Coeli' (*Zalmoxis*, vol. ii, 1939 [reprinted in *SP:1*]). The second issue of this new journal opens with this study by AKC, which we discuss more fully elsewhere. There follow two articles on the Thracian god *Zalmoxis*, from whose name the journal takes its title. In the first article, Carl Clemen seems to want to see *Zalmoxis* first and foremost as a 'god of vegetation', in conformity with the 'naturist' concepts made fashionable by Frazer. In the second article, Jean Coman examines the question whether *Zalmoxis* is really a god, or a 'prophet', and is inclined to conclude that originally he might have been a man and only subsequently was 'divinized', which seems to us to turn things upside down, as it were, for there is nothing surprising in the fact that the 'prophet', or more exactly the supreme chief who was both 'king and high-priest' before the separation of the two powers, should have been given the name of the principle (designated, according to the most probable etymology, as 'Lord of men', which could be compared to a divine name, the identical expression being found in the last *sūrah* of the Koran) of which he was the representative and which he 'incarnated' in a certain fashion in the human world. This name, applied secondarily to a man, thus properly speaking referred to a function, and not to an individual, which also explains how there could have been not only one man, but quite a succession of men, bearing the name *Zalmoxis*. In connection with a publication by N. Cartojan, *Les livres populaires dans la littérature roumaine*, Mircea Eliade presents some reflections on the origins of folklore, which are fundamentally correct, even though the manner of expression is not above reproach, for to speak of 'laicization' of the 'fantastic' seems rather strange; but when he adds that this 'laicization' is a 'degradation', we understand that he means a degeneracy due to the 'popularization' of something that was originally of a completely different order, which, although it is not sufficiently precise, at least conforms to the truth (keeping all reservations on the subject of the 'fantastic', however, which, strictly speaking, only appears as such because of a failure to understand its symbolic significance). But what is truly astounding to anyone who possesses any traditional notions is that the accusation of 'infantilism' can be leveled at legends such as that of the 'Wood of the Cross', which we transcribe here because its transparent symbolism seems likely to interest our readers:

After Adam had been buried with the crown on his head, there grew from the crown a tall and marvellous tree whose trunk divided into three great branches. These joined together, only to separate and rejoin seven times in succession. It is from the wood of this tree that the cross on which the Savior was crucified was made.

Is it not clear that the three principal *nādīs* and the seven *chakras* of Hindu tradition can be seen in the description of the growth of this mysterious tree (which, it goes without saying, is essentially 'axial')? — Mircea Eliade also contributes 'Notes sur le symbolisme aquatique', which seems to be but a beginning, for it concerns only shells and pearls, and their ritual use based on the sense of 'fecundity' or 'fertility' generally associated with them, which is related to birth not only in the ordinary meaning of the word but also to the 'second birth' in the rites of initiation, and even, in funerary rites, to 'resurrection' and consequently with immortality.

'Līlā' (*Journal of the American Oriental Society*, June 1941 [reprinted in *SP:2*]). In this article AKC studies the meaning of the Sanskrit term *Līlā*, which properly means 'play', and is applied especially to divine activity, a conception in no way peculiar to India, for it is clearly expressed in Eckhart and Boehme for example. Plato, while not expressly describing divine activity as play, says at least that we are the 'playthings' of God, which can be illustrated by the movement of pieces in a chess game, and above all by the play of puppets (the string on which they are suspended and which makes them move being an image of the *sūtrātmā* which we discuss elsewhere). In all cases, 'play' differs from 'work' in being a spontaneous activity, not due to any need and implying no effort, which agrees as perfectly as possible with divine activity. In this regard, the author recalls that plays originally had a sacred and ritual character. He shows further, through linguistic considerations, that the symbolic prototype of this conception is found in the movement of fire or light expressed by the verb *lelāy*, with which the word *līlā* is connected. The 'play' of a flame or a flickering light is a fitting symbol of the manifestation of the Spirit.

'Play and Seriousness' (*Journal of Philosophy*, September 24, 1942 [reprinted in *SP:2*]). Here AKC returns to the same subject in a note headed 'Play and Seriousness'. The Spirit or 'Self' is not affected by the fortunes of the various kinds of vehicles by means of which it is manifested, and for the one aware of this, it naturally entails disinterestedness or detachment, in the sense understood in the *Bhagavad-Gītā*, with regard to action and its results. If this disinterestedness leads us to consider life as a game, it would be wrong to wish to oppose the 'seriousness' that characterizes work to this attitude. In a game there is nothing to be gained but the 'pleasure that perfects the operation,' as well as the understanding of what in reality properly constitutes a rite. This does not mean that we ought to play with unconcern, which would only be in accordance with the profane and abnormal point of view of moderns, who consider games as insignificant in themselves. We play a role determined by our own nature, and our only concern must be to play it well, with no view to the outcome. Divine activity is called 'play' because it cannot have any purpose whatsoever, and in the same sense our life also can become play. On that level, however, 'play' and 'work' can no longer be distinguished in any way from one another.

'Am I my Brother's Keeper?' (*Asia and the Americas*, March, 1943 [reprinted in *Am I My Brother's Keeper?* (London: Dennis Dobson Ltd., 1943) and *The Bugbear of Literacy* (Bedford, Middlesex: Perennial Books, 1979)]). This article is an excellent critique of the way modern Westerners attempt everywhere to impose what they call 'civilization'. AKC denounces this energetically, citing in support quite a number of corroborating opinions and the misdeeds of this 'Westernization' which makes itself more and more intrusive in all domains and tends only to destroy everything of really qualitative value in order to substitute what corresponds to its own exclusively quantitative and material 'ideal', so much so that it is no exaggeration to characterize it as a true 'murder'. It is certainly not through any sort of 'propaganda' aiming at an outward standardization, that a real reconciliation between peoples, and more particularly between East and West, can ever be achieved. Quite the contrary. This can be achieved only through an agreement on principles, and it is precisely the principles which, from all points of view, are entirely wanting in modern Western civilization.

'The Bugbear of Literacy' (*Asia and the Americas*, February 1944 [reprinted as above]). In this article AKC returns particularly to that aspect of Western proselytism which, starting from the prejudice that 'culture' consists above all in knowing how to read and write, desires to impose on the most diverse peoples a certain kind of elementary and uniform education that could not have the slightest value for them because in reality it is closely linked with the special conditions of the quantitative civilization of the modern West. This is yet another means of destroying civilizations that rest on very different foundations, by rapidly eradicating everything that has always been the object of oral transmission, that is, everything that constitutes for them what is essential. Far from furthering, however slightly, a profound understanding of any truth whatsoever, European 'education' only produces men totally ignorant of their own tradition (and ultimately every specifically modern enterprise is necessarily directed against tradition in all its forms). And so in many cases it is only among the 'illiterate', or those considered so by Westerners and the 'Westernized', that one can still find the true 'culture' (here taken otherwise than in its usual quite profane sense) of such or such a people before it is too late and Western intrusion has completely spoiled everything. The author makes an interesting comparison between the real significance of oral transmission and

the Platonic doctrine of 'reminiscence'; and he also shows, by appropriate examples, to what extent the moderns are unaware of the symbolic
and universal value of traditional language, and how alien it is to their
'literary' point of view, which reduces 'figures of thought' to no more
than simple 'figures of words'.

'The Reinterpretation of Buddhism' (*New Indian Antiquary*, December 1939). AKC here examines some principal points on which previously held conceptions of Buddhism must be rectified, a Buddhism
which in truth had been so much admired in Europe only because it
was poorly understood. The recent books of Mrs Rhys Davids have contributed to this rectification, particularly in dealing with the interpretation of *anatta*, which in no way implies a denial of *Ātmā*, as has been so
often asserted, but which can be truly understood only through the distinction of the 'Great *Ātmā*' and the 'lesser *ātmā*', that is to say, in short,
of the 'Self' and the 'I' (whatever terms one may prefer to adopt to
describe them in Western languages, among which 'soul' is especially to
be avoided since it gives rise to innumerable confusions); and only of
the second is it denied that it possesses an essential and permanent reality. When it is said of individuality viewed in its psychic as well as its
corporeal part, that 'this is not the Self', even this presupposes that there
is a 'Self' that is the true and spiritual being, entirely distinct from and
independent of this compound that serves him only as temporary vehicle, and of which it is not one of the composing elements. Buddhism
does not differ at all fundamentally from Brāhmanism in this. Also, the
state of the *arhat*, who is liberated from the 'I or lesser *ātmā*', can in no
way be considered an 'annihilation' (something that, in any case, is
strictly speaking inconceivable); he has ceased to be 'someone', but
thereby he 'is', purely and simply. It is true that he is 'nowhere' (here
Mrs Rhys Davids appears mistaken about the sense in which this must
be understood), but this is because the 'Self' obviously cannot be subject to space, any more than to quantity or to any other special condition of existence. Another important consequence is that in Buddhism,
just as in Brāhmanism, there can be no place for 'so-called reincarnation': the I, being transitory and impermanent, ceases to exist in the dissolution of the compound that constituted it, and there is then nothing
that could truly be 'reincarnated'. The 'Spirit' alone can be conceived as
'transmigrant', or as passing from one 'habitation' to another, but precisely because it is in itself essentially independent of all individuality

and of any contingent state. — This study ends with an examination of the meaning of the word *bhū*, for which Mrs Rhys Davids has insisted too exclusively on the idea of 'becoming' (although this idea is in fact often contained in it) and on the meaning of the word *jhana* (in Sanskrit *dhyāna*), which is not 'meditation', but 'contemplation', and which, being an essentially active state, has nothing in common with any 'mystical experience' whatsoever.

'*Ākiṃcañña*: Self-Naughting' (*New Indian Antiquary*, April 1940 [reprinted in *SP:2*]). This important study again relates to a subject connected to the question of *anatta*, and treats it above all from the point of view of the parallelism that exists in this respect between Buddhist and Christian doctrines. Man has two *ātmās*, in the sense pointed out previously, the one rational and mortal, the other spiritual and in no way conditioned by time or space. It is the first that must be 'annihilated', or from which man must succeed in liberating himself precisely through the knowledge of his true nature. Our real being is in no way engaged in the operations of discursive thought and empirical knowledge (by which philosophy usually tries to prove the validity of our consciousness of existing, which is properly anti-metaphysical). To this 'spirit' alone, distinguished from the body and soul (that is, from all that is phenomenal and formal), does tradition attribute absolute liberty, which, referring to time as well as to space, necessarily implies immortality. We cannot summarize the numerous quotations given to establish as clearly as possible that this doctrine is Christian as well as Buddhist (it is in fact universal), or the texts explaining more especially the concept of *ākimchannā* in its Buddhist form. We shall point out only that anonymity is considered an essential aspect of *ākimchannā*, something directly connected with what we ourselves have explained on the higher meaning of anonymity and its role in traditional civilizations (see *The Reign of Quantity and the Signs of the Times*, chap. 9, where, moreover, we have mentioned the article reviewed here).

'*Ūnātiriktan* and *Atyarichyata*' (also *New Indian Antiquary*, June 1943). By examining the meaning of these terms and the use that is made of them in the Vedic texts, AKC shows that *Prajāpati*, as Producer and Ruler of manifested beings, must be considered as 'a syzygy of conjoint masculine and feminine Principles' symbolically represented as a 'full' and an 'empty' and also linked with the Sun and the Moon. This is especially connected with the symbolism of the 'full vessel' or the 'vase of abundance', of which the Grail is one form, and of which the 'solar' character is more particularly manifest in Hindu ritual.

'The "E" at Delphi' (*Review of Religion*, November 1941 [reprinted in *SP:2*]). In this note AKC explains the '*E*' at Delphi in connection with initiatic rites and with the question 'Who are you?' put to the one who presents himself at the 'solar gate'. 'Know thyself' (*gnōthi seauton*) must, in this respect, be interpreted as an indirect expression of the question put by Apollo or the 'solar' god, and the '*E*', equivalent to *ei* according to Plutarch, gives the answer in an enigmatic form: 'You are,' that is to say, 'What You are [the Sun], I am.' Indeed, no other true reply could be given by whomsoever is 'qualified to enter into union with the Sun,' as is said in the *Jaiminiya Upanishad Brāhmana* (1.6.1).

'Eastern Religions and Western Thought' (*Review of Religion*, January 1942). In connection with a volume published by S. Radhakrishnan, AKC here emphasizes the similarities that exist between all the forms of tradition, whether Eastern or Western, and which are such that texts of any 'dialect of the language of the Spirit' may be used to explain and illuminate those of another, independent of any consideration of time or place. At the same time he also shows, through examples bearing on specific points, that unfortunately S. Radhakrishnan has 'by education or temperament, a mentality more European than Indian, even to the point of readily accepting the modern idea of 'progress', with all this implies, and of wanting to explain such things as the organization of castes, not by Hindu doctrine, but by current 'sociological' theories. It must not be forgotten that what essentially distinguishes the East from the modern West is the fact that the East still consciously preserves the metaphysical foundations of life, while the modern West is ignorant of traditional metaphysics (confusing it with 'philosophy', as does Radhakrishnan himself), and is at the same time actively and consciously anti-traditional.

'On Being in One's Right Mind' (*Review of Religion*, November 1942 [reprinted in *What is Civilisation?* (Great Barrington, MA: Lindisfarne Press, 1989)]). This article is an explanation of the true meaning of the Greek term *metanoia*, commonly and very inadequately rendered as 'repentance', although it really expresses a change of *nous*, that is to say an intellectual transformation. Fundamentally, this is also the original meaning of the word 'conversion', which implies a kind of 'turnaround' the scope of which far exceeds the merely 'moral' domain in which it has come to be considered almost exclusively. *Metanoia* is a transformation of the whole being, passing 'from human thought to divine understanding.' All traditional doctrines teach that the 'mind' in man is twofold, according to whether it is considered as turned toward perceptible things, which is the mind taken in its ordinary and individual sense, or whether it is transposed to its higher sense, where it is identified with Plato's *hēgemōn* or with the *antaryāmī* of Hindu tradition. *Metanoia* is properly speaking the conscious passage from the one to the other, from which results the birth of a 'new man', as it were; and the idea and the necessity of this *metanoia* are, with different but in reality equivalent formulations, unanimously affirmed by all traditions.

'*Ātmayajña*: Self-Sacrifice' (*Harvard Journal of Asiatic Studies*, February 1942 [reprinted in *SP:2*]). The principal idea of this important study, supported by many references to traditional texts, is that every sacrifice is really a 'sacrifice of oneself' through the identification of sacrificer with the victim or offering, as already will have been grasped from the quotations we have reproduced from it elsewhere. Moreover, since sacrifice is the ritual act par excellence, all the others partake of its nature and are somehow integrated in it, so sacrifice necessarily determines the entire structure of a traditional society, where everything can thereby be considered as constituting a true perpetual sacrifice. In this sacrificial interpretation of life, since acts have an essentially symbolic character, they must be treated as supports of contemplation (*dhiyālamba*), which presupposes that every practice implies and includes a corresponding theory. It is impossible to sum up here all that is said on *Agnihotra*, on *Soma*, on the 'murder of the Dragon' (symbolizing the domination of the 'I' by the 'Self'), on the significance of certain technical terms, on the 'folkloric' survival of traditional rites, and on many other questions. We shall merely cite some passages referring especially to the traditional conception of action:

> Acts of all kinds are reduced to their paradigms or archetypes, and so referred to Him from whom all action stems; when the 'notion that I am the doer' . . . has been overcome, and acts are no longer 'ours', when we are no longer any one. . . , what is done can no

more affect our essence than it can His whose organs we are. It is in this sense only, and not by vainly trying to do nothing, that the causal chain of fate . . . can be 'broken'. . . . If, in the last analysis, the Sacrifice is an mental operation . . . [this] by no means necessarily involves a disparagement of the physical acts that are the supports of contemplation. The priority of the contemplative does not destroy the real validity of the active life, just as in art the primacy of the free and imaginative *actus primus* does not remove the utility of the manual *actus secundus*. . . . It is true that, as the Vedānta consistently maintains, man's last end is unattainable by any means . . . but it is never forgotten that means are dispositive to that end.

'Perilous Bridge of Welfare' (*Harvard Journal of Asiatic Studies*, August 1944). As its heading indicates, this study by Doña Luisa Coomaraswamy refers to the symbolism of the bridge, which is found in one form or another in all traditions. We merely mention it for the moment with no further comment, for since we intend to devote a special article to this subject, we shall thereby have the opportunity to take it up more fully.

'Recollection, Indian and Platonic' and 'On the One and Only Transmigrant' (*Journal of the American Society* (supplement to the April–June issue 1944 [both reprinted in *SP:2*]). The first of these two essays deals with Platonic 'reminiscence' and its equivalent in Hindu and Buddhist tradition. According to this doctrine, what we call 'learning' is in reality 'remembering', which implies that our 'knowledge' is only by participation in the omniscience of an immanent spiritual principle, just as beauty is such only by participating in Beauty, and as all being is a participation in pure Being. This omniscience is correlative to the intemporal omnipresence, so that there should be no question of any 'foresight' of the future as such, by which our destiny could be arbitrarily decreed—a false conception from which stem all confusions in the matter. Here, knowledge is no more of the future than of the past, but only of a 'now'; the experience of duration is incompatible with omniscience, and this is why the empirical 'I' is incapable of omniscience. On the other hand, to the extent that we are capable of identifying ourselves with the omniscient 'Self', we rise above the sequence of events that constitute destiny; and thus this same doctrine of knowledge through participation is inseparably linked to the possibility of the liberation of the pairs of opposites, of which past and future, 'here' and 'there', are only particular cases. As Nicholas of Cusa said, 'the wall of Paradise where God resides is made of those opposites between which passes the narrow way that permits access to it.' In other words, our way passes through the 'now' and the 'nowhere' of which no empirical experience is possible, but the fact of 'reminiscence' assures us that the Way is open to those who understand the Truth.

The second study, 'On the One and Only Transmigrant', is in a way an explanation of Shankarāchārya's statement that 'there is truly no other transmigrant [*samsārī*] than *Ishvara*.' The process of contingent existence or of becoming, in whatever world it may be, is a 'reiteration of death and birth'; Deliverance (*Moksha*) is properly liberation from this becoming. In traditional doctrine there is no question of 'reincarnation', unless one means by this simply the transmission of the elements of the individual and temporal 'I' of the father to his descendants. Transmigration is something completely different: when a being dies, the 'Self', which is of the universal order, transmigrates (*samsarati*), that is to say continues to animate contingent existences, whose forms are predetermined by the sequence of intermediate causes. Deliverance is not for our 'I', but for the 'Self', which never becomes 'someone'; that is, it is only for us when we are no longer ourselves as individuals, but when we have realized the identity expressed by the Upanishadic formula 'That thou art' (*Tat tvam asi*). Incidentally, this doctrine is not at all unique to India, as is shown by numerous texts belonging to other traditional forms. Here, as in the case of 'reminiscence', is a doctrine that is truly part of the universal tradition.

'Note on the Stickfast Motif' (*Journal of American Folklore*, April 1944). This article deals with symbolic tales or narratives of which many appear in Buddhist texts, notably in the *Jātakas*, where an object coated with birdlime or some similar snare (which sometimes is, or appears to be, animated) is placed by a hunter representing Death. The being caught in the trap is usually attracted to it by thirst or some other desire leading it to stray into a domain not its own, which symbolizes attraction to things of the senses. The author shows by various comparisons that a story of this kind may very well have existed in India long before it adopted its specifically Buddhist form, and that it could even have had its origin there. It may not necessarily have happened like this, however, perhaps having possibly spread both to India and elsewhere from some common prehistoric source. In either case, it must be maintained that in order for his investigations to be valid, the historian of 'motifs' must take into account not only their 'letter' or outer form, but also their 'spirit', that is to say their real meaning, which 'folklorists' unfortunately seem too often to forget.

'Paths that Lead to the Same Summit' (*Motive*, May 1944 [reprinted in *The Bugbear of Literacy* (Bedford, Middlesex: Perennial Books, 1979)]). In this article bearing the subtitle 'Some Observations on Comparative Religion', AKC first shows why the comparative study of religions, as it is understood today, usually prevents any true understanding, whether the study is undertaken by those who consider their own religion to be the only true one, or on the contrary by those opposed to all religion, or even by those who simply adopt an 'ethical', and not a doctrinal, idea of religion. The essential aim of this study should be to permit the recognition of the equivalence of formulations differing in appearance and as it were accidentally, which are met in the various traditional forms. This would supply the respective adherents of these traditional forms with an immediate basis of understanding and cooperation through the recognition of their common principles. Of course, this has nothing to do with what is usually called 'tolerance', which really amounts to no more that indifference with regard to truth. On the other hand, such an understanding would naturally imply the renunciation of all proselytism and all 'missionary' activity, such as it is understood today. Moreover, the only true 'conversion', which all need equally, is *metanoia* understood in its original sense of intellectual metamorphosis, and which does not lead from one form of belief to another but in reality from the human to the divine. There follow characteristic examples of points of view expressed by the ancients and other 'non-Christians' when speaking of religions other than their own, bearing witness to the same understanding of those different forms. AKC also points out the benefit that the student of 'comparative religions' could and should draw, even for the understanding of his own religion, from the recognition of similar doctrines expressed in another language and by means which may seem strange to him.

There are many paths that lead to the summit of one and the same mountain; their differences will be the more apparent the lower down we are, but they vanish at the peak; each will naturally take the one that starts from the point at which he finds himself; he who goes round about the mountain looking for another is not climbing.

'Some Sources of Buddhist Iconography', in *Dr. B. C. Law Volume*, (Poona: Bhandarkar Oriental Research Institute, 1945 [reprinted in *Sources of Wisdom* (Colombo, Sri Lanka: Ministry of Cultural Affairs, 1981)]). Here AKC gives some new examples of the similarity of this iconography to Hindu symbolism prior to Buddhism. The representation of the Buddha as a 'pillar of fire' is closely related to the description of *Brahma* as the 'Tree of life', which is also a 'burning bush'. This axial pillar supporting Heaven is naturally also a symbol of *Agni*, and

it is clear that the representations of a pillar or of a tree of fire supported by a lotus are definitively based on the Vedic texts concerning the unique birth and archetype of *Agni Vanaspati*, the tree with the thousand branches, born of a lotus.

The prototype of the victory of the Buddha in his dispute with Kassapa whose firewood destined for the sacrificial fire will not burn, while his own ignites immediately, is found in the *Taittirīya Samhitā* (II.5.8). The flame over the Buddha's head finds its explanation in the passage of the *Bhagavad-Gītā* (xiv.11): 'Where there is knowledge, there the light flashes forth from the orifices of the body.' The struggle of the *Bodhisattva* with *Māra* immediately before the 'Great Awakening' has for prototype the fight of *Indra* against *Vritra*, *Ahi* or *Namuchi*, who are all likewise identified with Death (*Mrityu*). In both cases the hero, although alone, nonetheless has a 'following' or 'guard' which is in reality constituted by the 'breaths' (*prāna*) or the regenerated powers of the soul gathered in *samādhi*. This state of 'self-possession' in which the forms of Death (represented by the army of *Māra*) are overcome, is often described as a 'sleep', although in truth it is the most completely 'awakened' state there could be. Here, as always happens in similar cases, there is a reversal of the relations that exist in ordinary conditions between sleep and consciousness in the waking state:

that our present active life is a 'dream' from which we shall one day awake, and that, being thus wakened, we should seem sunk in sleep, is a concept that constantly reappears in the metaphysical doctrines of the whole world.

Finally, it is pointed out that headless demons are depicted in certain representations of *Māra's* army. This refers to a question which AKC has treated more fully in other studies which we shall discuss in the near future.

'"Spiritual Paternity" and the "Puppet-Complex"' (*Psychiatry*, August 1945 [reprinted in *The Bugbear of Literacy* (Bedford, Middlesex: Perennial Books, 1979)]). AKC here examines two kinds of facts among those that ethnologists interpret wrongly by reason of their preconceived ideas about the 'primitive mentality', and their tendency to consider as local peculiarities what are really only 'survivals', at times more or less degenerate, of theories found in all traditional doctrines. The first case is the 'belief' of certain peoples that the conception and birth of children has, in reality, not a physiological but a spiritual cause, consisting of the presence of an entity for whom the union of father and mother serves only to prepare the incarnation. Now in one form or another the same thing can be found expressed in all traditions, as is shown by many quite specific examples drawn from Hindu, Greek, Christian, and Islamic doctrines. The second case concerns what some people call the *puppet-complex*, that is to say the idea that the human individual is like a puppet, and his actions are not directed by his own will but by a superior will which, in the final analysis, is the divine Will itself. This idea, which fundamentally implies the doctrine of *līlā* and of *sūtrātmā*, exists explicitly in the Hindu and Buddhist traditions, and is also equally clear in Plato himself, whence it passed to the Western Middle Ages. As AKC says, 'the expression *complex*, which supposes a psychosis, is quite inappropriate to indicate what is in reality a metaphysical theory.' And also, 'it is impossible to claim to have considered "traditional teachings" in their true perspective if one ignores their universality.' Contrary to what the partisans of present-day 'anthropological methods' seem to think, simply observing facts, however carefully and accurately, is surely far from sufficient for a true understanding of them.

REVIEWS OF BOOKS & ARTICLES
BY OTHER AUTHORS

Reviews of Books: Other Authors

Sri Ramana Maharshi

Five Hymns to Sri Arunāchala [and other poems of Bhagavan Srī Ramana Maharshi] (Tiruvannāmalai: Srī Ramanāsramam, 1935 [New Delhi: Ramana Kendra, 1977]). The author of these hymns is none other than the 'Maharishi' of whom Paul Brunton speaks in his book *A Search in Secret India*, which we reviewed some time ago. *Arunāchala* is the name of a mountain considered to be a sacred place and a symbol of the 'Heart of the World'; it represents the immanence of the 'Supreme Consciousness' in all beings. These hymns breathe an incontestable spirituality. One might at first think that they concern only the *bhaktic* way, but this encompasses all the different but not at all exclusive ways in the unity of a synthesis that proceeds from a truly universal point of view. In the preface to this translation, Grant Duff felicitously contrasts Eastern spirituality with Western philosophy; it is only too true that the subtleties of dialectic do little more than waste time!

Truth Revealed: *Sad-Vidya* (Tiruvannāmalai: Srī Ramanāsramam, 1936, [1991]). We drew attention a few months ago to five hymns of the 'Maharshi'. We have here a work bearing more directly on doctrinal principles and condensing in a brief series of aphorisms the essential teaching concerning the 'Supreme Reality' or 'Absolute Consciousness' that must be realized as the 'Self'.

Five Hymns to Arunāchala, translated from the Tamil original (Tiruvannāmalai: Srī Ramanāsramam, 1938). When the first edition of the English translation of this text was published, we spoke of these hymns addressed to the sacred mountain *Arunāchala* considered as symbolizing the 'Heart of the World'. This second edition, which has just appeared, has been greatly improved both in regard to the correction of language and in fidelity of expression; furthermore, some commentaries which betrayed a certain influence of Western ideas have fortunately been rectified in a more traditional sense certainly more in conformity with the true thought of the author.

Upadesa Saram, tr. and notes B. V. Narasimha Swami (Tiruvannāmalai: Srī Ramanāsramam, 1938 [Madras: Tiruvannāmalai, 1965]). Upadesa Saram is a resumé in thirty short stanzas of Srī Ramana's teaching on the spiritual development of the human being. It defines the different 'paths' (mārgas) and shows that they all lead to the same goal, which is always 'absorption into the source or the heart of existence,' which is identical to the Supreme Brahma. Permanent absorption implies the 'extinction of the mind' (manonāsha) and consequently of the individuality as such; but far from leaving a void after it, this 'extinction' leads to a truly infinite 'plenitude' (pūrna), which is none other than the 'Self' and which is the perfect unity of Sat-Chit-Ānanda. This is the ultimate result of the 'enquiry' (vichāra) about the real nature of the being, corresponding to the 'That thou Art' (Tat tvam asi) of the Upanishads.

Who am I? tr. S. Seshu Iyer (Tiruvannāmalai: Srī Ramanāsramam, 1938, [1948]). This booklet contains explanations given by Srī Ramana in response to questions put by a disciple regarding the 'path of enquiry' (vichāra-mārga) he especially recommends: the being that in seeking to know its true nature asks itself what really constitutes its very essence, must first become aware successively that it is not the body, nor the subtle form, nor the vital force (prāna), nor the mind, nor even the totality of potentialities which subsist in the undifferentiated state of deep sleep. It can therefore only be identified with what subsists after all these adventitious elements have been eliminated, that is to say the pure consciousness which is Sat-Chit-Ānanda. It is the 'Self' (Ātmā) which resides in the heart (hridaya) and is the sole source of all manifestations, mental, vital, psychic, and corporeal. It can be attained by concentration and meditation. The state of 'absorption' in this 'Self' has nothing in common with the exercise of faculties or psychic 'powers' of any kind, nor, we will add—in order to anticipate another error of interpretation common in the West—with any 'psychological' state, since it is essentially beyond the mind. Indeed, this is a question of the path of Jñāna-Yoga, which is described very clearly in the Upanishads and which could be described 'technically' as a process of the gradual reabsorption from the outward to the inward, to the very center of the being. It finally ends in knowledge of the 'Self' and in the realization of its true nature (*svarūpa*), which realization is Deliverance (*Mukti*).

Who am I?, tr. Dr T. M. P Mahadevan (Tiruvannāmalai: Srī Ramanāsramam, 1940, [1969]). In the new edition of this booklet the translation has been improved and almost entirely reworked; perhaps it is to be regretted that fewer Sanskrit terms are explained than in the first version, for this is something that always helps greatly to clarify the meaning. On the other hand, at the request of one of his disciples, an English translation of a poem by Srī Ramana on 'Self-Knowledge' has been added at the end.

Crumbs from His Table, by Ramananda Swarnagiri (Trichinopoly, South India: Srī K. S. Narayanaswami Iyer, 1938 [Tiruvannāmalai: Srī Ramanāsramam, 1981]). This is the account of a series of meetings with Srī Ramana in which the method of *vichāra*, of which we have spoken, is as it were 'put into action' and which treats such questions as the 'faith' (*shraddhā*) necessary for the acquisition of knowledge, mind-control and the difference between the mind's temporary stabilization (*manolaya*) and its 'extinction' (*manonāsha*), and the obstacles to the realization of the 'Self' which can be overcome by constant concentration, deep sleep, and the different degrees of *samādhi*. What seems above all particular to Srī Ramana's teaching is his habitual insistence that one ought to undertake from the start the method of *vichāra* instead of beginning with some preliminary process of corporeal, psychic, and mental 'purification' (of which he recognizes the necessity), although a number of his principal disciples have expressly declared that the direct method is not suitable for all. As the author remarks, Srī Ramana never contested the legitimacy of other methods, but on the contrary, as we have seen above, he affirms more or less directly that they all lead to the final goal.

Sat-Darshana Bhashya and Talks with Maharshi, with Forty Verses in Praise of Srī Ramana (Trichinopoly, India, 1938, [1953]). The conversations recorded in the first part of this book deal again with subjects similar to those we have just mentioned: the relationship between *vichāra* and the 'Grace' which corresponds to it inwardly, the two movements exercised as it were correlatively in contrary directions; the identity of the *Satguru* with the 'Self'; the positive character of the state of silence (*mauna*), not to be confounded in any way with mere inactivity; the dwelling place of the 'Self' in the center designated symbolically as the 'heart'; the difference between *Siddhis* in the ordinary sense, that is, 'powers' sought for themselves and which are only obstacles to realization, and *Siddhis* occurring naturally and normally as contingent manifestations of a certain inward state; and the highest significance of the same term (*jñāna-siddhi*), which is the very realization of the 'Self'.

The second part is a translation with commentary of the *Sat-Darshana Bhashya*, which, first written in Tamil by Srī Ramana, and translated into Sanskrit by his disciple Vasishta Ganapati Muni, and which is as its title indicates a 'discourse on the perception of the truth'; starting from the discrimination of God, of the manifested world, and of the 'soul' (*jīva*), these must be left behind in order to reach the supreme Reality which, in its absolute 'non-duality', is the source and support of all that exists. This reality is the 'Self' that appears when the 'ego' and its limitations have vanished; the *jīvanmukta*, having realized the 'Self', is one with the Supreme, and his condition and his mode of action are incomprehensible to the mind. This state of realization is always the same, whether it be attained in this life or in some other world, and there is no distinction of degrees in Deliverance, which is the conscious identity of the being with the supreme Truth.

Self Realisation: Life and Teachings of Sri Ramana Maharshi, by B. V. Narasimha Swami (Tiruvannāmalai: Srī Ramanāsramam, 1938, [1962]). This biography of Srī Ramana relates his sudden 'vocation' at the age of seventeen years, his retreat to Arunāchala along with the difficulties he had to overcome in order to persevere there, his relations with his disciples and the instructions he gave them, the way he treats animals, and daily life at the *āshrama*—too much to be summarized in a few lines, so that we can only advise that those who would like to have a more complete idea of the Maharshi's 'personality' read the book itself. What seems especially important to note is that by virtue of its 'spontaneous' character Srī Ramana's realization represents a path that is rather exceptional, and also, doubtless for this very reason, that he seems to exercise above all what one could call an 'action of presence', for although he always replies willingly to questions, it cannot be said that he gives a regular teaching strictly speaking. Moreover, his disciples are quite different in many respects and he always gives everyone the utmost liberty, which, it must be said, produces very different results according to the individual. But, after all, is it not inevitable that each will reap only the benefits that correspond to his own capacity?

Maha Yoga, or the Upanishadic Lore in the Light of the Teachings of Bhagavan Sri Ramana, by Sarma K. Lakshman [under pseudonym 'Who'] (The New Light Publishing House, Pudukotah, South India [Tiruvannāmalai: Srī Ramanāsramam, 1973]). Not without reason, the author of this short book finds a confirmation of the doctrine of the *Upanishads* in the life and the teachings of Srī Ramana; but his point of view may appear somewhat odd when he declares that it is these that constitute for the disciple the most authoritative 'Revelation', and that the ancient doctrine is valid for them because it accords with these same teachings. Here there is a kind of reversal of relationships that does not indicate a very accurate idea of traditional orthodoxy. Thus we think that all of the responsibility for these interpretations ought properly to be left to the author alone, at least in the measure that they are affected by a certain 'modernism' and by various little justified comparisons with Western philosophical and psychological ideas, which also testify to the same spirit. While recognizing what his work contains that is very worthy of interest, it is to be regretted that the subject has not been wholly treated in conformity with the very doctrine to which it directly relates; and perhaps one must see here one of the less fortunate effects of that absence of a regular teaching to which we just alluded, and which does not allow us in such a case to give to the qualification 'disciple'—however lofty it may be—its full significance.

A Catechism of Enquiry (Tiruvannāmalai: Srī Ramanāsramam, 1940 [and later editions]). This small volume is the translation of instructions given by Srī Ramana to one of his disciples to guide him in the inquiry about the 'Self', an inquiry that must finally lead to the realization of the true nature of the being. Since the 'Self' is identical to the 'Supreme', all adoration of the 'Supreme' is in the end nothing else than a form of inquiry of the 'Self'; this, by whatever means it is pursued, is the sole method that allows one to gradually discard all obstacles and to reach 'Deliverance'. The essence of these teachings can be summarized in these words: 'Realize perfect Beatitude by constant meditation on the Self.'

A Catechism of Instruction (Tiruvannāmalai: Srī Ramanāsramam, 1940). This second book brings together teachings given by Srī Ramana in response to questions posed by his disciples. The principal subjects are the essential character of spiritual teaching (*upadesha*) and the distinctive qualities of the *guru*; the method of realization (*sādhana*) and its various modes, notably the *vichāra-mārga*, that is to say the inquiry about the 'Self' which we discussed above; 'experience' (*anubhava*), that is, realization itself at these different stages; and finally, the nature of the state of one firmly established in the state of 'Knowledge' (*ārūdha-sthiti*), an immutable state which is that of complete identity with or absorption in the 'Self'. We somewhat regret the use of the word 'catechism' in the title of these two volumes (of which only the second is actually written in the 'catechetic' form of questions and answers), for in the West it will almost inevitably call to mind the idea of a purely exoteric and even quite elementary teaching. Such word 'associations' must be taken into account if one wishes to avoid ambiguity, something against which Easterners who write in Western languages are unfortunately not always sufficiently on guard.

Maharshi's Gospel [*Being Answers of Bhagavan Sri Ramana Maharshi to Questions Put to Him by the Devotees*] (Tiruvannāmalai: Srī Ramanāsramam, 1940, [1994]). This little volume was published on the occasion of Srī Ramana's sixtieth birthday, December 27, 1939. It is, like most of its precursors, a collection of his responses to questions posed by different disciples. The principal subjects treated are the renunciation of the fruits of action, silence and solitude, mind-control, the relationship of *bhakti* and *jñāna*, the 'Self' and the individuality, the realization of the 'Self', and the role of the *guru* in his twofold 'outer' and 'inner' significance. We note in particular the teaching given on the subject of action: it is not action in itself which poses an obstacle to realization, but the idea that it is the 'ego' that acts, as much in the effort to abstain from action as in action itself. It is action accompanied by a perfect detachment that does not affect the being. Let us also point out the effects of what can be called an 'action of presence': communication of Knowledge can really only take place in silence by the influence of an inner force incomparably more powerful than speech and all the other manifestations of any outward activity. In sum, this is the true doctrine of 'non-action'.

Études sur Ramana Maharshi, vol. 1, by Swāmī Siddheswarānanda, Dr Sarma K. Lakshman, and Swāmī Tapasyānanda; intro. and tr. by Jean Herbert [Paris: A. Maisonneuve, 1940]. In the introduction Herbert apologizes for publishing only studies on Srī Ramana and not the writings themselves. These writings are certainly very few in number, and even the various compilations of his oral teachings published to date represent only something very fragmentary and incomplete, but we wonder whether these are Herbert's only reasons for abstention; and what might lead one to believe there must have been others is the rather bitter criticism he levels at Maharshi's entourage... It is moreover quite correct that Maharshi 'did not accept any disciples' in the true sense of the word, although many people all too readily claim this status. We even doubt that there is good reason to 'hope a day will come when he will agree to assume the role of guru,' for it seems indeed that if he exercises only what we have already called an 'action of presence', it may be in virtue of the very exceptional character of the way he followed. — The main part of this first volume consists of a translation, slightly modified on certain points, of the book by Dr Sarma K. Lakshman previously published as *Mahā-Yoga* under the pseudonym 'Who'. We have already reviewed this book, indicating certain reservations from the doctrinal point of view; we shall therefore not return to it except to remind the reader that it must be considered only as the expression of the author's own point of view. The translation is set between a preface and an appendix; in the first, Swāmī Siddheswarānanda calls attention to the path and the attitude of Srī Ramana, and he also notes quite appropriately the mistakes committed by a writer who professed to appreciate him from the point of view of the Western 'mystic'. As to his Appendix, Swāmi Tapasyānanda gives such a 'reticent' impression that one cannot help wondering why he wrote it!

Sri Ramana Gita, by Kavyakanta Ganapati Muni (Tiruvannāmalai: Srī Ramanāsramam, 1936, [1981]). This booklet contains a series of conversations of the 'Maharshi' with some of his disciples, among others the author himself, on diverse questions touching on spiritual realization and the means of attaining it. Let us particularly note the chapters concerning *hridaya-vidyā*, 'mind control', the relationship of *jñāna* and *siddha*, and the state of the *jīvanmukta*. All of this, which cannot be summarized here, can, like the contents of the preceding volume, furnish excellent starting points for meditation.

Sri Ramakrishna

Un des chemins... [*Tous les chemins de vérité mènent au même Dieu*], French adaptation by Marie Honegger-Durand; preface by Jean Herbert (Frameries, Belgium: Union des Imprimeries, 1936). The title of this compilation is explained by the first thought to appear there: 'There are paths which lead us to God by pure love, by study, by good works, and by contemplation . . . all these paths are different, but the Goal remains the same.' The concern to adapt things to a Western audience does not appear to us to be free from every inconvenience. In order to do safely, as Jean Herbert says, 'what Ramakrishna himself would have done had he addressed the French,' one would have to have reached Ramakrishna's own spiritual degree... Then there is the occasional vagueness or inaccuracy in expression; thus, to take just one typical example, why use the word 'tolerance' when what is meant is obviously 'patience', which is quite a different thing? But in spite of such imperfections, these thoughts are still worth considering by those for whom Unity and the Divine Presence are something else than purely verbal formulas. — From the point of view of outward presentation, we believe that it would perhaps have been better to put a little more 'substance' into this volume (one would surely have had only the difficulty of choice) rather than to write on each page a single thought which occupies only three or four lines...

Les Paroles du Maître (conversations recorded and published by Swāmī Brahmānanda, French translation by Marie Honegger-Durand, Dilip Kumar Roy, and Jean Herbert; preface by Swāmī Yatiswarānanda (Frameries, Belgium: Union des Imprimeries, 1937). In this collection the text has been followed much more faithfully than in the preceding translation, and the inclusion of a number of original terms also helps promote a better understanding (in the absence of the word *sādhana*, for example, one would be perplexed by an expression as manifestly inadequate as 'exercises of devotion'). This difference can be easily seen by comparing the passages found in both volumes. Moreover, the talks of Ramakrishna collected here have been methodically grouped by one of his disciples according to their subject. It is naturally impossible to summarize them or even give a sketch, and it is better to advise all whom it might interest to read the book. One must not stop at the apparent simplicity of the form, for one who possesses some traditional knowledge will often discover information of a much more technical nature than that which will come to the ordinary reader; but naturally, as in all teaching of this order, each gets what he can according to his own comprehension, and in any case this is always beneficial.

MARCO PALLIS

Peaks and Lamas (London: The Woburn Press, 1974). This work, to which Coomaraswamy has already devoted a note here at the time of its first appearance (June 1940 issue), has now gone through several editions, in which the author has refined various details. We come back to it here as a 'travel account', whatever its interest, but only to point out more particularly some points pertaining to the Tibetan tradition. Let us say first that Pallis does not accept the term 'Lamaism', which in English seems to carry a pejorative nuance. We must say that this does not seem to be the case in French, so that for our part we have not hitherto seen any drawback to its use on occasion. It is true that it is a purely conventional denomination, but there are others to which the case equally applies (that of 'Confucianism' for example), and which are used solely for reasons of convenience. One can doubtless be content to speak quite simply of Tibetan Buddhism, and this perhaps is the best expression. In any case it must be clearly understood that this form of Buddhism presents peculiarities which clearly distinguish it from other forms, not only of Buddhism in general, but even from the *Mahāyāna* of which it is a branch. — One chapter of quite special importance from the doctrinal point of view is entitled 'The Round of Existence', and it contains in an excellent exposé of the symbolism of the 'Wheel of Life' a schematic representation of the multiple states of conditioned existence. Here the author explains various fundamental points of Buddhist doctrine insofar as it aims essentially to bring beings out of the indefinite succession of these states in order to lead them to *Nirvāna*, on which subject he very justly corrects false interpretations current in the West, explaining that

> that which is extinguished is Ignorance and its train of consequences. A double negative . . . is the only way of even faintly suggesting its positive reality. . . . He who attains it, knows it. He who

has not attained it can only speculate in terms of his own relativity, which do not apply to it. . . . There is a complete discontinuity between that state and the Round of Existence. . . .

Let us also mention the considerations he offers on Method and Wisdom, envisaged as both complementary and inseparable and symbolized respectively by the *dorje* and by the hand bell or *dilbu*. Another chapter describes the symbolism of the *Tantras* which, besides explanations that they bring to the purely doctrinal order, notably concerning the idea of the *Shakti*, constitute as clear as possible a refutation of the inept assertions one meets almost everywhere on this subject, which is doubtless one where Western incomprehension has reached its apogee. Elsewhere we find explanations of the 'Three Refuges', of the formula *Om mani padme hum*, and of *mantras* in general as supports of meditation; and other points, which it would take too long to enumerate, are treated incidentally. The last part is dedicated almost entirely to Tibetan art; here Pallis speaks first of its present state, and one notes that this is one of the rare examples still extant of a truly living traditional art today. The author also introduces certain general views on 'popular art' inspired by pointers from Coomaraswamy, but he observes that in Tibet it is hardly possible to envisage a 'popular art' distinct from any other kind of art, 'because all the elements which have contributed to give its form to the Tibetan civilization, from whatever source they are derived, have been combined in a completely developed synthesis and adapted to the needs of men of every rank and capacity.' Pallis then shows the close connection of art with doctrine; from this chapter, which it is impossible for us to summarize here, we note only considerations on the essentially intellectual character of traditional art, on ritual regarded as 'a synthesis of all the arts placed in service of the doctrine and collaborating toward the unique goal' of preparing the spirit for metaphysical realization, and on the absence of all 'idolatry' in the usage thus made of symbolic figures. Finally, he draws attention to the danger that can result for art and for the indivisible whole of the traditional civilization from the penetration of Western influence which the interior of Tibet has thus far escaped, but which is already starting to make itself felt on its frontiers. We will also mention very justified reflections on the importance of custom in maintaining the traditional spirit. Those who wish to destroy tradition among a people know quite well what they are about when they start imposing on it European culture!

Although Marco Pallis's *Peaks and Lamas* has already been reviewed here twice (June 1940 and January–February 1947 issues) we must return to it again to point out an important chapter entitled 'The Presiding Idea' which the author has added expressly for the American edition and where he has made a particular point of defining as explicitly as possible the principle of unity proper to Tibetan civilization which distinguishes it from other forms of traditional civilization. That this principle is found in the Buddhist doctrine is not in doubt, but such an acknowledgment is insufficient, for in countries other than Tibet where it is practiced, the influence of Buddhism has produced very different results. In fact, what above all characterizes Tibetan civilization is the predominance given to one element of this doctrine, to a degree found nowhere else, this being the notion of the state of *Bodhisattva*, that is to say

> the state of the fully awakened being who, though under no further constraint by that Law of Causality which he has transcended, yet freely continues to espouse the vicissitudes of the Round of Existence in virtue of his Self-identification with all the creatures still involved in egocentric delusion and consequent suffering. [p303]

An apparent difficulty stems from the fact that the state of *Bodhisattva* is, on the other hand, commonly considered to constitute a lower and preliminary degree to that of *Buddha*, but this hardly seems apt when applied to the case of a being

> who not only has realized the Void, in a transcendent sense, but also has realized it in the World itself, in an immanent sense, this double realization . . . being for him not twofold but one and only, . . . the supreme unitive Knowledge. [p309]

The solution to this difficulty seems to reside in the distinction between two different uses of the term *Bodhisattva*: in the one case it is used to designate a saint who has not yet attained the ultimate degree of perfection, but who is only on the point of reaching it, whereas in the other case it means a being

> who is identical with Buddha by right of knowledge, but who . . . for the benefit of creatures *recapitulates* some of the stages of the Way for *exemplary* reasons, as a 'shower of the Way'. In that sense he redescends into the Round rather than remains in it, though the

latter may be the impression produced on the minds of beings, ever prone to be deceived by external appearances. [p308]

This way of envisaging the *Bodhisattva* therefore properly corresponds to what we have called 'descending realization' and naturally it also has an obvious connection with the doctrine of the *Avatāras*. In the rest of this chapter, which we cannot completely summarize here, Pallis tries to dispel the confusions which this conception of the *Bodhisattva* might raise if it were interpreted falsely in conformity with certain tendencies of the present mentality, in terms of 'altruistic' or so-called 'mystical' sentimentality; then he gives examples of its constant applications in the spiritual life of the Tibetans. One of these examples is the practice of invocation widespread among the whole population; another concerns in particular the mode of existence of the *naldjorpas*, that is to say those who are already more or less advanced along the way of realization, or whose aspirations and efforts are at the least definitively established in that direction, and whom even relatively ignorant Tibetans consider to be truly the protectors of humanity, without whose 'non-acting' activity it would soon be irretrievably lost.

HARI PRASAD SHASTRI

Teachings from the Bhagavadgita, tr., into., and comments (Luzac and Co., London, 1935 [London: Shanti Sadan, 1949]). There are already many translations of the Bhagavad-Gītā in various Western languages; this one is incomplete, its author having suppressed passages which seem to him to relate to conditions peculiar to India and keeping only those he considers to have the value of a 'universal' teaching. For our part, we think this mutilation quite regrettable. Moreover, dominated by an idea of excessive 'simplicity', he gives only a rather outward meaning that lets nothing appear of more profound meanings; his comments are reduced in sum to very little. One could also point to errors in terminology, which are not always without importance; in this connection we will point out a confusion of 'non-dualism' with 'monism'. This book will certainly bring nothing new to those who have any acquaintance at all with Hindu doctrines, but perhaps it will at least stimulate their study by bringing them to the attention of some of those still unaware of them.

The Avadhut Gita: translation and introduction (Chez l'auteur, 30, Landsdowne Crescent, London, W. 11 [London: H.P. Shastri, 1934]). This small volume is much more interesting than the preceding one, for the text concerned is not well known. The word *avadhut* is almost synonymous with *jīvanmukta*, so that the title could be translated as 'Song of Deliverance'. The author is Dattatreya, but no other writing is attributed to him and it is not known exactly where or when he lived. Without the original text at hand we naturally cannot verify the exactness of the translation in detail, but we can at least note an error regarding *ākāsha*, which is really 'ether' and not 'space' (in Sanskrit *dish*); and we also wonder why *Brahma*, in this book as in the other, is constantly spelled *Brhama*. Although we do not see how the translator can have discovered the idea of 'love' in a work of pure 'knowledge', the spirit of the text is in general noticeably well preserved and well rendered in translation. This is a remarkable account of *advaita* doctrine which, as is said in the introduction, 'breathes the purest spirit of the *Upanishads* and of Srī Shankārachārya' and reminds us especially of the latter's *Ātmā-Bodha*; and so its reading could not be recommended more highly.

Book of Ram, The Bible of India, tr. by Mahatma Tulsidas (London: Luzac & Co., 1935). This 'book of Rāma', written in Hindi in the sixteenth century of the Christian era, must not be confused with the ancient Sanskrit Rāmāyana of Valmiki. Although Tulsidas is said to have been inspired by Rāma himself, the appellation 'Bible of India' is quite improper, for obviously this would be much better applied to the *Veda*. In this book the path of *bhakti* is recommended above all, as is fitting in a written text addressed to the greatest number. However, the teaching is indisputably 'non-dualist' and clearly indicates 'Supreme Identity' as the ultimate aim of all 'realization'. The translation includes only extracts, but these are chosen in such a way as to give the essential from the doctrinal point of view; the accompanying notes are generally clear although there are some confusions, especially concerning cyclical periods. It is regrettable, on the other hand, that the author wished to translate all the terms, even those which, not having any equivalent in Western languages, ought to have been kept as they are with an added explanation. This results in some rather strange assimilations: need we point out, for example, that the *Trimūrti* is something quite other than the 'Holy Trinity'?

A Path to God-Realization (London: Shanti Sadan, 1935). The author declares that the ideas expressed in this short work came to him while meditating on the teachings of Lao Tzu. To tell the truth, we find in it nothing of specifically Taoist inspiration, but rather an elementary sketch of a 'preparatory' method which can be applied independently of any definite traditional form. 'Moral' and 'devotional' prescriptions hold a perhaps excessive place, whereas what relates to knowledge and should be the essential is reduced to rather little. There is also, at the beginning, a notion of 'spirituality' which seems to us rather vague and inadequate; but we can fully approve of the author when he declares that 'psychic phenomena' must not be associated with the 'spiritual life', recalling that in his *Rāmāyana* Tulsidas asks to be kept from the temptation of so-called 'powers', and that Shankarāchārya warns that they only constitute a trap from which it is difficult to escape.

Meditation, its Theory and Practice (London: Shanti Sadan, 1936 [1974]). This slim volume contains a simple but reasonably exact exposition of the nature of concentration and meditation, and how one can progressively train oneself in them. Moreover, the author justly notes that meditation is not a goal in itself but only a method of attaining Knowledge, which is basically nothing other than the 'realization of the Self'. He also emphasizes, with good reason, the necessity of traditional teaching; but a little more precision would have been desirable here, for many readers might believe it enough to attach themselves 'ideally' to a tradition, even by merely studying its teachings in books, whereas it is nothing like this, and it is necessary that the attachment be direct and effective. In the same order of ideas we note another omission: it is quite true that *mantras* are valid only if pronounced in the sacred language of the tradition to which they belong and not as translated into some other language, but why not also inform the reader that they can only be fully effective if they have been communicated by a regular transmission and according to the rites traditionally prescribed? Perhaps this is to avoid overly discouraging Westerners, for whom this condition cannot be fulfilled; nonetheless, we think that it is much better to warn them about the limitation of the results they can ordinarily hope for rather than to let them suffer more unfortunate disappointments later.

Vedanta Light: Teachings of Shri Dada (London: Shanti Sadan, 1936 [1956]). This booklet contains a translation of meetings with the author's *guru* about different subjects relating to the teachings of the *Vedānta*, in particular the means preparatory to spiritual realization. The form is simple and the contents quite elementary, but there is nothing here which can raise serious objections. We will point out only one somewhat contestable assertion: how and in what sense can the origin of *Karma-Yoga* be attributed to Zoroaster?

JEAN HERBERT

Quelques grands penseurs de l'Inde moderne [Talks given on 'Radio Geneva' in June 1937] (Frameries, Belgium: Union des Imprimeries, 1937 [Paris: Adrien-Maisonneuve, 1937]). The talks collected in this little volume, evidently intended for 'the general public', raise the fear of a tendency in its author to 'popularization', which necessarily imposes excessive simplifications that some subjects can hardly accommodate. Thus is it truly correct to present as 'thinkers' in the Western sense Srī Ramakrishna, Srī Ramana Maharshi, and Srī Aurobindo, who are mentioned here, or are they not rather, especially the first two, something quite different of which it is hardly possible to give 'the general public' in Europe an idea? It is wrong to say that Srī Ramakrishna 'abandoned Hinduism at a certain point' and 'became Christian,' then Muslim. The truth is altogether different, as Ananda K. Coomaraswamy has explained even here; but it would certainly be very difficult for unprepared readers to understand what it is. We shall not therefore dwell on this any further, and shall make only one more remark: Herbert says of Srī Ramana Maharshi that his teaching 'offers the remarkable peculiarity of claiming to say absolutely nothing new.' But this, far from being a 'peculiarity', is on the contrary the only normal and valid attitude in all traditional civilizations; it is precisely for this reason that in such civilizations there cannot be any 'thinkers', nor above all any inventors of philosophical systems, that is to say men who put individual originality above the truth.

Introduction à l'Etude des Yogas hindous (Frameries, Belgium: Union des Imprimeries, 1938 [Paris: Adrien-Maisonneuve, 1938]). This lecture was given at the 'International Institute of Psychagogy' of Geneva, which perhaps explains why from the outset the author defines the term of *Yoga* as 'meaning more or less a path leading to a goal, a discipline preparing us for something.' This is quite inaccurate since it signifies 'Union' and indicates on the contrary the goal itself, and it is only by extension that it is applied also to the means of attaining it. On the other hand, the author is entirely correct in denouncing the gross simplification by which Westerners consider the human body to be composed of only two parts, body and soul, this last including indiscriminately all that is non-corporeal; but why does he reverse the normal meanings of the words 'soul' and 'spirit'? He shows quite well the need for multiple paths in pointing out that one must not only consider the goal, which is one, but also the starting-point, which differs according to the individuals concerned; then he summarily characterizes the different kinds of *Yoga*, taking care to explain, as is again very just, that they are not at all exclusive and that in practice they are always more or less combined. What is also perfectly true is that *Yoga* has nothing to do with 'religion'; but he should have added that for the most part Hindu methods nonetheless have a ritual character by which they are linked to a determinate traditional form, outside of which they lose their efficacy; only, if one would understand this, one must obviously not follow the teaching of Vivekānanda... Finally, the author ends his account with a warning against charlatans who look to profit from ideas more or less vaguely inspired by *Yoga* for ends that have absolutely nothing spiritual about them. In the present circumstances, such a warning is timely indeed!

Caroline A. F. Rhys Davids

The Birth of Indian Psychology and its Development in Buddhism (London: Luzac & Co., 1936). It seems to us very doubtful, even after having read this book, that there has ever been something that can be called 'Indian psychology', or in other words that the 'psychological' point of view as understood by modern Westerners has ever been envisaged in India. The author recognizes that the study of the human being has always been made from the inward to the outward, and not inversely as in the West. This is precisely why psychology, which confines itself to endlessly analyzing certain superficial modifications of the being, could never hold the slightest interest there. Only in Buddhism, doubtless as a consequence of its tendency to deny or at least to ignore transcendent principles, does one find considerations which could to some extent lend themselves in some measure to an interpretation in psychological terms; but even here one ought not to push comparisons too far. As for wishing to find psychology in the *Upanishads* themselves, this gives proof of a perfect incomprehension, which moreover manifests itself only too clearly in incredible confusions of language: 'soul', 'spirit', 'ego', 'self', 'man'—these terms are constantly and indifferently employed as if they referred to one and the same thing! It hardly needs saying that here one sees constantly affirmed the bias common to all orientalists to reduce everything to purely human 'thought', which, beginning from a state of infancy, would then have progressively 'evolved'. Between such a viewpoint and that of tradition there is obviously no possible area of agreement... The so-called 'historical method' is in fact very far from ruling out such more or less fanciful hypotheses; thus Mrs Rhys Davids has imagined, under the name of *Sakya*, something she believes to have been the original Buddhism and which she thinks can be reconstituted purely and simply by eliminating as 'later' additions everything that does not agree with the concept she has of the beginning of what she calls a *world-religion*, and first, all that seems to have a 'monastic' character. What such a procedure really proves is only that she is affected with a violent 'anti-monastic' prejudice! We would never finish if we wished to note every trace in her interpretations of her own religious or philosophical preferences; but since she is really persuaded that whoever does not share them is thereby destitute of any 'critical spirit', this would surely serve no purpose... However that may be, after reading a work of this kind we are certainly much better informed on what the author thinks than on what those she means to study 'historically' truly thought; and that at least is not without offering a certain 'psychological' interest!

To Become or Not to Become (That is the Question!), Episodes in the History of an Indian Word (London: Luzac & Co., 1937). It is only too true that grammarians, philologists, and translators often do a rather bad job, and that it would take much to rectify their insufficiencies and errors. In this we entirely agree with the author; but is this to say that we should also agree with her on the special point in question here, namely regarding the verb *bhū* and its derivatives such as *bhava* and *bhavya* where, instead of the meaning of 'being' ordinarily attributed to them she wants to see almost exclusively that of 'becoming'? The truth seems to us somewhat different, nor do we think there is need for much discussion and meticulous analysis to prove it. The two roots *as* and *bhū* are certainly not synonymous, their relationship corresponding exactly to that between 'essence' and 'substance'. Strictly speaking, the word 'being' should be kept for the translation of the first and the terms related to it, while the idea expressed by the second is properly that of 'existence', understanding by this the totality of all the modifications deriving from *Prakriti*. It goes without saying that this idea of 'existence' in a way implies that of 'becoming', but also that it does not reduce entirely to it, for in the 'substantial' aspect to which it refers there is also the idea of 'subsistence'. Without taking this into account, we wonder how one could really translate, for example, a term such as *svayambhū*, which certainly cannot mean anything other than 'that which subsists by itself'. No doubt modern language commonly confuses 'being' and 'existing', just as it confuses many other notions; but one must apply oneself above all to dispel precisely confusions of this kind in order to restore to the words one uses their proper and original meanings. At root we cannot see any other means but this to improve translations, at least to the full extent allowed by the resources, rather restricted despite everything, of Western languages. Unfortunately, preconceived ideas all too often arise to complicate the simplest questions. Thus Mrs Rhys Davids is obviously influenced by certain more than questionable ideas, and it is not difficult to see that she prefers the word 'becoming'; in accordance with the theories of Bergson and other contemporary 'evolutionist' philosophers she considers 'becoming' more real than even 'being', that is to say she wishes to make what is only a lesser reality to be on the contrary the highest and perhaps even the sole reality. That she thinks so on her own account certainly concerns only her, but when she adapts the meaning of traditional texts to these wholly modern conceptions, this is something much more regrettable. Her entire view, moreover, is naturally affected by 'historicism'; she believes that such and such ideas had to appear at a given moment, then change from one age to another as if it were a matter of mere profane 'thought'. What is more, she has, as we have already had occasion to notice, an astounding faculty for 'imagining' history, if one may put it so, according to her own particular views; we even wonder whether this is only imagination, and to tell the truth certain rather clear allusions to 'psychic' experiences make us fear that there may be something even worse here!

SRI AUROBINDO GHOSE

Aperçus et Pensées, tr. from the English with preface by Jean Herbert (Frameries, Belgium: Union des Imprimeries, 1937 [Paris: Adrien-Maisonneuve, 1937]). This small book, the first work of Sri Aurobindo Ghose to be published in French, is a collection of aphorisms and short fragments on such different subjects as the real purpose of existence, the nature of man and his relation with the world and with God, the 'chains' which prevent the being from attaining liberation, and so on. All this, which it is obviously impossible to summarize here, should be read and especially meditated on. It is to be hoped that this translation will be followed by other more important works from a man who, although he perhaps sometimes presents the doctrine under a rather too 'modernized' form, has no less incontestably a high spiritual value. We certainly do not think it desirable, as the author of the preface says, that he find a Romain Rolland to write his autobiography... and to distort it by his uncomprehending and wholly Western sentimentality!

The Mother (Calcutta: Arya Publishing House, 1938). This little book treats of the divine *Shakti* and of the attitude that those who aim at spiritual realization must have toward her. This attitude is defined as a complete 'surrender', but one must not be mistaken about the meaning that should be attached to this word. Indeed, it is said expressly from the start that the collaboration of two powers is indispensable, 'a fixed and unfaltering aspiration which calls from below, and a supreme Grace which responds from above,' and, furthermore, that 'as long as the lower nature is active [that is, as long as the individuality exists as such] the personal effort of the *Sādhaka* is still necessary.' In these conditions it is evident that there could be no question of an attitude of 'passivity' such as that of the mystics, nor with all the more reason of any 'quietism'; this 'surrender' is much more comparable to, even if not basically quite identical with, what in Islamic terms is called *at-tawkīl ala 'Llah*. The last chapter, particularly important and interesting, explains the principal aspects of the *Shakti* and their respective functions in relation to the manifested world.

Lights on Yoga (Shrī Aurobindo Library, Howrah, 1938 [Pondicherry: Sri Aurobindo Ashram, 1981]). This book, composed of excerpts from letters written by Srī Aurobindo to his disciples in response to their questions, clarifies how he sees the path and goal of *Yoga*. For him, it is a question

> not only of rising from ordinary ignorant mundane consciousness to the Divine consciousness, but also of bringing down the supramental power of this Divine consciousness into the ignorance of the mind, of life, and of the body, and of transforming them, of manifesting the Divine even here below, and of creating a Divine life in matter.

This amounts to saying that the total realization of the being includes not only the 'Supreme', but also the 'Non-Supreme', both the unmanifested and the manifested aspects finally uniting as it were indissolubly as they are united in the Divine. Perhaps the author's insistence on showing a difference with 'the other *Yogas*' risks an incorrect interpretation; there is in fact nothing 'new' here, for the teaching has always been that of the Hindu tradition as well as of the other traditions (the Islamic *taṣawwuf* in particular is very explicit in this regard). If the first point of view seems more in evidence generally than the second in expositions of *Yoga*, there are several reasons, which we will perhaps examine some day. Let it suffice here to point out, first, that the 'ascent' must necessarily precede the 'redescent'; and then that the being that has truly realized the 'Supreme Identity' can therefore, and for that very reason, 'move at will' in all the worlds (this excludes, of course, that in the 'redescent' he must once again find himself enclosed in individual limitations). It is therefore a mere question of 'modality' and not of a real difference as to the goal, which would be strictly inconceivable; but it is worthwhile to stress it, since too many people tend to see innovations where there is only a perfectly correct expression or a legitimate adaptation of traditional doctrines and to attribute to individuals a role and an importance which they could never have. Another point to note concerns the method of realization (*sādhana*) recommended by Srī Aurobindo. It proceeds, he says, 'by aspiration, by concentration on the inward or on the higher, by an opening to the Divine influence.' This is indeed the essential in every case, and one can only ask if, in seeming to neglect means which, whatever their 'accidental' character may be, nonetheless constitute far from negligible aid, the difficulties of this realization would not be augmented, at least in the generality of cases, for there are very few (especially in the conditions of our age) to whom the most direct path is immediately accessible. One must not conclude that this path may not be suitable for some, but only that beside it the other *mārgas* retain their purpose for those for whose nature and aptitudes they are most suited. Besides, exclusivity regarding method has never been in the spirit of any tradition, and certainly no *Yogi* will contest that the path he has followed and in which he guides his disciples is really only one path among many others, which as we said elsewhere in no way affects either the unity of the goal nor that of the doctrine. We cannot dwell on details such as those relating to the distinctions between different elements of the being, but we must express regret that the terminology adopted here is not always as clear as one might wish; doubtless there is no objection in principle against such words as *Overmind* and *Supermind* for example, but since they are not in current use they demand an explanation. A simple reference to the corresponding Sanskrit terms might have sufficed to remedy this defect.

Lumières sur le Yoga (Frameries, Belgium: Union des Imprimeries, 1938 [Paris: Adrien-Maisonneuve, 1945]). This is the French translation, just out, of the first of the two volumes we spoke about above. This translation, approved by the author, is on the whole very precise, and we have reservations only on one point: the word *mind* has most often been translated by *esprit*, and also sometimes by *intellect*, when in reality it is neither but is instead the *mental* (*manas*). Since this was considered important enough to warrant a note here and there, would it not have been simpler and more satisfying to put the correct and exact term in the text itself?

Bases of Yoga (Arya Publishing House, Calcutta, 1938 [Pondicherry: Sri Aurobindo Ashram, 1981]). This work, composed in the same way as the preceding one, further clarifies various points, particularly the difficulties that can arise during the work of realization and the means of overcoming them. The author insists particularly on the need for mental composure (not to be confused with 'passivity') in achieving concentration and no longer letting oneself be troubled by superficial fluctuations in consciousness. The importance of these fluctuations must not be exaggerated however, for 'spiritual progress' does not depend as much on outward conditions as on how we react inwardly.

What is no less necessary is 'faith' (of course, this is something alto-gether different from a mere 'belief', contrary to what Westerners too often think), which implies firm and unvarying adherence of the whole being; whence the insufficiency of mere theories which require nothing more than mental adherence. Among the many other questions dealt with let us also note the regulation of desires and the way of life to fol-low in order to obtain control of oneself; and let us say that in this regard we do not find there any of the exaggerations that rule in certain pseudo-initiatic Western schools, but on the contrary a warning against the error of taking mere means for the end. The last part of the book examines the different degrees of consciousness, including the essential distinction between the 'superconsious' and the 'subconscious' that the psychologists are unaware of, and offers insights on sleep and dreams and their different modes, and on illness and the resistance that can be inwardly opposed to it. In the last section there are passages that have so close a connection with what we ourselves have written on the subject of 'psychology' that it seems worthwhile to cite them at some length:

> Freud's psychoanalysis is the last thing one should associate with *Yoga*; it takes a certain part, the most obscure, the most dangerous, and the most unhealthy part of nature—the lower vital sub-conscious—then isolates a few of its most morbid phenomena and attributes to them an action out of all proportion with their true role in nature. . . . I find it difficult to take these psychoanalysts seriously when they try to examine spiritual experience under the flickering light of their torches; however, perhaps it is necessary to do so, for half-knowledge can be a great obstacle to the manifesta-tion of truth. This new psychology reminds me of children learn-ing a basic and incomplete alphabet, confusing with an air of triumph their 'a b c' of the subconscious with the mysterious superconscious, and imagining that their first book of obscure rudiments is the very heart of real knowledge. They look from below above and explain the higher lights by the lower darkness; but the foundation of things is above and not below, in the super-conscious and not the subconscious. . . . One must know the whole before one can know the part, and the higher before one can understand the lower. The promise of a greater psychology awaits its hour, before which all this meager experimentation will disap-pear and be reduced to nothing.

This could not be more clear, and we would really like to know what the partisans of false assimilations, whom we have denounced on various occasions, think of this...

Les Bases du Yoga, preceded by a study by Nolini Kanta Gupta on the *Yoga* of Shrī Aurobindo (Frameries, Belgium: Union des Imprimeries, 1940 [Pondicherry: Sri Aurobindo Ashram, 1946]). We have already reviewed the English edition of this book; therefore we would only have to mention the publication of this French translation if there had not been preceded an introduction that it must be said calls for certain reservations. First, when Srī Aurobindo says 'our *Yoga*', that can mean in a legitimate sense the *Yoga* he practises and teaches; but when others speak of the '*Yoga* of Srī Aurobindo', they sometimes seem to attribute ownership to him or claim for him a kind of 'copyright' of a particular form of *Yoga*, which is inadmissible, for we are in a domain where individualities do not count. We wish to believe moreover that Srī Aurobindo himself had no part in this, and that he sees in it only the manifestation on the part of some of his disciples of a somewhat indiscreet and rather inappropriate zeal. What is perhaps fundamentally more serious is that the introduction is influenced strongly by 'evolutionist' ideas; we will cite only two or three characteristic phrases in this regard:

> Up to the present, death has been the principal director of life on earth; it will be replaced by the consciousness of immortality. Evolution has been effected by struggles and sufferings; henceforth it will be a spontaneous flowering, harmonious and happy.... Man is already one or two million years old; it is plainly time for him to be transformed into a being of a higher order.

How can such affirmations be reconciled with the least understanding of the traditional doctrine of cycles, and more particularly with the fact that we are presently in the darkest period of the *Kali-Yuga*?

La Synthèse des Yogas, vol. 1, *Le Yoga des Œuvres divines*. (Frameries, Belgium: Union des Imprimeries, 1939). This work, which appeared in English in the review *Arya* from 1914 to 1921, comprises four parts: (1) *Le Yoga des Œuvres divines*; (2) *Le Yoga de la Connaissance*; (3) *Le Yoga de la Dévotion*; (4) *Le Yoga de la Perfection*. The present volume contains only the translation of the first six chapters, reviewed and augmented by the author. As the title and the sub-titles show, it concerns a view of the whole in which the different forms of *Yoga* are reunited or combined in order to converge toward the perfection (*siddhi*) of the 'Integral Yoga' of which they are really only so many branches. The first part is devoted to *Karma-Yoga*. The author quite naturally insists principally on detachment from the fruits of works, according to the doctrine taught in the *Bhagavad-Gītā*. He presents this detachment especially as a 'gift of self' and as 'sacrifice', this last word being perhaps a little ambiguous, since its proper meaning essentially implies a ritual element that does not appear very clearly here, despite the allusion made to the 'sacrifice of *Purusha*', envisaged as the 'common divine action that was projected into this world at its commencement, as a symbol of the solidarity of the universe.' Furthermore, everything belonging to the properly 'technical' side of the question is left rather in the dark. It may be that this is intentional, but it nonetheless gives a certain impression of 'vagueness' that risks disconcerting the ordinary reader, that is, one who does not have the necessary facts to supply what is lacking. On the other hand, one must also be careful not to be led astray by the terminology adopted, for some words are taken in a sense far removed from what they had originally. What comes to mind is the expression 'to be psychic' which the author almost seems to take as synonymous with *jivātmā*. Such a use of the word 'psychic' is not only unusual but again is clearly contrary to its original meaning, and we cannot at all see how it could be justified. But of course none of this lessens the interest of the matters expounded in this book, even if they do not give a complete view of the subject, which would doubtless be impossible. But what we have said shows that it must not be read without precaution.

L'Isha Upanishad (Frameries, Belgium: Union des Imprimeries, 1940 [Paris: Adrien-Maisonneuve, 1939]). This volume contains the Sanskrit text and a translation of the *Isha Upanishad*, followed by a commentary. It had appeared in part in the French edition of the journal *Arya*, which had only a few issues in 1914–1915; the previously unfinished translation of the original English was completed by Jean Herbert. At the start of his commentary the author remarks that

the *Upanishads* are meant to illuminate rather than to instruct, and are composed for seekers who are already familiar, at least by and large, with the ideas of the Vedic and Vedāntic seers, and even for those who already possess some personal experience of the realities to which they refer. Their authors therefore refrain from expressing thought transitions and from developing implicit or secondary ideas. . . . Only the conclusions are expressed, and the reasoning on which they rest remains implicit—the words suggest it, but do not communicate it openly to the spirit.

This is perfectly correct, and we think moreover that in this way of preceding there is something inherent in the very nature of the traditional teaching in question. Srī Aurobindo thinks, however, that 'such a method is no longer applicable to modern thought'; but does this thought justify making concessions when insofar as it is specifically modern it shows itself all too obviously incapable of receiving and understanding any traditional teaching? One can assuredly try to make the ideas more explicit, which is at root the whole reason commentary exists; but it is clearly dangerous to wish to 'systematize' them, since one of the essential characteristics of ideas of the metaphysical order is precisely that they do not lend themselves to any 'systematization'. And what is more, should one suppose an 'implied reasoning' in a text expressing truths whose real source is purely intuitive? These observations bear above all on the 'arrangement' of the commentary in question; its division into different 'movements of thought' (an expression which is moreover very far from clear) might appear rather artificial, at least to one not habituated exclusively to the particular forms of 'modern thought'. Having made these reservations, however, the various paragraphs of the commentary, taken in themselves and independently of the overly 'rational' setting in which they are inserted, contain nonetheless a great number of very interesting points that one cannot read and meditate on without benefit as long as one already possesses some knowledge of Hindu doctrine.

L'Enigme de ce Monde (Paris: Adrien Maisonneuve, 1949). This pamphlet is the translation of an article written in English in 1933 in response to a rather 'sentimental' question raised by Maurice Magre regarding the reasons for suffering and evil in this world. He quite rightly answers that all possibilities must be fulfilled, and that it is division and separation that give birth to evil insofar as these possibilities are considered in isolation from each other and from their principle. In sum, what we consider as evil, that is to say as a negation, is such only in consequence of our ignorance and our limited horizon. What is more contestable is that Srī Aurobindo seems to admit not only a spiritual evolution for each being but also evolution in the sense of a 'progression' of the world in its totality. This is an idea which appears very modern to us, and we also do not see how it can agree with the very conditions of the development of all manifestation. On the other hand, if we sufficiently understand what is not expressed very explicitly, he appears to think that 'ascending realization' is insufficient in itself and that it requires completion by 'descending realization'; at least, some of his expressions allow this interpretation of his thought. But why then oppose liberation as he understands it to what he calls an 'escape from the world'? As long as the being remains in the Cosmos (and by that we mean not only this world but the totality of manifestation), however elevated the states he can reach, they are always only conditioned states which have no common measure with true liberation. Liberation can only be attained by leaving the Cosmos, and it is only thereafter that the being can 'redescend', in appearance at least, without any longer being affected by the conditions of the manifested world. In other words, 'descending realization', very far from being opposed to 'ascending realization', on the contrary necessarily presupposes it; it would have been useful to clarify this so as to leave no room for equivocation, but we want to believe that this is what Srī Aurobindo means when he speaks of 'an ascension from which one no longer falls back, but whence one can take flight in a winged descent of light, strength, and *Ānanda*.'

Swami Vivekananda

Jñāna-Yoga, tr. from the English by Jean Herbert (Frameries, Belgium: Union des Imprimeries, 1938 [Paris: Adrien-Maisonneuve, 1936]). Most of our readers doubtless already know what we think of Vivekānanda and of his desire to 'adapt' Hindu doctrines, particularly the *Vedānta*, to the Western mentality. They will not be surprised, then, that we have many reservations about a book like this present collection of lectures addressed to English and American audiences. This is not to say that it is wholly lacking in interest, but such material can only be read with many precautions and are without danger only for those able to make the necessary 'selection' and to discern correct interpretations from those more or less twisted by regrettable concessions to modern ideas, 'evolutionist', 'rationalist', or other. It is rather disagreeable, for example, that someone claiming to speak in the name of a tradition should cite with approval 'scholarly' theories on the origin of religion, or to rail continually against 'superstitions' and the 'absurd' stories of priests.' Some may admire this as evidence of what is nowadays called a 'broad outlook', but for our part, in the presence of such an attitude, we can only ask: with regard to the traditional truth, is this ignorance or betrayal? Indeed, there is obviously ignorance on some points; thus, Vivekānanda himself confesses that he 'understands very little' of the doctrine of the *deva-yāna* and the *pitri-yāna*, which nevertheless is of some importance; but one has the impression most often that he has been preoccupied above all with presenting things in a way that will please his 'public'. Moreover, for that very reason he has brought upon himself a curious posthumous punishment, if one may say so; in the letter which opens the book, Romain Rolland declares that the 'intuition of the Indian prophet [*sic*] rejoins without knowing it the virile reasoning of the great interpreters of communism.' Romain Rolland obviously sees things through his own 'spectacles', and one would be wrong to take what he says quite literally; but all the same it is rather sad, when one has desired the role of 'spiritual Master', to furnish a pretext for such a comparison! Be that as it may, in examining the book's contents, one sees that the title is somewhat deceptive; it is true that it is not Vivekānanda who is responsible for this, but rather the English editors who have compiled his lectures. These lectures skirt the subject, so to speak, rather than effectively addressing it; there is much talk of 'philosophy' and 'reason', but true knowledge (*Jñāna*) is certainly not at all philosophical and *Jñāna-Yoga* is not rational speculation but suprarational realization. On the other hand, it is almost incredible that while invoking his own tradition a Hindu could present it as constituted by 'philosophical' opinions which have passed through 'successive phases' beginning with 'rudimentary' ideas to arrive at more and more 'elevated' conceptions; might one not as well be listening to an orientalist? And, without even speaking of the formal contradiction between these 'progressive' views and cyclic doctrine, what is to be made of the 'nonhuman' character of the tradition? To take truths of different orders for 'opinions' that have replaced each other is a very grave error, and this not the only one; there are also ideas which, without being entirely wrong, are far too 'simplistic' and inadequate, such as comparing

'Deliverance' (*Moksha*) to a state of 'liberty' in the ordinary philosophical sense, which does not go very far; these are things which in reality have no common measure... The idea of a 'practical *Vedānta*' is also highly contestable. Traditional doctrine is not applicable to profane life as such; on the contrary, in order to 'practice' it there must be no profane life; and this implies many conditions not in question here, beginning with the observance of the rites that Vivekānanda affects to treat as 'superstitions'. What is more, the *Vedānta* is not something that was ever meant to be 'preached', nor was it formed to be 'put within the reach of all'; often one has the impression that this is what the author is proposing... Let us add that in general even the better parts remain rather vague, and the prejudice for excluding almost all technical terms is certainly largely responsible for this, although the intellectual limitations of the author are no stranger to this problem either. These are things which one cannot really say are incorrect but which are expressed in such a way that nothing appears of their profound meaning. Let us point out again that there are terminological errors which, because we cannot compare the French translation to the English original, we do not really know to which of the two they are to be imputed; thus *manas* is not 'spirit', *ahankāra* is not 'egoism', and *Ātmā* is not the 'self', even were it written with a capital; but we have said enough to show how far such a work is from being acceptable as an exposition of pure *Vedānta*, and beside this essential consideration all the rest amounts to only secondary details.

Karma Yoga, tr. from the English by Jean Herbert (Frameries, Belgium: Union des Imprimeries, 1937 [Paris: Adrien-Maisonneuve, 1943]). This book is on the whole better that the preceding one, no doubt because it touches less often on properly doctrinal and intellectual questions. It is, if you like, a commentary on the *Bhagavad-Gītā* which really considers only one very partial aspect of it, but it is on the whole acceptable within its limits. The idea of *svadharma*, 'detachment' toward the results of action, is expressed reasonably well, but action must not be taken only in the too restricted sense of 'work', and in spite of everything the author's 'moralizing' and 'humanitarian' tendencies are sometimes a little too apparent not to cause a certain embarrassment when one knows how foreign they are to the true spirit of Hindu doctrine.

Bhakti-Yoga, tr. from the English by Lizelle Reymond and Jean Herbert (Frameries, Belgium: Union des Imprimeries, 1937). There are some rather heterogeneous things in this collection, for the considerations on *Avatāras*, on the necessity of a *guru*, and on *mantras* and the *pratīkas* (not '*prātikas*', as is incorrectly written), do not have a direct and special link with the path of *bhakti* but in reality have a much wider scope, moreover, they are reduced here to very summary and rather superficial glimpses. As to the very idea of *bhakti*, ideas like 'love' and 'renunciation' perhaps do not suffice to define it, especially if, as here, they are not linked to its first meaning, which is that of 'participation'. On the other hand, it is perhaps not very accurate to speak of the 'simplicity' of *Bhakti-Yoga* when one recognizes that it is clearly distinct from inferior forms of *bhakti*; these may be intended for the 'simple', but one cannot say as much of any *Yoga*; and as for 'aspiration' toward some 'ideal', this is no longer even an inferior *bhakti* but pure childishness for the use of moderns who are no longer effectively attached to any tradition. We must also note as an error of detail the quite incorrect translation of *para* and *apara* by 'superior' and 'inferior', for they can only be rendered by 'supreme' and 'non-supreme', which indicate a totally different relationship; and considering what these terms apply to, it is not difficult to understand that this is far more than a mere question of words.

Raja-Yoga ou la Conquête de la Nature intérieure, tr. from the English by Jean Herbert (Frameries, Belgium: Union des Imprimeries, 1937 [Paris: Adrien-Maisonneuve, 1937]). In this volume which unlike the preceding ones has been written in this form by the author himself, we find some of the confusions current on this subject in the West, but which it is astonishing to meet in an Easterner; we mean the false assimilations to 'mysticism' and 'psychology'; in reality, 'mysticism' can be linked to *bhakti*, as long as one is clear that it is only a question of certain 'exoteric' forms of *bhakti* without any connection to *Yoga*; as for psychology, it could never be a path leading to 'Union', and indeed, it leads absolutely nowhere... In addition, the exposition is marred in many places by an unfortunate mania for seeking comparisons and parallels with modern science; this sometimes results in rather curious errors, like those of identifying *chakras* and *nādīs* with bodily organs. It is also strange that a Hindu should see in *Hatha-Yoga* only a kind of physiological 'training'; now *Hatha-Yoga* is a preparation for some of the forms of true *Yoga*, or it is nothing at all. The second part of the book contains a rather free rendering of Patanjali's *Sūtras* accompanied by a commentary, which of course represents no more than Vivekānanda's interpretation. This generally corresponds only to a very outward sense, striving at all costs to bring everything back to the 'rational' level. Does Vivekānanda really believe this possible, or does he only fear to offend Western prejudices by going further? It would be difficult to say, but it is in any case quite certain that he had a strong tendency toward 'popularization' and 'proselytism', and that if one yields to this tendency the truth will suffer... Moreover, one could here apply the notion of *svadharma* very aptly; Vivekānanda would have been a very remarkable man had he filled a function suited to his Kshatriya nature, but the intellectual and spiritual role of a Brahmin certainly did not suit him.

Conférences sur Bhakti-Yoga, tr. from the English by Lizelle Reymond and Jean Herbert (Frameries, Belgium: Union des Imprimeries, 1939 [Paris: Adrien-Maisonneuve, 1939]). This volume was meant to collect passages scattered throughout Vivekānanda's works and which though also relating to *Bhakti-Yoga* were not included in the book bearing this title whose translation appeared earlier in the same series. What is rather curious is that the sources are not clearly given, so that one does not know whether the passages come from different lectures or only from notes others took during those lectures; but this is only of secondary importance, since in any case the two collections complement one another.

The ideas expressed here naturally call forth the same reservations that we have expressedabout the preceding work. This is not to say, of course, that some interesting points are not found here, for example on the necessity of a *guru* or on the use of symbols, things moreover which do not relate exclusively to the path of *Bhakti*; but all this must be read with caution and by those who are sufficiently forewarned to distinguish what is only a modern 'adaptation' from what truly reflects something of traditional teaching. And one final observation: since this book is meant to complement *Bhakti-Yoga*, why reproduce in its entirety the part entitled *Parā-Bhakti*, which apart from the addition of some notes merely duplicates what is already found under the same title in another volume?

STELLA KRAMRISCH

A Survey of Painting in the Deccan (London: The India Society, 1938 [New Delhi: Munshiram Manoharlal, 1983]). This volume is a history of painting in the Deccan from the era of Ajantā up to our time, a period of more than two thousand years, accompanied by numerous plates showing characteristic examples of the different periods. The most interesting part from our present point of view is her exposition of the principles of the oldest painting, that found at Ajantā. This does not aim at representing space as it is perceived by the eye but space such as it is perceived in the 'mind' of the painter. It cannot therefore be interpreted either in terms of surface or in terms of depth; instead, figures and objects 'come forward' as it were and take their form in this very movement, as if they came forth from an undifferentiated 'beyond' of the corporeal world to reach their state of manifestation. The 'multiple perspective' under which the objects are represented, the simultaneity of the different scenes which is like a 'multiple perspective' in time, and also the absence of shading are equally characteristics of this mental space, by which it is distinguished from sensible space. The considerations on rhythm and its different modalities in this painting, on the character of the *mudrās* which are essentially the movements of the figures, on the symbolic value of colors, and on yet other points that we cannot summarize here, are no less worthy of interest; and the references to traditional texts clearly show the doctrinal and metaphysical basis on which such a conception of art entirely rests.

PAUL BRUNTON

A Search in Secret India (London: Rider and Co., 1935 [New York: Samuel Weiser, 1981]). This account of a journey in India and of meetings with individuals of very varied character is interesting and agreeable to read, although the tone, especially at the beginning, recalls rather too much the author's journalistic profession. Contrary to what is too often found in Western works of this kind, accounts of 'phenomena' do not take up excessive space. The author assures us, moreover, that this subject does not especially interest him, which is doubtless why he was able to establish contact with certain things of another order despite a 'critical spirit' which, carried to such an extent, seems rather incompatible with deep spiritual aspirations. We have here a curious example of specifically Western (more exactly, Anglo-Saxon) reactions in the presence of the East, the difficulty of admitting the existence and the value of a 'non-acting activity' being especially characteristic in this respect. The author's resistance, with the resultant struggles and hesitations, last until the day they are finally conquered by the mysterious personage called the 'Maharishi'. The pages devoted to him are certainly the most remarkable in the book and we cannot dream of summing them up here, but taken in its entirety this work is surely of more value than many more pretentious ones, and it can only contribute to awaking in some readers a sympathy for Eastern spirituality and perhaps among some of them a more profound interest.

A Hermit in the Himalayas (London: Leonard and Co., 1937 [York Beach, ME: Samuel Weiser, 1984]). This new book by Paul Brunton is a journalistic account of a 'retreat' he made in the Himalayas close to the Indo-Tibetan frontier after having failed to gain permission to stay in Tibet itself. One should not expect a unified narrative, for the description of the region and the accounts of different incidents and rare meetings with a few visitors are mixed with reflections on the most varied subjects, but the whole reads quite agreeably. What is probably most curious is the opposition one constantly feels between certain of the author's aspirations and his desire to remain in spite of everything 'a man of the twentieth century' (and we could add also, a Westerner). He resolves this as best he can by constructing for himself an idea of *Yoga* that he himself qualifies as 'heterodox' and by limiting his ambitions in the spiritual order to obtaining a state of calm and inner equilibrium, which is certainly a very appreciable thing in itself, but which is nevertheless far removed from all true metaphysical realization!

L. ADAMS BECK

Du Kashmir au Tibet: A la découverte du Yoga. tr. from the English by Jean Herbert and Pierre Sauvageot. (Paris: Éditions Victor Attinger, 1938). This novel, written in a spirit of obvious sympathy for

Eastern doctrines, may arouse some interest in these doctrines among those who do not yet know them, and may perhaps subsequently lead them to a more serious study. But this is not to say that the way in which things are presented is always exempt from defects, thus Hindu and Buddhist doctrines are sometimes mingled in a very unlikely way which risks confusing readers about their relationship. On the other hand it is quite laudable that, contrary to what usually happens in works of this kind, there is only very restricted place for more or less extraordinary 'phenomena', and their value is reduced even there to its just proportions; where they occur, one can consider them 'signs', but nothing more. From another angle, the goal of *Yoga* itself is perhaps not explained with enough precision to avoid all misunderstanding among those who are not already informed of it. The author should have shown more clearly that competence in an art, for example, can only be a quite secondary result, and also in certain cases a kind of 'support', on the condition that the spiritual orientation be invariably maintained. However, if one takes it as an end, or even if one simply seeks it for itself, it becomes on the contrary an obstacle and it will have from this point of view more or less the same disadvantages as 'powers' that are apparently more strange, for in the final analysis all of this always belongs to the same contingent order.

D. S. SARMA

Lectures and Essays on the Bhagavad-Gītā, with an English translation of the Gītā (London: Luzac and Co., 1938 [Madras, 1939]). The Bhagavad-Gītā has already been translated into Western languages many times and has also been commented on from very different points of view, which unfortunately do not always strictly conform to the traditional spirit. The present translation, although more or less exempt from 'tendentious' misrepresentations (a frequent occurrence in translations of orientalists and Theosophists), lacks perhaps all the precision one might wish. This failing seems due above all to a concern to avoid as far as possible the use of 'technical' terminology, something not without problems in such a case, for everyday language is necessarily vague and limited in its means of expression. There is moreover a bias here toward 'simplification', which nearly always allows so to speak only the outermost meaning, one which does not presuppose a knowledge of the many traditional data of different orders implied in the text. The six lectures preceding the translation further confirm this impression; addressing students who are more or less affected by the modern spirit, the author tries to render the teachings of the *Bhagavad-Gītā* 'acceptable', which can scarcely be done short of diminishing them by many regrettable concessions. Does he not go so far as to try, despite the doctrine of cycles which seems to cause him some embarrassment, to reconcile these teachings with the idea of 'progress'? Above all, there is an ambiguity he has not been able to avoid; it is perfectly correct that what is stated in the *Bhagavad-Gītā* can be applied to all actions comprised by human existence, but this is on the condition of envisaging this existence in a traditional way, which confers on all things an authentically 'sacred' character, and not under the profane aspect of 'ordinary life' in the modern sense. These two ideas are mutually exclusive, and one cannot embrace the first without entirely rejecting the second and considering it as the clearly illegitimate deviation that it really is. Nothing could be further from the truth than to present the *shāstras*, or traditional treatises on the sciences and the arts, as relating to 'secular knowledge', or to reduce the system of castes to an attempt by mere 'thinkers' to solve what are known today as 'social problems'. We wonder if the author's incomprehension really reaches this point, or whether he only means to make ancient Hindu 'culture' (!) agreeable to his too modern audience! This is not to say that in the course of his exposition he may not present 'orthodox' views more worthy of interest; but it remains true that the general intention of an 'adaptation' like this can only lead to a great misunderstanding of the value and import of everything that is most deeply traditional, namely all that is most essential. Not until one commits oneself to this path will it be possible to react effectively against the degeneracy of our time.

JEAN-MARQUES RIVIERE

Le Bouddhisme au Thibet (Paris: Éditions Baudinière, 1936). The first part of this work is an exposition of the fundamental ideas of Buddhism in general, and especially of the *Mahāyāna*; the second deals with the special form assumed by Tibetan Buddhism or Lamaism. The author very justly corrects certain erroneous ideas current in the West, particularly on the subject of 'Tantrism', and also regarding 'reincarnationist' interpretations; nor does he admit the idea that would make the *Mahāyāna* a 'corrupted Buddhism', which implies, he says, a total misunderstanding of the doctrines of the East and of their proper value. His book is therefore certainly better in many respects than the usual 'orientalist' works; and we must point out as among the most interesting the chapters devoted to meditation, to the symbolism of the 'wheel of life', and to the 'science of the void'. However, all is not perfectly clear, and from time to time he relapses into current confusions: Buddhism is not 'religious' in the Western sense of the word, and certainly none of this has anything to do with 'mysticism'; besides, this is why it has an initiation and a method, obviously incompatible with any 'mysticism', of which the author does not really seem to understand either the character or the import. Perhaps this is due in part precisely to that confusion as well as in part to the exaggeration of the importance of 'phenomena' and 'psychic development', which are very secondary things, even if they do not depend solely on 'a very advanced knowledge of human physiology'. However, this lack of perspective does not suffice to explain how one can speak of a 'wholly materialist and mechanical conception' where the very notion of 'matter' is absent, or qualify as 'purely human' what on the contrary essentially implies the intervention of 'supra-human' elements; here is an ignorance of the true nature of 'spiritual influences' which one may well find astonishing! But the truth is that the assertions we have just cited belong to a collection of 'tendentious' reflections which curiously do not seem to be part of the rest of the work, for they are almost invariably added at the end of chapters, and some of them bear witness to 'apologetic' and even 'missionary' preoccupations of a rather low order. In any case, could one not thus legitimately ask whether this ignorance is in a certain measure 'deliberate'? In any case, it is very regrettable that a work which otherwise has real merit should be so distorted by the intrusion of an attitude which we prefer not to qualify otherwise than as one of the forms of Western 'proselytism', although a more severe term would perhaps be more appropriate.

L'Inde secrète et sa magie. (Paris: Les Œuvres Françaises, 1937). This short volume is written in the form of a travelogue, not exclusively descriptive but accompanied by doctrinal notes, and to speak the truth it sometimes seems that the author has felt somewhat obliged to mix in with it recollections from his own readings. What prompts this remark is not so much that in the work as a whole there is something that reminds one of the 'allure' of Paul Brunton's book, which we reviewed when it came out and which in fact was translated into French under the rather too similar title of *L'Inde secrète*; it is especially because here and there among the remarks attributed to different speakers there are formulas and phrases already seen elsewhere. Indeed, there are also improbabilities; thus, a certain story of the 'Rose-Cross of Asia', which brings to mind at least two more than suspect affairs of which we know precisely that the author also had knowledge; an astrological correspondence of the different traditions also noted in the same chapter where there is not a single correct attribution. Nonetheless, beside these things there are others that are excellent, for example reflections how Europeans make it impossible for themselves by their very attitude to penetrate anything at all Oriental, on the real meaning of Hindu rites, on the erroneous opinions current in the West regarding Tantrism, or again on the nature of the only true secret, which lies in the 'incommunicable', something which most certainly has nothing to do with the so-called 'occult secrets' in question above. Nonetheless, when one thinks of the preceding 'fluctuations' of the author, one cannot refrain from a degree of inquietude in the presence of the sympathy he again shows for the East and its doctrines; will this return be durable? To be honest, certain rather tendentious confusions like speaking of 'mysticism' where there is really something altogether different make us think involuntarily of other sympathies as unexpected as they are hardly impartial that have appeared in certain circles in recent years and of which we have had to speak on different occasions. Let us hope nevertheless that this will be of a better quality and that there remain none of the ulterior 'missionary' motives that show through in certain passages from *Le Bouddhisme au Thibet*... However this may be, let us not forget as regards confusions to note a rather unfortunate comparison of Hindu methods of spiritual development with modern psychological methods (yet another false assimilation which definitely seems to be spreading more and more), and also the curious mistake that considers essentially psychic faculties as 'possibilities of the human *body*'; beside the very accurate views that we just pointed out, things like this impose a strangely discordant note; but at least it is fortunate that despite the title, there is not much mention of magic.

Le Yoga Tantrique hindou et thibétain (Paris: Collection "Asie", Librairie Véga, 1939). What is striking at first sight in this little volume is the complete lack of care with which it has been written and printed. It literally teems with mistakes of all kinds, and unfortunately they cannot all be taken for simple typographical errors... As to its content, despite its claims to provide 'direct information', it is really only a compilation, for the most important part is obviously taken from Arthur Avalon's *Serpent Power*, and there are many other borrowings as well; some of these are not acknowledged, but we have good evidence for recognizing them although in order not to appear to be purely and simply 'copying' the author has found it good to substitute for a precise terminology a singular collection of vague or inappropriate words. On the other hand, there is a chapter on 'reincarnation' from which it is absolutely impossible to conclude what the author thinks on this question, which is surely the best way not to displease anyone. Is it also to preoccupations of this kind that one must attribute the curious precautions he takes to point out the fanciful character of certain lucubrations of the late Leadbeater and certain others, or again a note that seems to admit the reality of spirit 'communications'? We will not dwell on the usual 'mystical' confusion, and we will not stop to note certain more or less bizarre assertions, which moreover do not all concern Hindu or Tibetan doctrines, witness the designation of 'puffers' given to the Alchemists, or the considerations on the 'baphometic idols'... We wonder precisely what end the author really has set himself, unless he simply wanted to try to arouse the curiosity of eventual readers of other works whose impending publication he announces.

Rituel de Magie tantrique hindoue: Yantra Chintāmani (Le Joyau des Yantras), translated for the first time into French and preceded by a study of Tantrism (Collection 'Asie', Librairie Véga, Paris, 1940). The author is said to have 'chosen the title of "Tantric magic" for want of a more adequate name, although this text far exceeds the customary idea of the science of magic in the West.' This is no doubt true, but leaving aside the distortions of this word's meaning due only to modern incomprehension, it is indeed magic that is in question here, that is to say a traditional science that is very real although of a lower order. This is then only of a secondary aspect of Tantrism, for as we have explained on another occasion, this is above all initiatic, and is consequently by no means 'magic' in its essence, contrary to the erroneous idea sometimes had of it. It remains to ask exactly what interest may properly be attached to this aspect of magic, and we for our part would prefer to see translators' effort focused instead on texts of a more properly doctrinal character. It is important moreover to observe that such a ritual, with all that it comprises, has a real and efficacious value only for someone who is effectively attached to the Hindu tradition; in these conditions, its complete translation represents hardly anything more than a 'curiosity', and a few examples would have sufficed to realize the nature of the procedures put into use, which is the only really interesting thing in such a case. In our opinion, the introduction is more important than the text itself, for it presents general ideas about Tantrism as well as the *Yantras*; these ideas are inspired in part by the works of Arthur Avalon and in part by what the author himself was able to see and hear during a journey through India. It is to be regretted that one sometimes senses a certain influence from Western 'sociological' theories. As in the previous works of the same author, there many oversights, some of which are rather strange. Thus, *Vishvakarman* becomes *Viskraharman*, which could be a typographical error, and, what is surely not one, *Marishi* is identified with *Maharshî*, whereas it is obviously the name of the 'Mahayanic' goddess *Marichî*! Let us also note that *Chintāmāni*, translated far too vaguely as 'jewel' (which only renders *mani*) is in reality the Hindu equivalent of the 'philosophers' stone'.

C. Kerneïz[3]

Le Hatha-Yoga ou l'art de vivre selon l'Inde mystérieuse (Paris: Éditions Jules Tallandier, 1937 [1945]). This book is more 'sensible' than Western publications claiming to treat the same subject generally are; it contains some very sound reflections on the useless agitation of modern life; the exercises it recommends are those that at least present no serious danger, and on questions such as diet it shows a moderation in happy contrast with certain Anglo-Saxon excesses... But none of this is *Hatha-Yoga*; it is, if one wishes, something inspired by its methods up to a certain point, but only to apply them to entirely different ends. In fact *Hatha-Yoga* is not at all an 'art of living'; it is one of the modes of

---

3. Pseudonym of Felix Guyot. ED.

preparation for true *Yoga*, that is to say metaphysical realization, and if it can produce results of a physiological order, it is no more aimed at these than it is, as others have imagined, at the development of psychic 'powers'; all of these are but 'accidents' in the most exact meaning of the word. That is to say that it can in no way be considered as a sort of 'therapy'; and besides, the best proof of this is that one of the conditions rigorously required of those wishing to embark on its practice is to be in a perfect state of health. Moreover, let us note in this connection a misunderstanding of the very meaning of the word *hatha*: it really means 'force', but in the sense of 'effort' or even of 'violence' as understood in the Gospel passage: 'the Kingdom of Heaven belongs to the violent' [Matt. 11:12]; and it contains many other things as well, for symbolically *ha* is the Sun and *tha* the Moon, with all their correspondences. Here we are certainly very far from physiology, hygiene, and therapy... And it is also a mistake to think that *Hatha-Yoga* as it really is can be addressed to those who are not connected in any way to the Hindu tradition. Here, as in everything not confined to mere theory, there is a regular transmission that plays an essential role. Of course, this question does not arise when one only has in mind, as is the case here, aims that are entirely foreign to traditional knowledge; but once again, it is no longer then a question of *Hatha-Yoga*, and there must be no illusion on this matter. We do not wish to dwell longer on this, but it seemed to us that these few clarifications would not be without use for bringing things into somewhat better focus.

Le Karma Yoga, ou l'action dans la vie selon la sagesse hindoue (Paris: Éditions Jules Tallandier, 1939). This book is certainly more 'harmless' than the same author's *Yoga de l'Occident*, of which spoke earlier; but this is not to say that despite its title it contains much more authentic 'Hindu wisdom'. On the contrary, we find in it all sorts of very Western things: 'reincarnationist' ideas, moral considerations in the most ordinary sense of the word, attempts at reconciliation with modern scientific theories, as well as the inevitable psychoanalysis. To grasp the author's degree of competence regarding Hindu doctrines it suffices to see for example his more than fantastic interpretation of the symbolism of the monosyllable *Om* (which for him is formed out of only two elements), or again the assimilation he claims to establish between *Ānanda* and 'sexuality'! And let us also point out a rather amusing misunderstanding: the Tibetan word *Bardo*, literally 'between two', designates the 'intermediary world', or in other words the psychic domain; but he believes that this word applies to 'the human personality after death', or to the 'discarnate entity', so that he speaks of the 'fate of the *Bardo*,' of 'communication between the *Bardo* and its surroundings,' and so on; but he refers nonetheless to the tradition of the *Bardo Thödol*; how then has he read it? These few examples seem to us quite sufficient, and we will not stress the point further. We feel sorry for those unfortunate readers who, having no other idea of Eastern doctrines, will confidently accept the 'presentation' given to them in works of this kind!

Count Gobineau

Les Religions et les Philosophies dans l'Asie centrale.[4] It was an excellent idea to republish one of the more interesting works of Count Gobineau, a writer who until now has remained too little known in France. He has been much spoken of, certainly, at least for some time, but usually without having been read. It is quite different in Germany, where his racial theories, which may contain some truth but are mixed with much fantasy, are exploited for political ends. The idea of an 'Indo-Germanism' cannot stand examination, for between India and Germany there is absolutely nothing in common, no more intellectually than from any other point of view. However, Count Gobineau's ideas, even when false or highly fanciful, are never indifferent; they can always furnish matter for reflection and that is already a great deal when reading so many other authors leads only to an impression of emptiness.

Here moreover it is not so much a matter of theories as of a description of facts that the author was able to experience at first hand during his sojourns in Persia. The title could lead to an error regarding the work's contents; it does not speak of the quite varied regions commonly joined under the name Central Asia, but speaks solely of Persia; and the 'religions and philosophies' he touches upon are reduced in sum to the more or less particular forms taken by Islam in that country. The principal and central part of the book is composed of the history of the Muslim heresy known as Babism. It is as well to read this history to see

4. Vol. 1 of *Bibliothèque des Lettrés*. This review appeared in 1929.

just how little Babism resembled its so-called successor, that is, the sentimental and humanitarian 'adaptation' made of it for Westerners, particularly Anglo-Saxons, under the name of Bahaism. This part is framed between two others, the first containing general considerations on Islam in Persia while the last is devoted to the theater in Persia; the latter's interest lies above all in that it clearly shows that here, as in ancient Greece and in the European Middle Ages, the origins of the theater are essentially religious. Indeed, we think that this statement could be applied more generally, and doubtless much could be said about it. The creation of a 'profane' theater seems to be a kind of deviation or a degeneration; and is there not something analogous for all the arts?

As for the general considerations in the beginning, they need to be discussed at far greater length than we can think of doing here; we must confine ourselves to noting some of the most important points. Among the most questionable views is explaining the particularities of Islam in Persia as a sort of survival of Mazdaism; for our part, we do not see any clear trace of such an influence, which remains purely hypothetical and even rather unlikely. These particularities are sufficiently explained by the ethnic and mental differences existing between the Persians and the Arabs, just as those observed in North Africa are explained by the characteristics proper to the Berber races. Islam, much more 'universalist' than is commonly believed, bears in itself the possibility of such adaptations, without any need to call upon foreign infiltrations. Besides, the division of Muslims into Sunnites and Shiites is very far from having the rigor attributed to it by the simplistic conceptions current in the West; Shiism has so many degrees and is so far from being exclusively proper to Persia that it could be said that in a certain sense all Muslims are more or less Shiites; but this would lead us to overly long explanatinos. As for Sufism, that is, Muslim esoterism, it exists as much among the Arabs as among the Persians, and in spite of all the assertions of European 'critics' it is linked to the very origins of Islam: it is said, in fact, that the Prophet taught the 'secret science' to Abu Bakr and to Ali, and it is from them that the different schools originate. In a general way, the Arab schools refer especially to Abu-Bakr, and the Persian to Ali, the principal difference being that in the latter esoterism assumes a more 'mystical' form, in the sense that this word has acquired in the West, whereas in the first it remains more purely intellectual and metaphysical. Here again, the tendencies of each of the races suffice to explain such a difference, which moreover is much more in the form than in the fundamentals of the teaching, at least insofar as this remains true to traditional orthodoxy.

Now, one may wonder how far Count Gobineau succeeded in penetrating the Eastern spirit; he was certainly what one may call a good observer, but we do not think we are unjust to him in saying that he always remained an observer 'from the outside'. Thus, he noted that Easterners pass easily from one doctrinal form to another, adopting this one or that one according to circumstances; but he saw this only as the effect of an aptitude for 'dissimulation'. That in certain cases prudence effectively imposes a sort of dissimulation, or what may pass for such, is undeniable, and one could find plenty of examples of this kind outside the East; the language of Dante and other writers of the Middle Ages would furnish an abundance of them; but in facts of this kind there is also an altogether different reason, one of a much more profound order, which seems to completely escape modern Westerners. The truth is that this detachment from outward forms always implies, at least to some degree, an awareness of the essential unity hidden under the diversity of these forms. This is something very different from hypocrisy, which in these conditions can no longer exist, even where the superficial observer sees its appearance, since to pass from one form to another has then scarcely any more importance than changing clothing according to season or place, or speaking different languages according to one's interlocutors. This was something Count Gobineau certainly did not understand, nor should we blame him for it; but a book which raises such questions, even if the author is unaware of them, cannot be an indifferent one, and this is the justification of what we said at the beginning, that one can always find in it something to reflect on, and this is, in the final analysis, the greater profit it can and must furnish us.

SARVEPALLI RADHAKRISHNAN

L'Hindouisme et la Vie, tr. Fr Paul Masson-Oursel [Paris: F. Alcan, 1929]. The East that is presented to Westerners often has only a very distant connection with the true East, even when the representation is made by people who are Easterners by birth but who are more or less completely Westernized. Such is the case with this little book; the 'critical' opinions of learned Europeans as well as the sympathies of Anglo-Saxon Protestantism with its 'moralism' and 'religious experience' surely hold a much greater place than does orthodox Hinduism in the ideas of the author, who scarcely seems to know what the traditional spirit is; and this will not surprise anyone familiar with the 'reformist' movement (Servants of India) in which he is involved. What is especially unfortunate is the fact that a work like this is signed with a Hindu name strongly risks leading an uninformed public into error and can contribute to all sorts of false ideas. The best part, or rather the least bad, is that which, toward the end, deals with the institution of castes; yet the profound reasons for this are far from emerging clearly. The translation is at times very defective; thus on p34 one does not say in French the *tenanciers* but the *tenants* of an opinion; on p40 the English word 'immaterial' should not be translated by *immatérielles* but by *sans importance*; on p47, one does not 'join' an argument, one 'refutes' it, and the words *intransigence* and *privation* are used quite unintelligibly; on p93, *occupationnelles* is a pure barbarism, etc.

François Arouet

La fin d'une parade philosophique: le Bergsonisme [Paris: J.-J. Pauvert, 1968; no publisher given by Guénon in this 1929 review]. Unsound as the Bergsonian philosophy may be, we do not think that it can be dealt with by questionable jokes or by opposing it with ideas that are even emptier and more nebulous than itself. The author of this brochure, who thought himself clever in taking the name Voltaire as pseudonym, seems to have such confused ideas that we have been unable to understand what he means by 'concrete' and 'abstract', even though these words flow constantly from his pen. At root, the real reasons for his hatred (the word is not too strong) toward Bergson are more political than intellectual, as one realizes by the end of his diatribe, for when all is said and done what he reproaches him for is being a 'bourgeois philosopher' and having played during the war the role of 'a puppet whose strings were pulled by the General Staff.' All this is of very little interest.

G. Dandoy, S. J.

L'Ontologie du Vedānta [*essai sur l'acosmisme de l'Advaita*], tr. from the English by Louis-Marcel Gauthier (Paris: Desclée de Brouwer et Cie, 1932 [see also *Vedānta Studies* (Calcutta: Light of the East series, 1950/59]). We had heard that Father Dandoy, who directs the revue *Light of the East* in Calcutta, studied Hindu doctrines sympathetically and without the usual orientalist prejudices; thus we expected to find in his book a truly comprehensive exposition of one aspect of the *Vedānta*, but we must say we were somewhat disappointed. It is not that alongside certain errors and confusions there are not some interesting views, although expressed at times in questionable terminology, but on the whole the author's point of view is distorted by the desire for controversy. The very fact of limiting himself to ontology (and it would still be necessary not to force into it things that in reality go beyond this domain) can only be explained by a determination to establish a comparison with scholasticism, which goes no further than this; and in this connection we must make a remark: if we wrote, as the translator recalls in his preface, that scholastic language is 'the least inadequate of all those the West puts at our disposal' to translate certain Eastern ideas, we in no way wished to imply thereby that it is perfectly adequate; and in any case it does not apply beyond a certain point where the correspondences that can be legitimately established stop. Father Dandoy discusses things as if it were simply a case of philosophy and theology, and although he quite explicitly admits his hesitation to 'refute' the *Vedānta*, it is understood that he will conclude in favor of scholasticism. However, as he cannot pass over the existence of 'realization' in silence, he himself writes that 'since it is a direct and independent intuition, it is not affected by limitations which are essentially philosophical and does not have to resolve difficulties of a philosophical order'; this one sentence should suffice to cut short all discussion and show its inanity. Curiously, in the commentaries placed at the end of his book, Maritain recognizes for his part that 'the deepest meaning of the *Vedānta* is not philosophical, rational, or speculative'; nothing is more true, but does not this reduce the author's entire thesis to nothing? Maritain himself attributes to the *Vedānta* a value that is essentially 'pragmatic', a word that is at least unfortunate when it concerns the purely spiritual order, which has nothing to do with action, and a 'religious and mystical' meaning, a confusion which is scarcely less serious than that of making it into a philosophy. It is always the same inability to go beyond Western points of view... But there is still something else. Maritain states that 'it would be a dupery [*sic*] to take, as proposed to us by some of the most zealous Western interpreters of Hinduism, Vedāntic thought for the pure type of metaphysics par excellence.' We do not believe that any 'Western interpreter' has ever said that; on the other hand, we ourselves have said something of this kind, although giving to the word 'metaphysics' a wholly different meaning than Maritain, who sees in it only 'pure speculation' and, at root, mere philosophy. We have explained many times that true metaphysics is essentially 'supra-rational', and that in the original sense, the only one we take into account here, 'metaphysics' is in sum synonymous with 'supernatural'; but 'supernatural' does not necessarily mean 'mystical', with all due deference to Maritain. If we insist on this, it is because we see only too clearly the profit some think of gaining from the publication of a book like this; Father Dandoy himself seems to be thinking of substituting in India scholasticism for *Vedānta*, for he writes that 'one only suppresses what one replaces,' which is a rather blunt confession; but among others there is perhaps a more subtle intention: could one not 'accommodate' the *Vedānta* in such a way that Thomism could absorb it just as it absorbed Aristotelianism? But the case is entirely different, for Aristotelianism is after all only a philosophy while the *Vedānta* is something else entirely; besides, Eastern doctrines in general are such that they defy all attempts at annexation or assimilation; but this does not mean that some may not try it, and the sudden interest they show for these doctrines is not of a nature to inspire unlimited confidence. Moreover, here is something that justifies these suspicions only too well: in its edition of last April 1st, the *R. I. S. S.* published a eulogy of Father Dandoy's book, claiming expressly to oppose it to our own works. It added that the book 'can be consulted with confidence' because 'it is the work of a Catholic,' which is a peculiar guarantee of competence concerning Hindu doctrines (would one accord preference to a Brahmin in explaining Catholic doctrine?), 'the whole being written with an impartiality to which the Hindu *pundits* themselves have paid homage.' And indeed they were careful to include in the preface the testimonial of a *pundit*; unfortunately, this commendation (whose real significance is moreover very much reduced for anyone acquainted with the customs of oriental politeness) refers, not to Father Dandoy's book, but to a work by his colleague Father Johannes published in the review *Light of the East*! Do we not have in all of this good reasons to maintain a reserve tinged with some mistrust? And let no one be surprised that we dwell more on these things than on what Father Dandoy wrote, who personally has undoubtedly nothing to do with it; the book has no great importance in itself; it has above all that which its 'promoters' wish to give it.

HENRI VALENTINO

Le voyage d'un pèlerin chinois dans l'Inde des Bouddhas [precedé d'un exposé des doctrines de l'Inde antique sur la vie et la mort] (Paris: Éditions G. P. Maisonneuve, 1932). This is the account of the celebrated voyage of Hiuen-tsang in the seventh century of the Christian era, an account that is organized according to the translation of Stanilas Julien, which is not a guarantee of perfect accuracy, and which, moreover, seems to have been clothed in a bit of 'literature'; however that may be, it reads well enough. Unfortunately, the work is 'preceded by an account of the doctrines of ancient India on life and death,' that is, in reality, by a sort of resumé of everything it has pleased orientalists to recount about it. One must see such interpretations 'in brief', so to speak, in order to fully appreciate their incredible fantasy; even when one is accustomed to it one cannot but feel a certain astonishment at the accumulation of 'isms' invented by Westerners for their own use and applied at random to things to which they in no way belong, or again at the innumerable confusions produced by using the single word 'soul' to designate without further distinction the most disparate elements of the human being. Besides, all question of detail aside, to appreciate the spirit in which this account has been written it suffices to say that the very idea of tradition is totally absent, that heterodoxy is put on the same footing as orthodoxy, the whole being treated as a collection of purely human 'speculations' formed during this or that age, which have 'evolved', and so forth. Between such a way of looking at things and one in conformity to the truth no compromise is possible, and perhaps this book's greatest utility is to make this so clear.

R. KRISHNASWAMI AIYAR

Thoughts from the Gītā (Madras: The Madras Law Journal Press, Mylapore, 1939 [Madras: Ganesh & Co., 1961]). In our time innumerable commentaries on the *Bhagavad-Gītā* have been written, most of which are far from conforming to the traditional spirit. This is certainly no cause for astonishment as concerns the works of orientalists, but what is odd and also most regrettable in a certain sense is that many contemporary Indian commentaries are also affected, either by a more or less accentuated 'modernism' or by political or social preoccupations which have led their authors to restrict or deform the meaning of the text in various ways. This book was written to counter these tendencies; in particular, against those who regard the *Bhagavad-Gītā* exclusively as a sort of treatise on *Karma-Yoga*, the author is at pains to show that it teaches on the contrary very clearly that the three paths of *Karma*, *Bhakti*, and *Jñāna* do not lead in reality to the same point, that their respective predominance corresponds rather to as many successive degrees, and that it is by *Jñāna* alone that complete and final realization can be attained. There is obviously no 'exclusivism' here in favor of one or another path but on the contrary rather the affirmation that each one of them has its own purpose and is even necessary, on the condition of situating it in the place where it truly belongs. This progression is very correctly observed throughout the exposition, which is presented in a language that is very clear and as simple as possible—we might even say a little too simple sometimes, for one must not be too afraid to use 'technical' terms when ordinary language does not furnish the equivalent, and the inclusion of a greater number of Sanskrit words would certainly have contributed to increased accuracy. Naturally we cannot give a summary of all the questions treated in the book; we will content ourselves with noting more particularly the correlation between the different ideas of the Divinity as so many more and more profound 'points of view' with the different stages of spiritual development, for we think it would be difficult to find a more easily comprehensible and more satisfying account than that presented here.

Thoughts from the Eternal Law (Madras: The Madras Law Journal Press, Mylapore, 1939 [*The Eternal Law: A Brief Outline of the Basic Principles of the Sanātana Dharma* (Madras: Ganesh & Co., 1965)—this seems to be the text referred to; the author was later known as Swami Jñānānanda Bharati]). In this book, conceived in the same spirit as the preceding, the subject is essentially, as the title indicates, the *Sanātana Dharma*; and the author, distinguishing what relates to the different constitutive elements of the human being, devotes himself to showing the true reasons for the different kinds of prescriptions that correspond to them. He very justly denounces the profound ignorance shown by those who misunderstand or reject these prescriptions, or some of them, solely because they are incapable of really understanding them and because they presumptuously believe that everything that they do not understand is worthless or even nonexistent. If some of those who now claim to govern India were not ignorant of almost everything in the Hindu tradition, they would not attack as they do institutions such as that of the castes, and they would know that 'untouchability' also has its justification, which pertains to the very nature of beings and that it is not in anyone's power to suppress it. The justification of properly ritual prescriptions, that of using the *pratīkas* or images representing divine aspects among other things (and these are also indeed among those that the so-called 'reformers' most willingly attack), is likewise excellent. There are other points about which one might have some reservations, in that they are interpreted with a 'literalism' that is a bit too outward to the detriment of the symbolic meaning which is at once deeper and more true, but this defect is only perceptible in certain passages which are not among the most important. As to the affirmation of the 'universal' character of the Hindu tradition, which will perhaps astonish some, it only needs to be clarified by some greater precision. For us this character is to be explained by the fact that the Hindu tradition proceeds directly from the primordial tradition and thereby it in a way represents; and it is the primordial tradition that truly constitutes the *Sanātana Dharma* in its very essence, all the rest amounting in sum only to a necessary adaptation to circumstances of time and place.

RAÏHANA TYABJI

L'Âme d'une Gopī, trsl. and pref. by Lizelle Reymond (Frameries, Belgium: Union des Imprimeries, 1935 [*The Heart of a Gopi* (New Delhi: East-West Publications Fund, 1977)]). This is the well-known story of Krishna and the *Gopīs* told in the form of a short novel. The title might lead one to fear that it is interpreted rather too 'psychologically', but it is not, and in fact the true meaning comes out quite clearly. The *Gopīs* represent individual beings who by the path of *Bhakti* come to have to one degree or another the perception of the Divine. Each believes that the aspect that they know is the only true one and that those who see other aspects are in error; but they must finally come to recognize, like Rādhā, the Divine under all its disguises, that is to say under the innumerable appearances of the manifested world. It is interesting to note that the author is an Indian Muslim, which does not prevent her from showing a real understanding of the Hindu tradition; and cannot one see precisely in this an application of what we just said about recognizing the one Truth under the multiple forms in which it clothes itself in the different traditions?

SRI KRISHNA PREM

The Yoga of the Bhagavat Gītā (London: John M. Watkins, 1939 [Shaftesbury: Element, 1988]). The author of this new commentary on the *Bhagavad-Gītā* is of English origin, which we must admit hardly shows except in a few places expressing certain very Western prejudices against 'priests' and 'dogmas' and also a tendency to diminish the importance and the value of rites. From the same point of view one can also regret references to Theosophical works and to 'metapsychic' experiments; on the other hand, it goes without saying that we find the comparisons with Plotinus and the Hermetic books perfectly legitimate, for here it is truly a matter of teachings which although pertaining to other traditional forms, nonetheless authentically conform to the same spirit. On the other hand, the author firmly refuses to take into account all the discussions of the orientalists, whose method he quite rightly denounces as incurably outward, which cannot lead to any true comprehension. Having started with the idea of explaining the meaning of the titles of the *Bhagavad-Gītā's* different chapters, he has largely gone beyond this framework to comment on the whole *Bhagavad-Gītā*; his point of view is that it constitutes a veritable manual of *Yoga*, taking this word in its 'total' meaning, that is to say as designating not just one or another of the particular 'paths' which also bear this name, but 'the

Path through which man unites his finite self with the Infinite' and of which these different *Yogas* are only so many aspects; and it is 'less a synthesis of these separated teachings than the original and undivided whole of which they represent partial formulations.' This point of view seems to us entirely correct, and the book, full of other interesting insights we cannot summarize here, is certainly one of those, unfortunately all too rare, that will not be read without real profit.

VASUBANDHU

Wei Shih Er Lun: or, the Treatise in twenty stanzas on Representation-only, translated from the Chinese version of Hsüan Tsang, Tripitaka master of the T'ang Dynasty, by Clarence H. Hamilton, (New Haven, CT: American Oriental Society, 1938). This treatise is the first of two fundamental classical texts of the *Vijnaptimātra* school (this designation being rendered here as *Representation-only*), one of the branches of the *Yogāchāra* Mahāyānic school. The two texts are the *Vimshatikā* and the *Trimshikā* of Vasubandhu, of which Sylvain Lévi made an almost entirely unintelligible so-called translation into French some years ago. Wishing to render each word of the text by a single word even when there were no corresponding French terms, he continuously employs neologisms such as 'inscience', 'mentation', 'thusness', and 'essenceness', which are true barbarisms, and still more unlikely expressions such as 'notation de tréfonds', 'imprégnation de concoction', 'révolution du récipient', 'mise-au-point de barrage', and so on, to which it is impossible to attach any meaning whatsoever.[5] This is certainly an example to show that we have never exaggerated in speaking of the insufficiencies of certain works of 'orientalists' and their perfect futility. The author of the present English translation seems too indulgent toward his predecessor in merely saying that he was unable to follow his 'specialized vocabulary,' and in attributing these oddities to a 'concern to preserve linguistic nuances.' The truth is that under the pretext of

5. Not having access to the translations employed in the English version of this text, these four expressions might be rendered as something like 'notation of the depths', 'concoctive impregnation', 'revolution of the recipient', and 'establishment of the barrier'. ED.

'exactly rendering the meaning' Sylvain Lévi has given absolutely none. Hamilton very happily has not fallen into the same error; doubtless this is not to say that his translation cannot be questioned on certain points, for this is certainly a very difficult text because of the very ideas expressed, and one must not rely too much on the capacities of Western philosophical terminology in this regard. But in any case it can at least be understood and presents on the whole a very plausible interpretattion. The translation, with the Chinese text of Hiuen-tsang on facing pages, is accompanied by notes offering numerous clarifications and is preceded by an introduction giving a history of the Chinese versions of the treatise and an analysis of its contents. Although this is perhaps somewhat influenced by the idea that it contains something comparable to Western 'idealism', the author does recognize that 'the idealist doctrine of Vasubandhu is finally in the service of a supra-intellectual realization'—we would rather say more exactly 'supra-rational'. But is this not precisely the essential point, that which profoundly distinguishes this doctrine from modern philosophical speculations and gives to it its real character and its true import?

A. M. HOCART

Les Castes, translated from the English by E. J. Lévy and J. Auboyer (Paris: Paul Geuthner, 1938 [*Caste: A Comparative Study* (New York: Russell & Russell, 1968)]). This work differs considerably from what is usually written in the West on the same subject, no doubt because the author (who unfortunately died before its publication) was not a professional orientalist, but had during the course of an administrative career in Ceylon and Polynesia the opportunity to observe directly what served as the basis of his work. This is what gives him the right to criticize with just severity the theories imagined by modern 'scholars' who 'were so intoxicated by their critical sense that they came to think they knew more about the ancients than the ancients themselves,' and who from prejudice rejected all the traditional explanations contained in the ancient texts for the sole reason that they were traditional, whereas an impartial examination of the facts confirms on the contrary the value of these explanations and shows the inanity of those meant to oppose them. One of the best examples of modern fantastic theories is that the distinction of castes had its origin in racial differences, on the pretence the word for caste is *varna*, which literally means color. The author has no trouble showing that the colors attributed to the different castes cannot represent those of so many races, that they are really purely symbolic, and that they are moreover like as taught in the traditional texts related to a division, found among the most diverse peoples, into four quarters corresponding to the cardinal points. This last point is so important that we propose to return to it in a special article. It is regrettable that the author did not think that *jāti*, another name for caste meaning 'birth', could also have a symbolic value; at root, this word designates above all the individual nature, for it is the virtuality proper to each individual that determines the conditions of his birth; and even if taken in the sense of 'lineage' it remains that this lineage can be understood above all in a spiritual sense, as shown by certain 'genealogies' which are manifestly nothing other than traditional 'chains'. Be that as it may, what emerges clearly from all this is that 'the system of castes is a sacrificial organization'—we would rather say 'ritual', which has a wider meaning, for there are obviously many kinds of rites other than sacrifices; and if the castes and their subdivisions seem to be identified in a certain measure with the professions, it is precisely because they are essentially ritual functions, for 'professions and rites cannot be precisely distinguished from each other', and the Sanskrit word *karma*, 'action', 'work', applies to them both; and let us add that in a strictly traditional society every occupation, whatever it may be, necessarily has a ritual character. However, this is no reason to qualify all these functions indifferently as 'sacerdotal', which implies an unfortunate ambiguity; and we will say as much in the case (for there is a certain vacillation in his ideas) where this same 'sacerdotal' designation is applied only to the first two castes. Each member of society necessarily has certain rites to perform, but what properly characterizes the sacerdotal function as such and distinguishes it from all the others is above all the teaching of doctrine. Even more serious is that the author constantly refers to the Kshatriyas as the first caste and to the Brahmins as the second, an inversion contrary to all tradition and which moreover renders certain things incomprehensible, as we will perhaps explain on another occasion. His idea is evidently to place royalty at the summit of the hierarchy and therefore above the priesthood (understood this time in its proper sense), but this is precisely what is untenable from the traditional point of view, and where such a thing does exist it only indicates a state of degeneration. Such is probably the case with certain Polynesian societies the author has studied, and even in Ceylon it is quite possible that the Buddhist influence has introduced certain alterations of the same kind, although the extinction of the upper castes there makes the thing more difficult to verify directly. On the other hand, the author does not seem to understand the profound purpose of rites, that which is their very principle, and more generally the 'non-human' element inherent in any traditional institution. If a society is ritually established, this is not for more or less 'psychological' reasons but because it really is by that very fact an image of realities of a higher order. Thus there are gaps here that can be filled only with the aid of a deeper knowledge of traditional doctrines; but it is no less true that this book contains much interesting information that we cannot of course summarize or enumerate in detail, many of which could serve as the starting-point for considerations going very much further than the author himself may have suspected. One can also point out certain inaccuracies of terminology, as for example the designation of the Vaishyas as 'cultivators', which is too narrow to apply to the whole caste, the erroneous use of the word 'initiation' to designate admission into a caste, or the confusion of the 'Titans', corresponding to the *Asuras*, with the 'Giants', which are something very different; but we will not dwell on these defects, which have on the whole only a quite secondary importance. And if it is permissible to think that the remarks about the exercise of certain occupations in modern Egypt have only a very questionable connection with the question of castes, there are many more valuable points of comparison to show that this institution, far from being unique to India as is too often believed, is on the contrary really something quite general that is found in one form or another at the basis of all traditional societies, and, we can say, because it rigorously conforms to the very nature of things and to the cosmic order in its entirety.

RABINDRANATH TAGORE

Sādhanā, translation and preface by Jean Herbert (Frameries, Belgium: Union des Imprimeries, 1945 [most recent English edition, *Sādhanā: The Realisation of Life* (Tucson, AZ: Omen Press, 1972)]). The first chapter of this book is the best in our opinion; the author very rightly protests against the artificial opposition the West claims to establish between man and nature, an opposition which implies a negation of the fundamental unity of all that exists; in India, on the contrary,

> the state where one has realized his kinship with the whole and has penetrated into all things by union with God [which, as he says elsewhere, has nothing to do with the 'pure abstraction' of the modern philosophers] was considered as the ultimate goal and accomplishment of humanity.

What follows is unfortunately less satisfying. It is understandable that a poet should be reluctant to renounce the world of forms, and we even willingly admit that in order to follow his proper path he must, more than any other man, take forms as a support; but this is only one path among many, and indeed, to be even more exact, it is only the starting-point of one possible path. If one goes no further one will never go beyond the level of 'cosmic consciousness', which represents only a transitory stage far from the supreme goal, and where it can even be dangerous to remain too long. We greatly fear that the author sees nothing beyond this, and the way in which he translates certain terms in the citations that he makes from the *Upanishads* bears the mark of this restricted point of view. Is it tenable for example that *Ānanda* means 'joy'? In any case, the title of the book is rather deceiving, for there is no question of 'realization' in the metaphysical sense, or of the 'technique' which can effectively lead there. Tagore may be a great poet, but he certainly cannot be considered a 'spiritual Master'.

F. J. ALEXANDER

Le Royaume Intérieur, tr. Marcel Sauton, preface by Swāmī Siddheswarānanda (Frameries, Belgium: Union des Imprimeries, 1946 [Paris: A. Maisonneuve, 1948, translation of *In the Hours of Meditation* (Mayavati, Almora: Advaita Ashrama, latest ed., 1951)]). The author of this book was an American with an enthusiasm for the works of Vivekānanda who after reading them made his way to India in order to meet other disciples of Srī Ramakrishna; but it is obviously the posthumous influence of Vivekānanda that predominates in him. The style of the book is rather disagreeable, with its continuous and perfectly useless repetition of words, its exclamations for any reason and for no reason. We will not dwell on the extreme vagueness of the terminology and the impropriety of many words, for not having read the original we cannot know exactly what part the translation plays in this, although our impression is that it aggravates these defects even further. As to its substance, as one might well expect it is very 'mixed'; alongside certain formulas borrowed from the Hindu tradition there are many others that are specifically Western; there are even passages that speak of 'purity' in a way which reminds one a bit too closely of certain 'obsessions' of Protestant moralism; there is also much talk of the 'ideal' and of 'character formation', which hardly takes us away from ordinary modern banalities; and on the whole it would certainly be difficult to take away anything that is even a bit distinct. It is moreover generally 'inoffensive' enough, although there is somewhere the advice to 'cultivate passivity', which is terribly dangerous; but what always astonishes us in writings of this kind is the lack of 'substance', so to speak, and the complete absence of useful details. On the other hand, from beginning to end the author makes the *Guru* speak in such a way that one wonders what idea he has of one, and in his preface Swāmi Siddheswarānanda indeed seems to have felt that there is a rather regrettable ambiguity here, but which he does not succeed in dispelling. It is certainly not a question of a real human *Guru*, nor can what is described pass for a stage advanced enough for the true 'inner *Guru*' to appear. It is therefore likely that this 'voice' represents only so to speak the 'idealized' memory of Vivekānanda, or even a 'fiction' meant to express the thoughts which came to the author during his meditations.

ROBERT BLEICHSTEINER

L'Eglise jaune, tr. Jacques Marty (Paris: Payot, 1937). First of all, the title of this book calls for some remarks: on the one hand we think it would have been better to avoid using the word 'Church' in such a context because of the specifically Christian meaning that is attached to it and that can hardly be separated from it. On the other hand, the term 'yellow Church' cannot in any case be applied except to the branch of Lamaism (the author, in contrast to Pallis, willingly uses this last term) that follows the reform of Tsongk-khapa in order to distinguish it from what could then be called the 'red Church', which has remained as it was before the period of this reform. But the work really deals with both, that is to say with Tibetan Buddhism in general as well as the Mongol Buddhism directly derived from it; it is perhaps even the only comprehensive work on this subject, or at least the only one readily accessible, and it is this above all that makes it of interest. We mean 'documentary' interest, for as to the 'spirit' in which it is written, there are assuredly many reservations to make. It contains first of all a fairly complete historical account, but unfortunately even this account is affected by a sort of skepticism toward anything that seems unable to be explained in conformity with modern Western ideas, and one has too much of a sense of the tendency to 'rationalize'. One point that remains rather obscure concerns the *Bon* religion which preceded the introduction of Buddhism and of which very little is known; as for what is said of an allegedly still more ancient 'popular belief', it is scarcely possible to understand what this is; perhaps he means to speak of a kind of 'Shamanism', which would moreover have to be anterior to its present degeneration and which in any case could not be 'popular' except for the sole fact of its partial survivals consisting as it were of a kind of 'folklore', after it had been replaced by other traditional forms. In this regard, let us point out (although it is found in another part of the book) a remark that is rather interesting, or at least one that could be if one knew how to draw all its consequences. The points of contact between Lamaism and Shamanism

> are not explained by the influences that Buddhism underwent in Mongolia and in Tibet from the theories prevailing there; it is exclusively a question of traits already attested to in Indian Tantrism and which in this country went forth to join with the ideas of Lamaism.

But instead of seeing in this indications of a common traditional source, which might moreover go back quite far, the author is content to declare that 'the explanation of these remarkable meetings must be left to later research. . . .'

After the historical section there follows a series of studies on monasteries and temples, the different categories of 'gods' in Lamaism, the hierarchy of the monks (among whom those following the 'direct path' are inappropriately qualified as 'mystics'), the 'magical arts' (under which are indistinctly ranged many things which certainly do not all pertain to magic in the true sense of the word), rites and festivals (whose symbolic dances hold an important place, and here the author raises with good reason the error all too frequently committed by those who have described them and who have taken 'terrible' divinities for diabolical entities), then cosmology (whose symbolic side is hardly understood), the sciences (notably astrology and medicine), and finally the arts and literature. Let us say again that all this is interesting as documentation, but only on the condition of disregarding the author's judgments, for he loses no occasion to inveigh against what he calls 'Tantric horrors' and to treat as 'absurd and lamentable superstitions' all that escapes his understanding!

We do not know exactly in what measure certain errors of expression must be attributed to the translation; this is probably the case in phrases whose meaning is very unclear, of which there are unfortunately a rather large number; but it seems difficult not to impute to the author himself the use of some rather extraordinary terms, as for example 'thundering stone' to render *dorje*, or again 'reincarnations' to designate *tulkus*, whom most Europeans very improperly call 'living Buddhas' and who are really nothing else than the human supports of certain spiritual influences. On the other hand, it is regrettable that the translator felt obliged to adopt for the Tibetan words a bizarre transcription that seems to be the German transcription somewhat modified and which sometimes makes it rather difficult to recognize for those used to seeing them under another form. The absence of any indications for long vowels in the Sanskrit terms is also rather annoying, and these are imperfections that could nonetheless have easily been avoided, for this at least obviously requires no great effort of comprehension.

Swami Pavitrananda

Common Sense about Yoga (Almora, Himalayas: Advaita Ashrama, 1948 [Calcutta: Advaita Ashrama, 1978]). The title of this short volume seems rather unfortunate, for we do not understand how one could think of reducing *Yoga* to the limits of the narrow and purely profane point of view that characterizes what is customarily called 'common sense'. The book as a whole moreover does not appreciably modify the impression that we had had on reading a translation of the first chapter, entitled *The 'Mysteries' of Yoga*, published in a special issue of *Cahiers du Sud* on India (see the December, 1945 issue). This is not to say, of course, that everything in it is bad. We can only approve the author when he denounces certain false ideas and suspect phantasmagoria, and the all too numerous charlatanical enterprises which in our day cover themselves with the usurped name of *Yoga* and which owe their success only to the complete ignorance of the immense majority of Westerners concerning the things of India (and we could just as well say of the East in general); but even if all of this is far from being useless, it is still only 'negative', as it were. The ensuing chapters successively consider *Bhakti-Yoga*, *Karma-Yoga*, *Jñāna-Yoga*, and *Raja-Yoga*; we think we can give a sufficient idea of how these subjects are treated by saying that it conforms entirely with the ideas of Vivekānanda, under whose patronage moreover the book is placed. The author expressly declares that his intention has been to 'explain the science of *Yoga* as simply and rationally as possible,' but the truth is that his views seem rather too 'simplistic', and he seems not to fully understand that there are realities that are supra-rational. What we find most striking in writings of this kind is, as we have already noted, that one finds nothing there of the initiatic character of *Yoga*, a character which is however what constitutes its very essence, although it is obviously incompatible with the modern tendency to 'popularize' everything.

MIRCEA ELIADE

Techniques du Yoga (Paris: Gallimard, 1948 [1975]). In this short volume, which treats in turn of the doctrines, the techniques properly so called, the connection of *Yoga* with Hinduism in general, and finally the particular technique of *Yoga* in Buddhism and in Tantrism, one incontestably finds far more evidence of understanding than in most Western works dedicated to the same subject. One sees this immediately by the care its author has taken in constantly putting in quotes any words which rightly appear to him to be inappropriate or inadequate for what they are to express and which the orientalists on the contrary habitually use without the least hesitation and without realizing to what extent they falsify the explanation of doctrines. But we still would have preferred to see him renounce at least some of these words, for example 'philosophy', 'religion', and 'magic', when they are applied to things for which they could not possibly be suitable. Why did he seem obliged to stop halfway from a kind of fear of departing too far from the commonly accepted terminology? On the other hand, he does not shrink from certain neologisms, which, even if they are not perhaps all equally useful, nevertheless include at least one which seems to us excellent and cannot be commended too highly: this is the word 'enstasy' used to render *samādhi*, which is perfectly correct, whereas 'ecstasy', besides implying an erroneous assimilation with mystical states, constitutes in itself an enormous misinterpretation; indeed, ecstasy is literally a 'going out of oneself' whereas quite to the contrary it is a 'return to oneself' that is really in question here. It is impossible for us to point out all the accurate opinions met with in the course of this account, and if it sometimes raises questions which it does not resolve, perhaps this is a virtue in a case like this, for one must see in this a very laudable concern not to simplify things excessively and not to conceal the real difficulties, as do the all too numerous propagators of '*Yoga* for everyone'. In spite of everything there are also points that call for certain reservations, as for example a manifestly insufficient idea from the traditional point of view of Hindu orthodoxy and of the way it has been able to incorporate doctrines and practices initially foreign to it; this remains much too outward and rather gives the impression of syncretism than of synthesis, which is certainly very far from the truth; and so it will always be as long as one does not clearly and unambiguously affirm what the tradition includes of the essentially 'non-human'. On the other hand, the care taken to distinguish the different varieties of *Yoga*, while certainly justified in itself, perhaps risks making one lose sight of their unity of principle; and when some of those varieties are called 'popular', it is necessary to know exactly how this is to be understood, for this may appear in contradiction with the properly initiatic character which in other respects is recognized in *Yoga*. We also regret some concessions to the ethnologists' theories on the 'cult of vegetation' and other things of the same kind; but on the other hand we do find here and there, particularly in the conclusion, some of the truly remarkable ideas we had already noted recently in an article by the same author (see the July–August 1948 issue). In concluding we will cite some phrases taken from the last pages:

The archetype of 'action' is the Creation of the worlds, cosmogony. In a certain sense, the yogi repeats upon his own being the transformation of chaos into Cosmos; again, an interiorization of the cosmogonic Creation. Before detaching himself from the Cosmos, he identifies himself with it, repeats it and appropriates to himself its rhythms and its harmonies. But this 'repetition' is not a goal in itself; the 'cosmization' which follows upon psychomental chaos is only a step toward the final liberation. The yogi must isolate himself from matter and withdraw from the Cosmos; this retraction is equivalent to the conquest of immortality. . . . . Reality can only belong to immortality; the being only recognizes itself insofar as it is eternal. So that the *yogi* who has succeeded in withdrawing himself from the Cosmos and from the ceaseless and painful cosmic cycle, by the very fact of having abolished his human condition, obtains immortality, which is freedom, autonomy, bliss, and eternity; he has liberated himself from death through the death of his very humanity.

In sum, this book most certainly deserves to be read by anyone seriously interested in these questions, and there are very few of which we can say as much.

P. B. Saint-Hilaire
& G. Monod-Herzen

Le Message de Srī Aurobindo et son Ashram (Adrien-Maisonneuve, Paris, n.d. [*The Message of Srī Aurobindo and his Ashram* (Pondicherry: Srī Aurobindo Ashram, 1947)]). This small volume, very well edited, is divided into two parts, of which the first is a kind of resumé of the principal teachings of Srī Aurobindo. It appears that great pleasure has been found in emphasizing above all their 'adaptation' to the conditions of the moment, an adaptation that definitely seems to us to go too far sometimes in the direction of concessions to the present mentality. The second part is a description of the Pondicherry Ashram and of its different activities; this description and especially the accompanying photographs also give an impression of 'modernity', which it must be said is somewhat disquieting. One sees immediately that Europeans have been there...

GEORGES BARBARIN

Je et Moi, ou le dédoublement spirituel (Paris: Librairie Astra, 1949 [Montreal: Du Roseau, 1991]). Mr Barbarin writes a great deal, perhaps too much, for what he has to say is usually of limited interest, and in this as in all things we for our part would prefer quality over quantity. This new volume, at least in its first chapters, is in the form of a kind of psychological autobiography; he thinks he has discovered in himself two distinct and even opposed elements which he calls 'I' and 'Me', and which he connects respectively with the 'individuality' and the 'personality', inverting the normal meaning of these two words in conformity with Theosophical terminology. His principal originality here is thus to call 'I' (one is not sure why) what others call 'Self'; but in reality he is greatly deluded about the import of these findings, for all of this is certainly far more psychic than spiritual, and in fact there is nothing here that goes beyond the individual human level, so that it really seems to be simply a matter of two parts of the 'Me', and in any case we remain very far from that transcendent principle which is the true 'Self', which moreover could never in the least lend itself to such analysis. The author then generalizes these discoveries by applying them to the human collectivity, then he comes to the 'Man-God'; the pages where he interprets the double nature of Christ in this way are even more contestable than the rest, although he claims to support them with Gospel texts from which he eventually tries to draw a 'Charter of Unity'. This is at root all rather 'simplistic' and can only contribute to maintaining certain confusions in the mind of our contemporaries who are already all too inclined to imagine that they will find 'spirituality' where there is not even a shadow of it. Psychological and sentimental banalities are, alas, much more 'within the reach of everyone' than true spirituality.

HUBERT BENOÎT

Métaphysique et Psychanalyse, essais sur le problème de la réalisation de l'homme (Paris: Éditions Mazarine, 1949). We wish we were able to speak favorably of this work because the author's intention was certainly very commendable in itself, but he has most unfortunately undertaken to apply it to something which by its nature does not in the least lend itself to it; and since he says that it was thanks to our works in particular that he discovered traditional metaphysics, we cannot but feel some anxiety about what some may try to draw from them... It is certainly very good to try to connect a science to principles of the metaphysical order, and this is indeed the only means of giving it or restoring to it the 'legitimacy' which it lacks in its present state; but it is also necessary that the science really be susceptible of being 'legitimized', and not specifically a product of the modern mentality, which in the final analysis are but elements of subversion pure and simple, as in the case of psychoanalysis. One might as well try to give a traditional basis to spiritualism or to any other aberration of the kind! Curiously, although the author does not appear to have a very clear idea of initiation (does he not go so far as to speak of 'initiation by frequenting books'?), has remarked that there is a resemblance between initiatic transmission and psychoanalytic transmission, but he has not noticed in the least that the latter constitutes in this respect a truly satanic 'counterfeit', acting 'in reverse' like certain operations of sorcery. And since he mentions our books, we can only urge him to refer to what we have written on this subject, which is quite clear. We shall hardly stress the contents of the work, which is in sum what it can only be in these circumstances, and we will limit to two or three remarks which we cannot really dispense with, for it is necessary not to let certain confusions gain credibility. In the beginning there is indeed an appeal to certain ideas of metaphysics and especially of traditional cosmology, but subsequently they disappear almost entirely except for some considerations of 'polarity' for which however there was no need to refer to psychoanalysis and its special language; everything finishes by being drowned if one may say so in the mythology of 'complexes', 'inhibitions', 'compensations', 'fixations', and so on. On the other hand, when one meets in the midst of all this some term borrowed from traditional metaphysics, it must not be thought that this is always taken in the sense that it normally ought to have; in fact, even where he speaks of the 'total being', what is so conceived never goes beyond the domain of individual possibilities. The author (and this is also quite astonishing for someone who has read our books) appears not to have the least idea of the multiple states of the being, so that he reduces everything to the proportions of the human individuality alone; and if it is rather difficult to say what exactly the 'realization' he envisages might be, it is in any case certain that in spite of his final allusion to the 'opening of the third eye', it is not an initiatic realization, just as when the 'Self' is conceived as 'pure thought', this is something rather too much like the Cartesian 'spirit' and which assuredly is very far from the unconditioned *Ātmā*; and as to the 'independent Intelligence', also called rather oddly the 'divine Reason', it is at most, to put things in their best light, a mere reflection of *Buddhi* in the individuality. As far as we are concerned, all these observations compel a conclusion: we cannot be too much on guard against the applications anyone else may claim to make of our expositions, without our knowledge and without our approval, and that we do not mean to accept responsibility for these to any degree; like all the other distortions of badly understood traditional doctrines, these are obviously things that cannot be prevented, but at least it is always possible as soon as one has knowledge of them to formally disown them, and, as disagreeable as this can sometimes be, it is an obligation that we shall not shirk.

E. TECHOUEYRES

A la recherche de l'Unité, essais de philosophie scientifique et médicale (Paris: Baillière, 1937). The first 'essay', which gives its title to the volume, carries the rather significant subtitle: *The aspirations of a Hindu soul and the tendencies of contemporary Western science*; this is therefore one of those attempts at reconciliation which we have often said to be illusory. Moreover, here the attempt implies a complete misunderstanding of the nature of the Hindu doctrines; the author sees 'philosophy' only as purely human 'research' and 'thought', which he believes tend toward the same ends as profane science. It must be said that he seems to have been led into error in this regard by what he calls the 'modern and syncretic thought of India', that is, by the writings of certain authors affected by Western ideas that have hardly anything Hindu about them save their origin. There are many confusions in this work, some of which are rather strange, such as taking the 'mind' for the 'spirit', believing that the 'heart' represents feeling for the Hindus as it does for modern Westerners, and, even more serious, seeing in India a 'philosophy of becoming' whose main ideas are very similar to those of William James and Bergson! Of the other 'essays', which are especially devoted to questions of scientific 'methodology', we will say only that they are on the whole very 'Bergsonian' in their inspiration; it is certainly not by mingling everything that unity is achieved; on the contrary, one has to know how to put each thing in its place, and 'antagonisms' are not themselves 'errors' so long as their scope is limited to the domain where they really apply. But how can one understand true unity when one sees nothing beyond 'becoming'?

REGINALD REYNOLDS

The White Sahibs in India, with a preface by Jawaharlal Nehru (London: Martin, Secker & Warburg Ltd., 1937). The long account of mercantile rapacity by British 'imperialism', based sometimes on vice, sometimes on violence, from the establishment of the *East India Company* up to our own day, that is to say for more than three centuries, is truly most edifying, all the more so since it was written for the most part according to the testimony of the English themselves. We cannot enlarge here on a subject well beyond the limit of our studies, but this book is recommended for all who are naive enough to believe in the so-called 'benefits' that modern Western civilization is supposed to bring to the peoples of the East. Tenacious as their illusions may be in this regard, it is still very doubtful that they can resist such an accumulation of precise facts supported by incontestable evidence!

HENRI-LOUIS MIEVILLE

Vers une Philosophie de l'Esprit ou de la Totalité (Lausanne: Éditions des Trois Collines, 1937). We would certainly have ignored the publication of this large book of Protestant philosophy had we not been advised that the author had thought it a good idea to make an excursion into foreign territory in order to attack the Brāhmana tradition... and ourselves; a rather unfortunate incursion, let us say immediately, but one that all the same merits a few words of clarification. What is most striking is that the criticisms he formulates rest almost entirely on false interpretations of the terms we use. Thus, he refuses to admit that one can 'confine rational thought within the individual' because, he says, it 'applies in principle to every thinking being'; but, unfortunately, this 'every thinking being' is precisely, for us, something that belongs to the purely individual domain, and it seems to us that we took enough precautions to explain it without leaving room for any ambiguity. 'Nondualism' for him is the 'doctrine of the non-duality of spirit and matter,' whereas we took great care to explain that it is not that at all, and that the very idea of 'matter' is not met with anywhere in Hindu doctrine. Brāhmanic metaphysics, or indeed metaphysics without further qualification, certainly does not 'consist' in 'propositions affirming the relations between concepts'; it is absolutely independent of all 'verbal imagination' as well as all 'discursive thought'. He evidently confuses it with the pseudo-metaphysics of the philosophers! That he is incapable of conceiving Non-Being beyond Being, or unity without multiplicity, or again 'intellectual intuition totally distinct from reason,' we admit quite willingly, and in any event we can do nothing about it; but let him at least not try to impose his own limitations on us. That it pleases him to give words a different meaning than we do is also acceptable, but what is not at all acceptable is that he also gives them this meaning when he wants to describe what we ourselves have said, to the point that he comes to give the impression simply of someone who cannot read... What is frankly amusing is his final reproach of 'never being where the adversary would like to engage in combat'; does he therefore imagine that traditional doctrine consents to acknowledge 'adversaries' and that it can lower itself to 'combats' or to any kind of discussion? These are strange illusions; in this domain, let it be said clearly, one understands or one does not, and that is all; perhaps it is regrettable for philosophers and other profane people, but it is so. In these conditions it is quite evident that the so-called 'adversary' will never be able to do anything but flounder in the void, and that all his arguments will inevitably miss their mark. We are certainly not displeased to have been given the occasion to point this out once more.

REVIEWS OF ARTICLES: OTHER AUTHORS

ACTION ET PENSÉE

[SEPTEMBER 1937] The review *Action et Pensée* of Geneva begins a section devoted to 'modern Hindu philosophy', under the direction of Jean Herbert. In the measure that this is 'modern', it cannot be truly 'Hindu', and it is mostly the product of a Western influence; but it must also be said that here we meet once again with the confusion we also noted in connection with Herbert's lectures. Srī Ramakrishna, who is particularly in question this time, is certainly in no way a 'philosopher', any more than the methods of spiritual 'realization', which truly are what is most foreign and even contrary to the 'modern' spirit, are a 'practical philosophy'; and what can be said about the foreword by the editors, which tends to assimilate these methods to those of the contemporary psychology to which the review is particularly consecrated, including 'psychoanalysis', and to identify with the 'unconscious' what is really the 'superconscious'? More interesting is the translation from the sayings of Srī Ramakrishna; but what a pity that his centenary had to serve as a pretext for the humanitarian declamations of Romain Rolland! On the other hand, a short note from Masson-Oursel (who, let us note in passing, appears to feel a curious repugnance to using the word 'Hindu') especially shows that he does not understand how certain things can be paths of 'realization', notably the exercise of the arts and crafts, which he is furthermore surprised to see are regarded as truly one and the same. It is to be hoped that he is aware of the article by A KC about which we have spoken, and which might clarify this subject a bit, about which moreover—even without having to leave the Western world—the most illiterate Compagnon surely knows more than he!

[SEPTEMBER 1938] This issue inaugurates the publication, under the title 'Ce que la Gītā peut nous donner' ['What the Gītā can give us'], of a translation of the first chapter of *Essays on the Gītā* by Srī Aurobindo. Here he clarifies the point of view at which he means to place himself in that work in order to study the *Bhagavad-Gītā*, leaving aside what has only a so to speak 'local and temporary' value, that is to say what represents only an adaptation of the traditional doctrine to certain particular conditions of time and place, in order to retain only what, since it entirely independent of these contingent circumstances, remains everywhere and always applicable; no doubt we shall have occasion to return to this when publication is completed. We wonder why, in the 'introduction' preceding this translation, the *Bhagavad-Gītā* is called 'the most important text of Hindu philosophy'; first, it is certainly not 'philosophy' that is in question, and then, without in any way contesting or diminishing the great importance it really has, we must point out that a text belonging to *Smriti* is in every case less important than the *Shruti* on which this *Smriti* is based and to which it is consequently always subordinate.

[DECEMBER 1939] This issue ends the publication of the chapter of Srī Aurobindo entitled 'Ce que la Gītā peut nous donner'. The author points out that even where it refers to things which 'seem at first sight purely local and temporary,' there is nonetheless always 'a deeper truth and principle implied in the structure of thought, even if they are not expressly stated by the words,' which is the very idea of the *Sanātana Dharma*, of which all the traditional institutions are only more or less particular adaptations. He also emphasizes the essentially 'synthetic' character of the *Bhagavad-Gītā's* teaching, where 'the *Sānkhya* and *Yoga* are only two convergent parts of the same Vedāntic truth, or rather two concurrent paths leading to its realization,' and where all the conceptions of the Divine find their place and are integrated in the total truth. 'The *Gītā*,' he says, 'is not made to serve as a weapon in a dialectic dispute; it is a door open onto the whole world of truth and spiritual experience; the view that it allows embraces all the provinces of this supreme region; it draws the map but does not cut it into fragments and neither builds walls nor hedges in order to limit our vision.'

[JUNE 1940] Let us draw attention to a resumé of talks on *Meditation* given by Swāmi Siddheswarānanda; it is regrettable that the idea of 'qualification' remains rather vague and without any 'technical' precision, and especially that the author seems to accept the 'evolutionist' and even 'transformist' theories of the moderns. It is furthermore quite true that 'method is only accessory' and that 'the essential is Liberation'; but for the method to be really valid and not 'arbitrary', and for it to truly lead to the goal, it still must conform to the data of traditional doctrine, of which it is in the final analysis only an application to the development of the possibilities of the human being.

[DECEMBER 1940] Swāmi Siddheswarānanda speaks here of Srī Aurobindo in connection with the recent publication of French translations of several of his books, which we have recently reviewed. From the way things are presented he seems to have a certain tendency to try to strip *Yoga* of its properly Hindu character, which is rather dangerous, for most Westerners are only too easily tempted to conclude from this that spiritual development can be undertaken and pursued outside of any traditional attachment, and this error is already too widespread to be encouraged. Besides, in wanting to appear 'accommodating' to an extreme, he sometimes goes beyond the goal he had proposed; thus, when he says, doubtless to appear benevolent, that 'Europe possesses the organization and the hierarchy,' is there not the risk that this will appear as a rather bitter irony to all those (and there remain a few among Europeans) who understand how things really are at present?

LE LOTUS BLEU

[APRIL 1938]   This issue includes a lecture by Jean Herbert entitled 'Notes sur la philosophie contemporaine de l'Inde' ['Notes on the contemporary Indian philosophy']. The author states justifiable reservations on the use of words such as 'philosophy' and 'thinkers', where the East and particularly India are concerned; but as soon as it is recognized that these terms can only give rise to ambiguities, why should one feel obliged to use them at all? On the other hand, if it is certainly very important to make a distinction between Hindus who adhere exclusively to their tradition and those who have been more or less influenced by Western 'culture', it is no less so also to distinguish among the latter those in whom this influence has hardly affected anything except the form and the means of expression, and those in whom it has on the contrary affected the very foundation of their mentality and their most

essential ideas. It seems to us that between Srī Aurobindo and Vivekānanda, to take as example the very names cited in this lecture, there is
a very great difference to make!

[JANUARY–FEBRUARY 1940] This issue contains an article by G.-E.
Monod-Herzen entitled 'Tendances modernes du Yoga', and this title is
rather significant. For our part, we would say instead that some have
wanted to associate *Yoga* with modern tendencies that are obviously
alien to it, and the example of Vivekānanda shows this only too well. As
for Srī Aurobindo, we do not really think he can be considered a 'modernist' in spite of certain ambiguities in his language and the regrettable
indiscretions of some of his disciples'. What is well to note on the other
hand is the declaration that the Theosophists have 'an attitude opposed
to that which *Yoga* requires'; here at least is a truth that seems to us
incontestable! Another article, signed by J. Charpentier, is devoted to
the *Mānava-Dharma-Shāstra*, and here one first finds a rather strange
essay explaining certain points, notably the institution of castes, in
terms of Theosophist theories about 'planes of evolution'. But there is
next something even more curious: it would seem that there presently
exists 'a current of propaganda in the European West favoring the Laws
of *Manu*'! This is very unlikely, and we wonder if this is not once again
some new 'counterfeit'; but if it is true, we would be fully in agreement
with the author in judging it to be an impossible undertaking; only it
would be for reasons diametrically opposed to his own. The Laws of
Manu are no longer applicable, not because they belong to 'a past which
has lost its educative value for us'(?), but because we live in the confusion of the final times of the *Kali-Yuga*. The author, who all too obviously is ignorant of cyclical laws, admires the 'progress' by virtue of
which 'laws are no longer of divine origin' and 'science is no longer a
revelation.' We say on the contrary, in conformity with all the traditional doctrines, that this is precisely the clearest mark of a profane
degeneration such that it is hardly possible to fall any lower!

ATLANTIS

[SEPTEMBER 1948] Beginning 'A la recherche d'une doc-
trine' ['In Search of a Doctrine'], Paul le Cour (he has decided to sign

himself 'normally' this time), starts with a would-be exposé of Brāhmanism which, as could be expected on his part, is really only an odious caricature; besides the usual fantasies about the 'aryan race' or the
'arganne', and on *Aor-Agni*, there are almost as many errors as there are
words, and there are even some that do not relate to Brāhmanism, witness the truly monstrous assertion that 'the Sufis are the upholders of
Mazdaism'! The principal aim of this nice piece of work seems to be not
only once more to denigrate India, but more particularly to persuade
readers that it has borrowed everything from the West, especially from
Greece and... from Nestorian Christianity (evidently this is not quite
an anachronism). All this certainly does not warrant stopping to treat it
in detail, and it would be no more than laughable were it not rather sad
to see so much malignant incomprehension on display. As concerns
ourselves, we are concerned, we must point out that in spite of all our
corrections, he persists obstinately in attributing to us, perhaps for the
twentieth time, a phrase, always the same, that we have never written.
In these conditions is it still possible to admit that he does this with
wholly good faith? Furthermore, we must again explicitly declare to
him that we have never meant to make ourselves the 'propagator' of
anything, and also that we have never had any 'disciple'. In a derisory
review of a book by our colleague F. Schuon (he has again amused himself as is his habit by counting the words of certain phrases) he let slip a
statement that is worth noting: he writes that 'intellectual intuition is
the spirit of invention, the technique, the instinct of insects, of beavers'
[how 'intellectual' this is!], which amounts to saying that in spite of all
our precise explanations he confuses it purely and simply with Bergsonian intuition, or that he confuses the supra-rational with the infra-
rational; does this not suffice to measure rather exactly the understanding he is capable of? Here is someone truly well qualified to denounce
so-called 'errors' in others... which are only so for those who like him
are wholly ignorant of the true meaning of traditional doctrines!

Following 'A la recherche d'une doctrine', Paul le Cour began what he
was pleased to call an 'objective study' by a pitiful diatribe against Brāhmanism which we spoke of above, and he has continued by occupying
himself with Buddhism. We were unaware of the issue devoted to Buddhism in general, but only of the following (January 1949) issue, which
deals more particularly with Lamaism. Naturally one finds there most
of the opinions found almost everywhere in the West: declamations

against 'gross and superstitious practices' directed especially at Tantrism; a confusion which takes *mantras* for 'magical formulas'; the attribution of a 'mystical' character to what is really something altogether different, even going so far as to speak of a 'mystical initiation' that moreover must be distinguished from a 'mystical intuition' that has the aim simply of 'acquiring powers'! Let us leave this fine mess, and state only that in his conclusion the author triumphantly declares that Lamaism 'only goes back to the seventh century,' as if anyone had claimed the contrary; it is true that this allows one to suppose without too much improbability that it was 'influenced by Christianity,' which perhaps explains his satisfaction. Apart from that, we scarcely find anything worthy of notice other than the amusing reproach that Buddhism is 'not concerned with the demiurge'! As for ourselves, Paul Le Cour still treats us as a 'propagandist for Hinduism'; we must therefore point out to him again that we have never been a 'propagandist' of anything, and that given all we have written as explicitly as possible against propaganda in all its forms, this assertion is a very characteristic calumny.

P.S. It has been pointed out to us that there is a passage concerning us in *Histoire de la Littérature Française* recently published by Henri Clouard. We were greatly astonished at this, for from any point of view our work certainly has nothing in common with literature. But it was true nonetheless, and the passage bears witness to a rather remarkable incomprehension! Since it is not very long we will reproduce it here in full so that our readers can judge for themselves:

René Guénon, the erudite author of *Introduction to the Study of the Hindu Doctrines* (1921), and who believes he has found in the East of Tagore and even of Gandhi the sole refuge possible for a pure and disinterested intellectuality (*East and West*, 1924), has constructed in *The Multiple States of the Being* a metaphysics of ascension to God by a series of purifications which are equivalent to a protracted mystical experience. The reader has the right to ask whether the God of Guénon is anything other than a subjective state of serenity; he agrees in any case in seeing Science and Progress treated as dangerous idols; he allows himself to teach a philosophy of detachment. But he recalls with skepticism and melancholy those first years between the two wars, when one heard defeated Germany prophesy the decline of the West, when the translation of the English book of Fernard [*sic*] Ossendowski, *Beasts, Men and Gods* (1924), was all the rage, and when Europe seemed to abandon itself to the pernicious appeal of the ancestral countries of Asia, so true to themselves, so mysterious, and whence Genghis Khan can always arise again.

First, we have never paid attention to anything except the traditional East, which is surely very far from the 'East of Tagore and even of Gandhi'; this is the last thing in the world to interest us, and none of our works makes the least reference to it. Next, we do not very well see what is meant by 'a metaphysics of the ascension to God,' or how what is metaphysical could be equivalent to a 'mystical experience'; besides, we have not 'constructed' anything since we have always limited ourselves to expressing the traditional doctrines to our best of our ability. As for a God who is a 'subjective state', this seems to us entirely bereft of meaning. After having explained so often that everything 'subjective' or 'abstract' has absolutely no value for us, how can such an absurdity be attributed to us? We do not know where the comparison at the end is meant to go, but what we do know is that it is based on nothing; this is all hardly serious... Finally, we wonder who has decided the choice of the three books mentioned in preference to all the others, unless perhaps these are all Clouard has had the occasion to read; in any case, connoisseurs of 'literature' who rely on him will be truly well informed!

CHRISTIAN SOCIAL ART QUARTERLY

[DECEMBER 1937]   The *Christian Social Art Quarterly*, journal of the *Catholic College Art Association* (Saint-Mary-of-the-Woods, Indiana), publishes in its first issue (December 1937) a lecture by Graham Carey entitled *What is Catholic Art?* Carey denounces 'laicism' and 'individualism', which dominate the modern world in all domains as essentially anti-Christian (and they are indeed so necessarily, we would add, by the very fact that they are in a quite general way anti-traditional). He examines the false ideas about art to which they have given birth and opposes to these the Christian idea of art, which is at root the application to the special case of Catholic art of the 'normal' or traditional idea which he and AKC have already explained in various other studies which we reviewed when they appeared.

[JANUARY 1937]   In the same journal, Félix Guyot (the author, under the pseudonym of C. Kerneïz, of a book on *Hatha Yoga* of which we spoke at the time), has published an article on 'Hindu Yoga and its Psychological Basis', which contains many more than debatable statements, beginning with the one that 'Western idioms are capable of expressing all the concepts of the human mind,' and that 'there is no Sanskrit term that cannot find its equivalent there'; nothing could be less exact, and it must be believed that the author is not very familiar with Eastern 'concepts'. As for the claim that yoga is 'linked only in appearance and artificially' to the Hindu tradition as a whole (and even for the Kabbalah in regard to the Hebrew tradition), this is to give proof of a remarkable ignorance of the constitution of traditional forms, which is not moreover a matter of 'religious beliefs'. If things of this order, which furthermore are in no way mere 'productions of the human mind', are 'independent of any confessional basis,' this is solely for the good reason that the very idea of reducing the link to the tradition (be this even in the exoteric domain) to the pitiful mediocrity of a 'confession' (even indeed of a 'denomination', as the Protestants say) could only take birth in the modern West! It is no more true that *Yoga* is a 'system of thought', which basically does not seem to us to differ much from a 'philosophy', nor that it has as its starting-point a 'postulate' that could be expressed as a 'succinct resumé of Kantism' (!), a comparison that is not very flattering for *Yoga*... As for the rest, here we find especially, as the very title of the article indicates, the 'psychological' interpretation whose erroneous character we have recently explained with sufficient elaboration that it is senseless to dwell upon it again; let us only say that even if one can in a certain sense speak of the 'movement of the luminous beam of the psychological consciousness,' there is in this very movement a point from which this consciousness ceases precisely to be psychological, and that it is beyond this point and not on this side of it that all that truly matters is situated.

MISCELLANEOUS JOURNAL REVIEWS

[FEBRUARY 1933]   In *Psyché*, A. Savoret dedicates to D. G. Mukerji's last book, *Le Visage du Silence*, an article which shows an incredible bias: in essence, he especially reproaches the Hindu doctrines for not being 'mystical' (who said they were, if not Westerners who understand nothing of them?), and initiation for having definite methods; evidently he prefers fantasies in the air! This diatribe has not even the merit of coherence, for after having mocked Ramakrishna as much as he can, the author writes at the end, 'Who would not feel awkward before such a giant?' Let him understand who can...

[JUNE–JULY 1935] *Yoga* is the journal of a *Yoga Institute* whose organization seems very 'modern', and which though based in India includes on its board a very strong proportion of Western elements. In this issue we find a rather elementary article on 'Self-Realization' whose terminology is not perfectly clear, particularly in its use of the words 'metaphysics' and 'mysticism'. Another article lists texts permitting women to study *Yoga*, which is a very controversial question; there is also instruction about certain exercises, with a visible concern to adapt them to the capacities of the *lay students* (*lay* could fairly well be translated by 'profane'); and it appears that the physiological and therapeutic points of view also play an important role here.

[OCTOBER 1935] The *Le Larousse mensuel* has published a rather long article on 'La pensée indienne'. In reality, it expresses the thought of orientalists on the Indian doctrines, for it is in sum only a conscientious summary of their most current opinions on this subject. Here one finds their 'evolutionist' idea, their more than contestable chronology, their philosophical labels applied without rhyme or reason, and numerous fantastic interpretations which we cannot discuss in further detail. At the outset the author states that 'in order to understand the philosophers [*sic*] of India it is necessary to renounce the intellectual habits of the Christian West'; it would have been much more accurate to say that it is especially necessary to renounce those of the modern West, which is certainly not Christian! The illustrations accompanying the article are better than the text, from which the reader will unfortunately draw very few correct ideas about Hindu and even Buddhist doctrines.

[FEBRUARY 1940] *Nouvelle Revue Française* has published Jean Grenier's 'Réflexions sur la pensée indienne' in reference to some recent books; they are, like the books themselves, of a very academic spirit, and present something like a 'summary' of the reactions of circles of this kind toward India. It is understandable that it must be 'discouraging' (and shall we say even irritating) for people imbued with 'historicism' to think that 'the greatest men and the most important facts of India are unknown or only vaguely attributable to a span of several centuries'; is it in order to reduce this 'vagueness' that they always strive to diminish its antiquity as much as they can? It appears that 'it is Europeans, working for only a century, who have taught the Hindus who their great men and their great works were.' As for the 'great works', the claim is rather extravagant; as for the 'great men', non-'modernized' Hindus willingly leave such a superstition to Westerners, who are incapable of understanding the value of traditional 'anonymity'. We will not dwell on the reflections about doctrines, which often amount to an admission of pure and simple incomprehension (for example: 'Emptiness in our eyes is Nothing,' or again the identification of the neuter *Brahma* to 'Being'); but let us also note as a curiosity that the author believes that the Theosophists, 'in order to draw closer to the Hindus, seek to follow their path,' whereas in reality their mentality is no less typically Western than that of the most 'official' orientalists... In the midst of all this there is nonetheless a declaration that we can only record with satisfaction: it is that although 'India has only been Buddhist for very few centuries of its long history [and it would be appropriate to say that it was never so entirely], up to now it is Buddhism which Europe has been particularly aware of, and that very badly through all sorts of deformations, from Schopenhauer to Deussen.' It is really time that one starts to realize this!

[FEBRUARY–APRIL 1940] An article by Dr P. T. Raju in the *Visva-Bharati Quarterly* entitled 'Traditionalism and Interpretation of Experience' studies the point of view of the Hindu doctrines, or the *Sanātana Dharma*, principally referring to our works. While the author states that he agrees with us in substance, he has no objection to the use of a word like 'philosophy' for the *Vedānta*, for example; he seems not to have understood the reasons that oblige us to avoid the use of certain terms because of the ideas they evoke in fact in current usage, and which, even if they were not attached to them originally, have become inseparable from them. This is equally true for the very word 'traditionalism', which as we have explained is very far from being synonymous with 'traditional spirit', and which we reject absolutely. As for 'proving the truth of tradition by the same methods that modern philosophy employs,' as the author hopes in his conclusion, enough is known of what we think of such concessions to the profane mentality. They are quite incompatible with the transcendent character of true traditional doctrine, and we can say without the least exaggeration that they are directly counter to what we really have in mind.

[JUNE–JULY 1941] *Les Cahiers du Sud* has published a voluminous special number entitled 'Mélanges sur l'Inde'; perhaps the title is not a very happy one in itself, but it must be acknowledged that it does in fact express rather well the character of the contents, which are 'mixed' indeed; this is what happens almost inevitably in an 'open' review that lacks a unified doctrinal direction. Even the 'presentation' shows a bit too much of this 'eclecticism', and as for ourselves, we must say that in spite of the complimentary way we are spoken of, there seems to be a certain incomprehension of our point of view, and moreover we are not very flattered to see our name connected to certain other representatives of 'diverse' attitudes, all very Western though, which certainly have nothing in common with our own! The introductory article, 'Le Message de l'Inde' by Jacques Masui, certainly shows the best of intentions, but the impression that emerges is somewhat confused, as if the author had tried to combine points of view that are rather difficult to reconcile. Most of the translations and some of the articles are owed to Jean Herbert and his usual collaborators; since the subjects treated here are for the most part found in his recent publications, of which we think we shall be able to speak shortly, we will not examine them in detail here. Among the other articles, 'Inde et Occident', signed by Satyanārāyana, is a very sound appreciation of modern Western civilization and the rather disagreeable effect it produces on Easterners entering into contact with it for the first time. The lengthy article 'Aperçu du développement religieux et philosophique de l'Inde brāhmanique', signed only with the initials G.B., is merely, as the title itself might anticipate, a sort of resumé of the orientalist notions that are most contrary to the traditional Hindu spirit. In 'Les "Mystères" du Yoga', Swāmī Pavitrānanda has good reason to oppose the more or less extravagant fantasies of the lovers of 'powers' and 'phenomena', but not for wishing to substitute for them a rather too modern oversimplification. In 'Les fondements philosophiques du yoga', Professor Akshaya Kumar Banerji confines himself to a far too 'philosophical' point of view to be truly able to give an account of things that are really of an entirely different order; in all this, the properly initiatic character of *Yoga*, which is nonetheless the essential, is completely lost from view. In its own particular domain we much prefer René Daumal's study entitled 'Pour approcher l'art poétique hindou', which explains briefly but clearly the general principles of this art. 'La science d'aujourd'hui et la pensée traditionnelle de l'Inde', by F. Le Lionnais, is truly summary and very weak on this subject, on which there would certainly be many other things to say. On the contrary, the article by Emile Dermenghem on 'L'Inde et Islam', is very interesting, and one can only regret that the setting in which he had to present it did not allow him to develop certain considerations that it contains as fully as they would merit. With Jean Grenier's 'Réflexions sur la mentalité indienne dans ses rapports avec la nôtre' we return for the most part to the current opinions of the orientalists. Toward the end of the book, under the title 'Au seuil de l'Inde', Benjamin Fondane begins by very correctly protesting against the ignorance which the more or less 'official' historians of philosophy display toward many of the ancient doctrines of the West, and precisely those that would be most worthy of interest, which can be excused in our opinion by pointing out that these doctrines are effectively beyond the viewpoint of philosophy, at least as it is understood today, so that they do have to figure in its history. Unfortunately, all this is only to arrive at the claim that, contrary to what his own colleagues think, the West has no reason to envy India from the intellectual standpoint, as if in the present state of things a still-living tradition could be compared with traditions long dead and by the author's own admission almost entirely forgotten by modern Westerners!

[OCTOBER–DECEMBER 1944]   We were given a number of issues of a review called *France-Orient*, published in India, where among articles that are mostly purely literary or even political, we were surprised to find in a section called 'Oriental Letters' a few of an altogether different character. We mean especially those by Alain Daniélou related to the sciences and traditional arts of India, in which, without touching directly on the properly metaphysical side of the doctrine, the author nevertheless gives proof of very interesting knowledge inspired by a truly traditional spirit. In 'La science des symboles et les principes de l'art religieux hindou' (October 1944 issue), Daniélou stresses the need, 'in order to understand the basis of traditional Hindu art, to first know the meaning of the symbols it uses,' and this understanding 'implies a profound knowledge of the laws which govern the Universe.' After

explaining how the science of symbols 'forms part of the cosmic interpretation of Vedic texts,' he gives several examples of its application to
iconography, including the description of *Kālī*, who is, as he says, 'one
of the most misunderstood Hindu deities'. — In 'La théorie hindoue de
l'expression musicale' (December 1944 issue), after explaining the technical incompatibility between modal and harmonic music, Daniélou
gives a glimpse of the effects that can be obtained by the first, including
its therapeutic application. 'Like all the Hindu sciences, musical science
is essentially the application to the world of sounds of a metaphysical
theory of numbers and their correspondences; Hindu musical theory is
only experimental within its boundaries, never in its principles.' Then
come some particularly noteworthy considerations on the 'spiral of
sounds' and the theory of the *shrutis*, as well as on the principle of correspondence, through whose use 'the Hindu science of sounds far
exceeds modern science.' Moreover, the author seems to have 'specialized' in the study of Eastern music, for there is an announcement of the
publication of a work of his, *Introduction à l'étude des gammes musi-
cales*,[6] based on the same traditional principles. 'La danse classique hindoue' (February 1945 issue) succinctly explains the principles of this art
according to the *Nātya-Shāstra* and the *Abhinaya-Darpana*.

[APRIL–MAY 1945] 'L'alphabet sanscrit et la langue universelle' is
perhaps the most important of Daniélou's articles, or at least those we
know of, for he presents previously unpublished information about the
Maheshvara-Sūtra and the symbolic value of the letters of the Sanskrit
alphabet. We cannot summarize this here, and we must be content with
noting his reflections on the manifestation of the word, which 'repro-
duces the very processes of universal manifestation,' and on the 'true
language' composed of sounds whose

> relationships form an exact representation in vibratory mode of
> certain principles, of certain cosmic entities, which, descending
> gradually into manifestation, are indefinitely subdivided into
> 'words', corresponding exactly to the changing forms of the natural
> world. . . . This true language always remains the standard by

---

6. See Danielou's *Music and the Power of Sound: The Influence of Tuning and
Interval on Consciousness* (Rochester, VT: Inner Traditions, 1995), first published in
English as *Introduction to the Study of Musical Scales* (London: India Society, 1943).

which are measured the spoken languages, which are its more or less corrupted forms and which are beautiful, intelligible, only insofar as they remain in agreement with the principles of the original language, which the Hindus identify with the form of 'Eternal Knowledge', the *Veda*.

It is only to be regretted that, carried away by the idea (very true in itself, moreover) that the same principles are applicable to all languages, toward the end of his article he believed he could give examples from modern Western languages; some of these are correct for the simple reason that from the etymological point of view they really have the same root as the corresponding Sanskrit words (which he does not seem to have noticed), but others are more than contestable and are based only on various confusions (for example between the secondary elements of composite words and their essential elements). If one wants to avoid all 'fantasy', one can never be too careful about applying traditional principles to languages which are as remote in all respects as these, but of course this reservation about a particular point does not in any way lessen the value of this remarkable study.

[JUNE 1945]   Also in the same review, an article published under Srī Aurobindo's signature has caused us painful astonishment; we say 'under his signature' because until further notice we refuse to believe it is really from him, and we prefer to regard it as no more than some 'scheme', if we may put it so, due to the initiative of some ill-advised disciple. In fact this article, entitled 'La Société et la spiritualité', contains hardly anything except deplorable 'progressivist' banalities, and if there were not here and there a few Sanskrit terms, it would give exactly the same impression as a sermon from some 'liberal Protestant' pastor, imbued with all the latest modern ideas! But, to tell the truth, we have wondered for some time now just what part Srī Aurobindo himself has is in all that appears under his name.

[JULY–DECEMBER 1948]   The *Revue de l'Histoire des Religions* contains an article by Mircea Eliade entitled 'Le "dieu lieur" et le symbolisme des noeuds' ['The "harvest god" and the symbolism of knots']. In the first instance it concerns *Varuna*, but in Vedic India itself he is not the only 'harvest god', and on the other hand we find in the most diverse traditions concepts corresponding to the same 'archetype', as well as rites utilizing the symbolism of 'binding' and applying it moreover in multiple domains that are very different from each other. Eliade very rightly points out that these similarities do not necessarily imply an 'historical' affiliation like that suggested by proponents of the theory of 'borrowings', and that all of this is far from being reducible exclusively to a 'magical' or even 'magico-religious' interpretation, and is connected with a whole series of other symbols, such as 'the weaving of the Cosmos, the thread of human destiny, the labyrinth, the chain of existence, etc.,' which in the final analysis refers to the very structure of the world and to the situation of man within it. It seems to us particularly important to point out here the connection between the symbolism of knots and that of weaving, and to add that, at root, all these symbols are more or less connected to that of the *sūtrātmā* of which we have often spoken. As regards 'labyrinthic' symbolism, let us recall our article entitled 'Encadrements et labyrinthes' (October–November 1947 issue [see also 'Frameworks and Labyrinths' in *Symbols of Sacred Science*, chap. 66]) and AKC's study, to which it refers and that Eliade also mentions. It is possible that we will have to return to this question again in future. — M.E. Lamotte's article 'La légende du Buddha' is in fact primarily a description of the discordant views held on this subject by orientalists, and particularly of the discussions between partisans of a 'mythological' explanation and those of a 'rationalist' explanation. After what is said of the present state of the question, the impossibility of separating authentically biographical elements from legendary elements seems to be generally recognized. No doubt this does not have a very great importance in the end, but it must be rather painful for those in whose eyes the historical view is almost everything; and how can one make clear to these 'critics' that the 'mythic' or symbolic character of certain facts does not necessarily exclude their historical reality? Lacking anything better, they are reduced to comparing texts in order to try to extricate the 'successive states' of the legend and the various factors presumed to have contributed to its development.

[DECEMBER 1948]   In the review *Études*, Fr Jean Daniélou has published an article entitled 'Le yogi et le Saint' in connection with various works concerning the Hindu doctrines, including ours. We must frankly say that, after having had the occasion to see him write earlier on other subjects, we would have expected more understanding on his part. It is true that at the outset he is careful to mark a difference between authentic traditional doctrine such as we have expounded it, and 'modern'—we would almost say 'modernist'—Hinduism that others persist in presenting, and that is certainly very good; but later he hardly maintains this essential distinction rigorously, so that one no longer always knows exactly to whom or to what his criticisms are addressed, and in the end they lead to a complete misunderstanding of the very idea of the tradition. He renews the confusion of speaking of 'mysticism' in connection with India, and he even feels the need to revive the idea of a so-called 'natural mysticism' started long ago by the 'neo-scholastic' philosophers in *Études carmélitains*, who themselves have now come to adopt a new attitude rather different from this one, as can be seen from what we have recently said about them... We will not go into the details of errors of interpretation that for the most part are only more or less direct consequences of this ambiguity. Thus, to give an example, *Yoga* cannot at all be assimilated to 'mystical union', and any comparison claimed to be established on the basis of such an assimilation will necessarily be false by this very fact. Moreover, we do not understand how in writing that 'Hindu mysticism is a mysticism of impersonal unity' the author was able to add a simple note of reference to one of our works, which greatly risks leading his readers to believe that we ourselves have said this or something equivalent. Such a procedure seems to us at the least strange, and it is also difficult to conceive how one can push incomprehension so far as to describe as 'subtle syncretism' the affirmation of the transcendent unity of all traditional forms! But what is perhaps most strange is this: all that Fr Daniélou says of the shortcomings of any 'human wisdom' is perfectly correct in itself, and not only are we fully in accord with him on this but we will readily go even further in this direction. But we cannot protest too much against the application he wants to make of this, for when it comes to the Hindu tradition, and moreover equally to any tradition whatsoever, it is not this that is in any way involved, for tradition is precisely such by reason of its essentially 'supra-human' nature. The most 'conciliatory' intentions, if they do not imply recognition of this fundamental point, fall as it were into the void since what they address has nothing in common with what really exists, and they can only provoke suspicion; the allusion to a current attempt to create a Christian mysticism of 'Hindu' structure leads one to think indeed that some have not renounced the 'annexationist' aims we have denounced in the past. Be that as it may, the clearest conclusion to be drawn from all this is that no agreement is

really possible with anyone who claims for one single and unique traditional form to the exclusion of all the others a monopoly on revelation
and the supernatural.

[1949]   In the second number of a review called *Hind*, which seems
to indiscriminately gather very disparate things (it appears that this is
called 'being objective') but whose dominant tendency is clearly 'modernist', an orientalist, Louis Renou, has given under the title 'L'Inde et la
France' a sort of historical account of works on India produced in
France from the eighteenth century to the present. Obviously, such a
project does not as a whole present any special interest from our point
of view; but there is a paragraph that merits being reproduced here in
full (it refers to the utility there might be of 'pursuing a certain contact
with this anonymous mass of readers, in whose midst a vocation can
one day arise'; and which no doubt is none other than what is commonly called the 'general public'):

> this contact must not, however, be pursued to the detriment of the
> truth. There is always some abuse of power to resolve in the arena
> of delicate questions, especially in a domain such as Indology,
> where many problems await their solution. But everything is a
> question of measure. What is patently dishonest is to use India and
> Indian spirituality to build ambitious and vain theories for the use
> of the Enlightened Ones of the West. Through the profusion of
> systems, through the strangeness of certain conceptions, Indian
> thought has offered, it must be confessed, some temptation here. It
> is from beginnings in more or less distorted Indian notions and
> images that the Neo-Buddhist sects and Theosophical movements,
> with which the West teems, were born. The success of René
> Guénon's elucubrations, these so-called revelations of the Tradi-
> tion whose keeper he believes himself to be, clearly illustrates the
> danger. People want to distinguish beside the official or university
> Indology (devoted, we are told, to grammar) an Indology which
> alone realizes the essence of things. In reality, this is an Indology of
> superficial travelers, of journalists (when it is not a question of
> mere exploiters of public credulity), who pride themselves on
> informing an ignorant public about *Vedānta*, *Yoga*, or Tantrism.

All who have the least knowledge of our work can appreciate at its
worth the 'fairness' of a process (what exquisite politeness they will also

admit) that consists in placing the phrase aimed at us between mention of the Theosophists and of travellers and journalists; as uncomprehending as an orientalist may be, it is all the same hardly possible that he should not be aware at all of the enormity of such comparisons. We only wish Louis Renou, or any of his colleagues, had done the thousandth part of what we ourselves have done to denounce the wrongdoing of those he calls the 'Enlightened Ones of the West'! On the other hand, we certainly have nothing in common with travellers, superficial or otherwise, or with journalists, and we have never pursued, even occasionally, either of these trades; we have never written a single line meant for the 'general public', with whom we do not concern ourselves in the least, and we do not think anyone can push further than we have the contempt for all 'popularization'. Let us add that we do not claim to be the 'keeper' of anything at all, and that we limit ourselves to that which we have been able to know in a direct fashion, and never through the distorting 'elucubrations' of the orientalists. But evidently in their eyes it is an unpardonable crime not to place oneself in their school and to maintain above everything else one's complete independence in order to be able to say 'honestly' and 'sincerely' what one knows, without being obliged to distort it in order to accommodate it to their profane opinions and their Western prejudices. Now, that we should have come to be considered a 'danger' both by 'official or university' orientalists and by the 'Enlightened Ones of the West', Theosophists and occultists of every kind, this is a fact that can certainly only please us, for it proves that both feel themselves harmed and fear to see the credit they have enjoyed until now with their respective 'clientele' seriously compromised... Let us also note that the article in question ends with an encomium by Romain Rolland, which is a very significant trait as regards the mentality of certain people. Following this attack, even more ridiculous than it is odious, that Louis Renou saw fit to launch against us without even trying to support it with the least shadow of a precise critique, we feel a certain satisfaction to see him declare that 'this study could not be better concluded than by evoking the memory' of this person whose foolish sentimentality is rather closely related to that of the Theosophists and other 'neo-spiritualists', and is just what is needed to please the 'ignorant public', which lets itself be taken in by journalists and travellers' gossip. Finally (a really amusing detail), the article is accompanied by way of illustration with a photograph of a fragment of a Sanskrit manuscript whose negative was inverted; this was doubtless only an accident in the layout, but it nevertheless has in some way a symbolic value, for it happens only too often that the orientalists interpret texts upside down!

[APRIL 1950]   This issue of the review *Témoignages*, published by the Benedictine Abbey of Pierre-qui-Vire, contains a lengthy article entitled 'Sagesse hindoue et sagesse chrétienne', by Dom Irénée Gros, which in many ways resembles that which Fr Jean Daniélou devoted to the same subject in *Études* and we reviewed earlier (see the June 1949 issue). First of all, our works are mentioned at the very outset, but not later; it seems to us that this can only have been done with the aim of creating to our detriment, or rather to that of the doctrines we expound, a confusion with the 'neo-Vedāntists' who are more or less affected by modern ideas, as well as with the various 'popularizers' frequently cited in the course of the article. At root, it is always the same thing: the affirmation that Christianity has a monopoly on the supernatural and that it alone possesses a 'transcendent' character, and consequently that all other traditions are 'purely human', which in fact amounts to saying that they are not traditions at all but rather comparable to 'philosophies' and nothing more. 'The Divine Wisdom,' it is said expressly, 'has no common measure with this human wisdom that the East offers us; Christianity is of a different order'; in other words, Christianity alone is an expression of the Divine Wisdom; but unfortunately these are only affirmations, and in reality, for authentically traditional doctrines, whether of India or anywhere else, including Christianity itself, it is never a question of 'human wisdom' but always of 'Divine Wisdom'. We have also noticed something curious, which confirms an impression we have already often had in similar cases: this is that the Non-Supreme is called 'the transcendent God' while the Supreme is considered to be 'immanent', although it is exactly the opposite that is true. We are unable to explain this reversal, and we are forced to recognize that it stems from a mentality that escapes us; but could this not throw some daylight onto the way in which Christian 'transcendence' is understood? Of course, we here again find 'natural mysticism', an expression which, at least as regards India and more generally the East (for we do not know whether it corresponds to some reality in the West), is applied to something which is precisely neither mystical nor natural. The Hindu doctrines are all the more considered to be merely 'human' to the extent that this greatly facilitates the 'annexationist' enterprises that we have spoken of on various occasions and which again are in question here, for one can then 'win over the Hindu philosophy to the service of Christianity as the Middle Ages were able to conquer Greek philosophy'; however, what one is dealing with here is altogether different from Greek philosophy and is indeed not even a 'philosophy', so that the comparison is entirely false. If this intended result can be obtained, one could condescend to give the Hindu doctrines, or rather a certain part of them (for what might be 'useful' would have to be chosen carefully) a 'subordinate place', on the condition that India 'renounce its metaphysics,' that is to say that it cease being Hindu. Western proselytism certainly lacks no confidence, and we have known this for a long time already; but since these are in fact two traditions which as such are in essence equally supernatural and 'non-human', and consequently can only be related on a footing of strict equality or else mutually ignore each other, it goes without saying that this is an impossibility pure and simple. We shall add only that all this is accompanied by a purely verbal argumentation, that can appear convincing only to those who are already persuaded in advance and which is worth exactly as much as that used by modern philosophers with other intentions when they claim to impose limitations on knowledge and wish to deny everything of the supra-rational order. Things of this kind, whatever their origin, irresistibly remind us of the reasoning of a blind man who would undertake to prove that light does not exist!

Appendix

АKC Reviews

REVIEWS OF OTHER AUTHORS

with India attempting to create a Christian mysticism of 'Hindu' structure... 227

[1949]

In *Hind* Louis Renou writes on historical works on India produced in France. He attacks René Guénon and ends with an encomium by R. Rolland... 229

[APRIL 1950]

Témoignages has an article 'Sagesse hindou et sagesse Chrétienne' on the superiority of Christianity... 231

GENERAL INDEX

Buddhism Index

Sanskrit Index

Printed in the United States
1366200006B/111

9 780900 588693